Sailor of Fortune

Jack Arnot

Sailor of Fortune

Ian Jackson

The Pentland Press Limited
Edinburgh · Cambridge · Durham

First published in 1993 by
The Pentland Press Ltd.
1 Hutton Close
South Church
Bishop Auckland
Durham

ISBN 1 85821 005 4

Typeset by Elite Typesetting Techniques, Southampton.
Printed and bound by Antony Rowe Ltd., Chippenham.

To Jack Arnot,
whose life was the subject of
Sailor of Fortune,
and who wrote a large part of it

Contents

Acknowledgements   ix
List of Illustrations   xi
Author's Foreword   xiii

 1. *Kasenga*   1
 2. *City of Harvard*   17
 3. Jack goes to school in Liverpool   23
 4. 'One and a half years as third of three watchkeeping officers'   29
 5. First Mate (Foreign-Going)   38
 6. *City of Salisbury*   41
 7. *City of Lille*   49
 8. *City of Barcelona*   56
 9. *Pedrinhas*   62
10. Burmah Oil   76
11. Burmah Oil, second tour   82
12. Burmah Oil, third tour   86
13. M.V. *Sabari*   92
14. *Badarpur* and *Yenangyaung*   97
15. The chance presents itself   100
16. In search of a vessel   105
17. Getting to know her   111
18. Trouble   118
19. More trouble   126
20. Fitting out   132
21. Away to a false start   140
22. Westward Ho!   145
23. Madeira and the Atlantic crossing   151
24. Caribbean Interlude   156
25. To the Isthmus of Panama   166
26. The Panama Canal   172
27. Four thousand ocean miles   180

28. Isles Marquesas   189
29. Isles Marquesas to Tahiti   197
30. Pacific Rendezvous   204
31. Auckland is our destination   213
32. The Pacific   220
33. T.S.M.V. *Altair*   225
34. M/V *Nukalau*   230
35. *Ai Sokula* and *Altair*   237
36. *John Williams VI*   241
37. *John Williams VI* at work   245
38. More of missionary ships   252
39. Yet more *John Williams VI*   261
40. *John Williams VII*   268
41. *John Williams VII*, Jack's final year   284
42. Tarawa   288

Acknowledgements

To Ellerman Lines, plc, for the use of extracts from the log of *City of Lille*.

To the Brooklyn *Daily Eagle*, for quotations from their pieces by O. R. Pilat.

To the Arnot and Jackson families, for the use of letters and papers.

To Harry Rome, for his help with the *Pedrinhas* chapter.

For photographs: The National Maritime Museum
                    The World Ship Society
                    Cia De Cabotagem De Pernambuco
                    Mr. J. V. Bartlett
                    The Burmah Oil Co. Ltd.
                    Fulleylove
                    The London Missionary Society
                    The Daily Telegraph

List of Illustrations

Frontispiece   Jack Arnot

World map – Indian sub-continent   2
Map of India   18
City of Harvard (National Maritime Museum)   19
City of Hong Kong (National Maritime Museum)   19
City of Cairo (National Maritime Museum)   30
City of Dunedin (World Ship Society)   30
Map of Japan and China   32
Branksome Hall (World Ship Society)   34
City of Nagpur (National Maritime Museum)   43
City of Salisbury (World Ship Society)   43
City of Durban (National Maritime Museum)   45
Map of The East Indies   46
City of Lille (National Maritime Museum)   51
Map of Grand Banks and Nova Scotia   53
City of Barcelona (National Maritime Museum)   58
City of Barcelona at Manchester – funnel top and topmasts
struck (World Ship Society)   58
Pedrinhas (Cia De Cabotagem de Pernambuco)   69
Captain J. McK. Arnot; J. F. Lindell, 2nd Mate; M. E. C. Miller,
Mate; H. M. Rome, 3rd Mate; J. W. Close, Wireless Officer
(Cia De Cabotagem de Pernambuco)   70
Highland Monarch (National Maritime Museum)   77
Masimpur (Jack Arnot)   77
Map of Arabia and the Gulf   78
Badarpur (J. V. Bartlett)   84
Singu (J. V. Bartlett)   88
Beme (Jack Arnot)   88
Sabari (Jack Arnot)   94
Yenangyaung (Burmah Oil Co. Ltd.)   98

Buzz, Kim and Jack   168
Panama Canal Clearance certificate   175
Jack in *Kimballa*, Buzz in forecabin   183
Kimballa (Jack Arnot)   205
Jack and Buzz at Rarotonga (Fulleylove)   206
Kimballa at Rarotonga   208
Off the Jetty, Rarotonga   210
Party time, Rarotonga; Jack and Buzz   211
Kimballa at Auckland   216
Map of The Central Pacific   223
Altair (Jack Arnot)   226
'Brats' aboard *Altair*   228
Nukalau (Jack Arnot)   233
John Williams VI (Jack Arnot)   242
Captain Jack Arnot and Mate Rosea, *John Williams VII*   269
Map of The Cook Islands cruise   271
John Williams VII (London Missionary Society)   280
John Williams VII (*Daily Telegraph*)   281

Author's Foreword

My Uncle Jack, officially John McKenzie Arnot, was born on 4th January 1907 in Koslin, then in Prussian Pomerania, now in Poland, the son of a Scottish paper maker and an Orcadian daughter of the manse. He only ever sought one career, the sea, which might partly be explained by the almost gypsy nature of his parent's life.

His father's work, designing, managing and consulting with the owners of paper mills, caused him to move from place to place with some rapidity in Jack's early years. Indeed, John Melrose Arnot's marriage to Johanna Graham Young Robb took place in Calcutta in 1897, after she had, in days when it was not an ordinary thing to do, travelled out by steamer, alone, for the express purpose of marrying him. John Melrose Arnot's wanderings took him and his growing family to Hendon, Farncombe, Penicuick, Inverkeithing, Jamaica and finally to Bury in Lancashire, which all the family came to recognise as home. Not content with shifting his residence with disconcerting frequency he seemed to have a propensity for changing employers at the drop of a hat, probably because he was such a well-known and skilled paper maker. In today's parlance, he was 'head hunted' a number of times before he settled in Bury. So the family certainly had a touch of the wanderlust built into their natures.

Not quite born into the Victorian era, Jack Arnot was none the less born into a time when Britons ruled, counselled, worked in, traded in, built bridges and sewage works and railways and cities and towns and hamlets in, wrote law for, administered the laws of and officered the military forces of vast tracts of the globe. The first Industrial Revolution had produced its best fruit and its application worldwide gave opportunities without number for Europeans in general and Britons in particular to make their lives abroad, and the servicing of the world's industrial demands and the transporting of the horde of expatriate Britons nurtured the greatest merchant fleet seen so far.

In today's terms the ships were tiny, with the average tramp steamer some 3,000 tons, the cargo liners a little bigger at some 5,000 tons and the great passenger liners, apart from the monsters of the North Atlantic, not much over 10,000 tons. So to carry the volume of trade generated by the Empire and world economies and to move all the expatriate managers, entrepreneurs, district officers and the like, and their families, out to work and home for leave, or childbirth, or school, required a lot of ships and a lot of ships' Masters, mates and engineers. Shipping companies were, therefore, much bigger in terms of ship numbers then than now and firms with fifty ships were not uncommon, though they are almost unknown today. This is not surprising when one considers that the annual carrying power of a modern 40,000 ton container ship is twelve times that of a high class 10,000 ton cargo liner of the late fifties, which was itself five times that of a cargo liner at the turn of the century. That means that for the same volume of cargo we need today one sixtieth of the ships which we needed at the turn of the century. Aeroplanes have removed passengers from the equation, abolishing the need for the large number of liners which moved the expatriates about the world.

So at the time that Jack Arnot was considering how to turn his desire to go to sea into an actual apprenticeship there were a vast number of ships and shipping companies to provide berths for lads such as he, though by 1922 when he was ready to leave the *Conway* and go to sea, the rosy postwar glow was fading and the opportunities were fewer. But there were still a lot of ships at sea and their dramatic explosion of size and carrying power was to await the conclusion of the Second World War.

Not only were there so many more ships and men in those days but the life and conditions were also very different. Wireless was in its infancy and ships' Masters, when they dropped their pilots at the Bar Lightship, or in the Downs or at Plymouth, were very much on their own until they reached their next port of call, at which cabled messages could well be waiting. Tramp masters were even more on their own, for they were often expected to find their own homeward cargoes, or cargoes for destinations other than home and thus might be away for years before finding a homeward freight. Far cry from today's conditions when a modern, well-equipped ship need never be out of range of a telephone call, a telex or a fax message from the owners at home. Diversions and re-directions need no longer await the vessel's arrival at some port at the end of a wire but can be communicated instantly. The Master remains in command, but is infinitely more subject to continual instruction and supervision. Big Brother can always be watching these days.

The equipment of the ships was very different, too. Even as late as 1931, when Jack Arnot gained his Master's ticket, the Gyro compass, the echo sounder and the simpler radio direction-finding equipment were rarely to be found, even in high-class cargo liners, and the radar set, the radio telephone, the auto pilot, the weatherfax machine, the telex and the satellite navigator had not even been invented. Chronometers were clockwork with quartz accuracy only a dream in the physicist's mind.

The ports were different for the carriers of the bulk of the world's freight. The people of today's container ships will visit only container terminals, briefly. The people of today's tankers, particularly the monsters known as Very, or Ultra, Large Crude Carriers can expect to see only oil terminals, extremely briefly, and many of those are out of sight of land. Even today's break bulk cargo liners, which carry an ever-reducing proportion of world trade, can expect to visit only modern ports equipped with cranes and gear for swift cargo handling, with the lesser ports served by smaller vessels into which their cargoes are transferred. Contrast this with the work of the cargo liner of the thirties whose itinerary would include ports with wharves and cranes, with wharves and no cranes requiring the use of the ship's own derricks, ports with neither wharves nor cranes necessitating working with the ship's own gear into lighters and sampans and barges, and even ports with nothing, where the ship would be put aground on the tide and discharge into carts at low water. In those days the cargo liner herself did a lot of the work now done by the smaller feeder ships which meant that the ports were not only different but far more frequent. Two and three ports in a day was not uncommon in some trades and it takes no great flight of the imagination to discern the enormous workload which that imposed on the ship's people of those days by comparison with today.

All of which meant that seafaring, before the container and supertanker revolution, offered a man enormous variety of experience, be it variety of experience within one ship or one company, or variety gained by moving from one ship or company to others. One who hated heat could stay on the North Atlantic run. One who hated heat and liked company could opt for passenger ships on that run. Sun lovers could find companies which traded solely or mainly in sunny climes, again with the options open for the convivial and the solitary to find the right berth. In all but the least desirable of tramp steamers the people were well fed and the officers, at least, reasonably housed though the concept of a hot fresh bath or shower, let alone those facilities for private use, had to await the Second World War and the Liberty Ship. Leave was appalling, voyages could be years long, and the pay would have been unacceptable to a competent clerk, but it was a life of interest and variety, if of hardship and a degree of deprivation.

Today it is very different. The equipment is modern, the living conditions are in the main excellent, the pay is first class and the leave is perhaps over abundant. Six-month voyages are deemed long enough and crews are changed by air as and when necessary. The food is still good but because crews are much smaller there is less company. It is a different world altogether by comparison with life at sea in the thirties and even up to the fifties. Much better in most of the important facets and in the material aspects of the job, but less rewarding in terms of variety and, dare I say it, 'adventure'.

It is because the comparison of conditions then with conditions now is so stark that I have thought it worthwhile to put together this pastiche covering my Uncle Jack's seafaring life which, though it never yielded him a fortune, contented him and contributed to the world's welfare. Large parts of it, particularly the section concerning *Kimballa's* voyage to New Zealand, are his own writings. Other parts come from reports and documents prepared by others who had to do with him. Some background derives from my own time at sea, first as an apprentice, then as a mate in cargo liners. The title is his own. After the voyage to New Zealand Jack wrote a book about the voyage, but never published it. He called it, for reasons which will become obvious, *Sailor of Fortune*.

Chapter 1

Kasenga

The basic training was over. The raw schoolboy John McKenzie Arnot had left North Manchester Grammar School in December 1920 after passing the entrance exam for H.M.S. *Conway* the previous month, at which time the seafaring die could be said to be cast for, in those days, not too many of the lads entering the *Conway* went on to initial careers other than the Merchant Navy. A few would find that two years in the old wooden wall anchored off Rock Ferry in the Mersey cured them of the desire to venture into the wider waters beyond the Bar Lightship. A very few would go on to Dartmouth and the Royal Navy but the vast majority 'went to sea' in the ships of British shipowners.

The *Conway* was the result of collaboration between the Educational Committee for the Mercantile Marine Service Association of Liverpool and the government of the day who provided the ship. The Committee originally sought to set up a school for the training of orphan and destitute children of seamen for the sea, an objective quickly modified to training boys to become officers in the Merchant Service. The Admiralty made a frigate, H.M.S. *Nile*, whose name was changed to *Conway*, available to the association which modified her to fit her new role and moved her to Rock Ferry, where she arrived in February 1859. There she and her two successor ships, also named *Conway*, remained until the Second World War when she was moved to the Menai Straits for safety's sake. She remained there until April 1953 when she went ashore and broke her back, becoming a total loss.

The two years which Jack spent in *Conway* provided a basic training for boys going to sea as deck apprentices. The physical regime was hard in a wooden ship anchored in the Mersey with its none too perfect weather and swift tides. Everything needed to sustain life and education had to be fetched from the shore and the cadets manned the boats which, in all

1

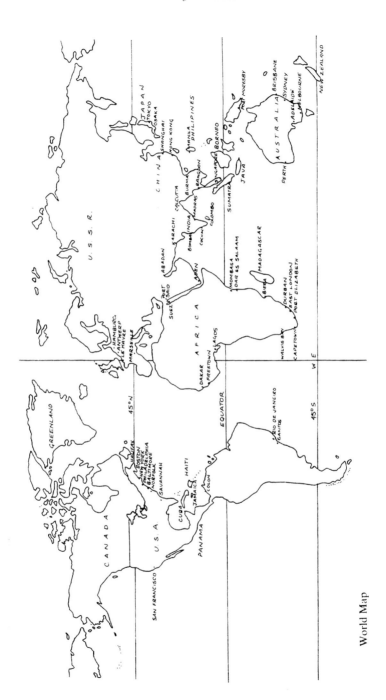

World Map

weathers, did the fetching and provided training in sailing, boat handling, boat pulling and all those aspects of seamanship connected with ships' boats. On board, in addition to the ordinary schoolwork covering the three R's and History and Geography and the like, there was training in Navigation, Chartwork, Signalling with flags, lamps and semaphore, Knots and Splices, Seamanship, Cargo handling, Ship Stability and a myriad other things appropriate to the needs of a budding ship's officer. The ship was kept clean and maintained by the cadets, there were fire and emergency drills and physical jerks. A thoroughly demanding existence with a remarkably high survival rate, at the end of which a boy went to sea as an apprentice, the subject of a degree of mockery at worst or scepticism at best by those without the advantage of *Conway* training but with the paramount advantage of the remission of a part of the sea time required before the first professional exam, that for the Board of Trade Second Mate's Certificate, could be attempted.

So when Jack Arnot, at the tender age of sixteen, arrived in Newcastle on a cold and dreary 3rd April 1923 to join the Ellerman and Bucknall line's S.S. *Kasenga* as a first voyage apprentice, he had some small idea of what he was letting himself in for, and some basic training to help him cope with his first seafaring days. Enough at least to know not to expect a *Mauretania* or *Aquitania*, for in *Conway* the pattern of cargo shipping would have unfolded constantly before his eyes on the waters of the Mersey which, in the twenties, was a river filled with vessels of all nations using the twin ports of Liverpool and Birkenhead. But he would certainly have been unprepared for the chaotic state of a moderate-sized cargo liner completing her cargo and preparing to sail for Hull and India. All the hatches were open with the last of the cargo being lifted aboard by the ship's derricks and clattering steam winches. The decks were cluttered with hatch beams and neatly piled hatch boards and whilst the holds were well populated by stevedores stowing the cargo the decks were relatively uninhabited, with just the winch drivers and the hatch man, conducting them as a conductor conducts an orchestra, directing their operations. The third mate was to be seen supervising the cargo work on the foredeck and the second mate doing the same for the after holds. The decks were a dangerous place when the ship was working cargo, with slings of cargo swinging over the rail and across the deck before disappearing through the hatches and into the holds. Sharp eyes and ears were needed for safety on the onshore side of the deck which was avoided by the experienced who kept to the offshore side, except where cargo was coming aboard from lighters moored alongside.

This was not yet of too much concern to Jack who, as instructed by his mentors in the *Conway*, sought out the Mate and reported his presence on board. The mate's distraction from the flood of paperwork which attends the completion of a cargo and preparations for sailing was brief, merely long enough to summon the senior apprentice to show Jack to the 'half deck', the traditional name for the apprentice's room no matter where in the ship it was situated, show him which bunk was his and where he could stow his gear, and tell him to get into his dungarees and turn to as quickly as possible. No niceties of introductions even to his fellow apprentices, let alone to the Captain and mates; just straight into the work, getting to know who was who as time went by. With the ship preparing to sail the unknown quantity, the brand-new, first-voyage apprentice, was put to work not too demanding of the knowledge gained in two years in the *Conway* and far removed from boyhood dreams of watchkeeping, of navigating in close waters, of conning the ship through stormy seas or even of taking part in the seamanlike activities of getting the derricks down and lashed for sea, or singling up the mooring ropes in preparation for departure. Not this time. Sweeping the boat and accommodation decks to clear them of the debris of a stay in port is a very necessary task and nicely within the capabilities of a newcomer. And after that, as the ship moved down the Tyne and past Tynemouth to sea, the rather heavier debris on the main deck, the broken bits of dunnage and packing cases, the fag packets and matchboxes, the scraps of spunyarn and bits of rope have all to be gathered up and put over the side to adorn the beaches on the next tide. All this to be done with only one eye and half a mind on the job, the other eye and half of the mind observing the work of getting the derricks down, of covering the hatch-boards with tarpaulins, of fitting the battens into the cleats around the hatch coaming and hammering the wedges home to secure them. All this while the senior apprentice, up on the bridge, worked the engine room telegraph to the pilot's orders and noted the engine movements in the engine movement book, while the other two apprentices worked with the sailors in getting the ship battened down and ready for the open sea.

Thus, after years of dreaming, after two years of what would today be called vocational training, Jack Arnot went to sea to begin a life's work of seafaring which, with a short interval of three years or so during which he spent time at sea for recreation, was to span a little over forty-one years. The first passage of all the hundreds of passages which he made in those forty-one years was a mere 138 miles down the East Coast of England to Hull, *Kasenga*'s final U.K. loading port. And Jack did not see much of that passage because in that ship the apprentices mainly worked days, so having sailed at evening the time between departure and arrival the following morning was spent getting to know his fellow apprentices, sleeping, living again in his mind the events of the day and pondering his future over the three years of apprenticeship which he must serve to get in his sea time for second mate; three years counted in days spent at sea with leave, which was in any event minimal, excluded. Years during which he would progress from his present status of lowest form of animal life in the ship, at the beck and call of all who chose to whistle for him, to senior apprentice entirely capable of standing in for the third or fourth mate should the occasion demand. Moving, too, from the starting salary of one pound ten per month for the first year and two pounds ten for the second to the princely sum of four pounds for the third, but bound over the whole period by indentures which obliged the shipowner to teach him the business of a ship's officer and which bound him to serve the shipowner diligently and faithfully, conducting himself as a properly brought up young man should and, specifically, agreeing 'not to enter taverns or alehouses except on the company's business'. Nor was he to embezzle, or to play illegal games.

With a service agreement set in terms such as these, and with no guarantee of employment on obtaining a second mate's ticket at the end of the apprenticeship, it is small wonder that apprentices especially and the public in general were of the opinion that the system provided cheap labour for the shipowners on a continuous basis, and so it did. Sea time for second mate could just as well be served on deck as a seaman at rather better rates of pay but it must be said that the chances of qualifying by that route were a great deal less. Reputable shipowners did teach their apprentices the business of a ship's officer and, whilst large lumps of time were spent in chipping and painting, in cargo watching and cleaning bilges and all the other essential routine jobs which have to be done to keep a ship as a going concern, there was instruction in navigation both coastal and with the sextant in the deep seas, in signalling, what there was of it, in the rule of the road at sea, both theoretical and practical when keeping a watch with one of the mates. Steering was taught to apprentices and seaman alike, and practised by both alike, but the combination of the direct educational advantage of an apprenticeship with the distancing from the rough and ready life of the fo'c's'le where habits, lifestyle and attitudes militated against study of any sort, made the likelihood of the apprentice gaining his certificate infinitely greater than that of all but the most determined of able seamen.

As a vehicle for serving an apprenticeship *Kasenga* was typical of the hundreds, no, thousands, of middle-sized cargo liners and tramp steamers which formed so large a part of the British merchant fleet in the 1920s. Of typical cargo liner size, 7,150 tons, she was built on the Tyne in 1899 for German owners and handed over to Ellerman and Bucknalls in 1920 as part of the reparations programme, changing her name from *Drachenfels* to *Kasenga* in the process. Bucknalls kept her until 1929 when, with a building programme in full swing, she was sold. She was a 'three island' steamer with two hatches forward of the bridge, two on the afterdeck and one on the poop, with one pair of derricks to each hatch served by steam winches. She steamed at ten knots which was typical of the time; not until the thirties did cargo liner speeds rise much beyond twelve knots and only at the end of that decade were the first of the eighteen-knot ships going into service, and they were few and far between. Oil lighting was used throughout the ship and, whilst flushing W.C.s were installed, everyone from the captain down had to take his bath out of a galvanised bucket, filled by dipper from a cauldron on the galley stove and placed on a board across the bathtub, which existed, but which had only a cold saltwater tap. Fresh cold water was also transferred by bucket except that that for the captain was carried up to his own freshwater tank, filled on the monkey island above the wheelhouse, this particular transfer being the responsibility of the apprentices. Woe betide them if the old man's freshwater tank ran dry.

Kasenga was to be home to Jack Arnot for sixteen months during which time he grew from green hand to confident seaman, visited his parent's home once when the ship called at Birkenhead, steamed 57,019 miles, visited thirty-two different ports, many of them more than once so that she entered and left port fifty-eight times. She passed through the Suez canal six times, three times southbound and three northbound; visited three continents, two islands, two oceans, four seas and one bay. By the time Jack came home and paid off in Tilbury on 30th August 1924 he had served nearly half the sea time he needed for second mate.

On 14th April 1923 *Kasenga* sailed from Hull and Jack's foreign-going seafaring life began in earnest, for she was bound for Oran and beyond and Jack was bound for blue water for the first time, on what was to be a typical Ellerman voyage ranging as far east as Calcutta in eighty-eight degrees of easterly longitude and as far west as Baltimore at seventy-six degrees west, and from Dondra Head in Sri Lanka with less than six degrees of northerly latitude to the Pentland Firth with nearly fifty-nine. Through a climatic range which encompassed the heat of the Red Sea and the Indian subcontinent to winter in the North Atlantic. The 57,000 miles steamed occupied 237 days at sea, or 1,422 four-hour watches, 474 for each watchkeeper, all to move the ship through her 276 days in fifty-eight ports; and those days in port were the hard days of the voyage. On each arrival the derricks had to be got up and the hatches opened and on each departure the hatches had to be covered and battened down and the derricks lowered and lashed. On intermediate days in port the hatches had to be covered, though not battened down, at the end of the day and opened up again next morning. Throughout the working days the cargo work and stowage was supervised by the mates with the apprentices assisting or sitting in the holds watching pilferable cargo, or chipping and painting or doing other ship's work. It did not take Jack much of this voyage to concur with the view that, as distinct from working cargo in port, you 'went to sea for a rest', though this would not become a working philosophy for some time yet, not until long after the novelty of being at sea and visiting a succession of foreign ports in a variety of foreign countries had worn off. Even after the novelty has gone the true sailor, and Jack was certainly that, continues to regard the business of being at sea and working in foreign ports as a continuous adventure for many a hard-working year.

Spring in the Mediterranean. First sight of the Rock of Gibraltar in the sunshine. Arrival at Oran on 21st April, then onwards to Port Said and the junior apprentice's first passage, of forty-one in all, of the Suez canal. First sight of the desert, of feluccas, of the undeniable sight of the earth's curvature, so clearly seen as the ruler-straight first thirty miles of the canal arches away over the horizon. First encounter with the bumboat men and assorted villains who will steal anything which is not locked up or nailed down, causing portholes to be screwed shut and cabin doors locked despite the heat. It matters not today, air-conditioning cures all, but it mattered then. First impression of the desert at night after the change of pilot at Lake Timsah, with the canal and its banks lit by the ship's searchlight, hung from a davit over the stemhead. In the night the ships debouch into the Gulf of Suez, the pilot is dropped, the searchlight is dumped into a lighter and courses are set down the Gulf, past Mount Sinai, past Ras Gharib and into the narrows by Gezr Ashrafi where the navigable channel narrows to a shade over five miles, and where the southbound canal convoy all arrives together and meets all the tankers and freighters making up towards Suez for a canal passage. It can be an exciting place and has been the scene of some notable collisions.

The Red Sea is not at its hottest in April and May so Jack's first passage of it was relatively comfortable and the passage through the Gates of Hell by Perim island produced a pleasant change in the atmosphere, but not the dramatic improvement which can occur when the Red Sea is really hot. Once out of the Gulf of Aden and into the Indian Ocean the south-west monsoon, blowing strongly over the starboard quarter, made itself felt, made steering more difficult and caused the ship to roll considerably whilst giving pleasant though humid weather for the passage to Bombay where the whole of the outward cargo was discharged. A fortnight's hard work in temperatures which, though not summer temperatures, were hot enough for a lad away from northern European climes for the first time.

Then more cargo work, this time loading the homeward cargo of rice and rattans, of tea and plumbago and desiccated coconut. Woven cotton fabric for dyeing and printing in Lancashire. Palm oil in the deep tanks and then the two-day passage to Karachi to load more of the same. Then westwards again, now punching into the monsoon across the Arabian Sea, past Socotra and Aden and Perim to Port Sudan on the west coast of the Red Sea for raw cotton. And onwards from there to Suez and through the canal again and into the Mediterranean for the first European discharging port, Marseilles, whence through the Strait of Gibraltar and into the Atlantic again. Past Cape St. Vincent, Lisbon, Finisterre and Ushant and into the English Channel to Dunkirk, discharging part of the cargo before moving on to complete discharging at Hull and Middlesbrough where loading for the next voyage, or as far as Jack was concerned, the continuation of this one, began. Northwards to the Pentland Firth, southward through the Minches, round the Mull of Kintyre and northward again past Ailsa Craig and the Cumbraes before rounding Cloch Point and sailing up the Clyde to Glasgow. More loading, more cargo work and down the Clyde again, past the Isle of Man to the Bar Lightship off Liverpool to embark the Liverpool pilot, and under his guidance through the Queen's channel, up the river and into the West Float at Birkenhead whence, while the outward cargo was being completed, Jack got home for a couple of days. The sailor home from the sea, briefly! His time in his first ship was nearly a third done, and though in those six months *Kasenga* had covered 15,000 miles there were 42,000 more to be steamed before she was to see home again, the next voyage being more extended than that just completed, though it too was typical of Ellerman voyages.

The leaves were beginning to turn when, in October 1923 *Kasenga*, with Jack still aboard, still the junior apprentice of four, still under the same Captain James though with a new Mate, Mr. Watkins having been relieved by Mr. Henry, locked out of the West Float into the river bound for Naples and India, down the river and out to drop the pilot by the Bar Lightship where the engines were rung 'full away' for Naples, 2,225 miles away. Down the Irish Sea, past Land's End and Ushant and into a Bay of Biscay racked by equinoctial gales. Past Gibraltar into the relative peace of the Mediterranean, south of Sardinia, Cape Tuelada and Cape Carbonara, past Capri and Ischia and into the Bay of Naples. More cargo work then southwards again through the Strait of Messina with Etna smoking gently to cheer *Kasenga* on her way to Port Said and the passage of the canal once more. From Suez she went once again direct to Bombay, this time punching into the north-east monsoon as she cleared the Gulf of Aden. And now Jack began to see more of India as *Kasenga* went by way of Karachi south round Dondra Head and up through the Bay of Bengal to Sandheads, that named piece of sea, out of sight of land, where the Hooghly pilot comes aboard from the trim white yacht which is the pilot cutter to take the ship up that very difficult river, past Diamond Head where the currents are strong enough to spin a ship out of control should the pilot make a serious mistake and up the long river to Calcutta and into the Kidderpore docks, where discharging is completed and loading begins, this time not for home but for the United States. Tea and rattans, cashews and desiccated coconuts, palm oil and plumbago and cotton, both raw and woven. Down the river and out to sea at Sandheads. Four days to Madras and two and a half to Colombo. Eleven across the Arabian Sea into the Red Sea to Port Sudan once more for cotton. Northwards to Suez and the canal again, bunkers at Port Said then westwards through the Mediterranean to Oran before crossing the wintry Atlantic to Boston.

The Atlantic crossing was typical for the time of year. Cold, grey and wet, with gale following gale putting up seas which the bows shattered into clouds of spray but whose weight flooded the well decks from time to time. The motion of the ship made all normal activities, even the simple matter of getting about the ship, akin to an assault course and maintaining a sleeping posture in a bunk took as much effort as a modest walk. By now, when the opportunities for chipping and painting were so much diminished by the weather Jack was standing watch as part of the three man group who were on duty with the mate of the watch; one steering, one on lookout on the fo'c's'le head in suitable weather or on the bridge if not, as in the North Atlantic, and one on stand-by, keeping warm and making tea, at all times ready to respond to the mate's whistle, one blast of which would bring him to the bridge if not at a run, then swiftly. The call might be to secure a rope or piece of gear which had come adrift, to investigate an unexplained noise, to trim the ventilators which governed the air circulation in the holds so, that spray and rain were kept out but the flow of air was maintained. This was a particularly important task with a rice cargo which is stowed so that tunnels are left among the bags in the form of a noughts and crosses frame, with vertical spaces at the intersections. A good circulation of air is essential if the cargo is not to sweat and swell with disastrous consequences. Turning ventilators could be a wet and hazardous job involving crossing decks occasionally swept by the seas, climbing to the tops of mast houses and working the ventilators round as the motion of the ship tried to fling one back to the deck. Nor was steering a light task for *Kasenga* did not have the luxury of a telemotor system of pipes containing oil under pressure to transmit the movements of the wheel to the steering engine beneath the poop. Chains transmitted the movements of the wheel down to the main deck where iron rods running in rollers carried the messages onward to the steering engine; all these rods and chains had to be physically moved by the action of turning the wheel. No light task when the seas, constantly throwing the ship off course, demanded continuous movements of the wheel. A period on stand-by after a two-hour trick at the wheel was a welcome relief, provided that one wasn't called out to grub about among the rods and chains on the seaswept deck to seek out some bit of cargo matting, or loose rope or whatever had jammed the steering gear, a fortunately not too frequent occurrence, particularly after the decks had been swept clean by the sea for a few days.

Westwards went *Kasenga* pursuing her Great Circle course into higher latitudes, passing north of the Azores before running down past Sable Island and Nova Scotia, and onto the Gulf of Maine and Massachusetts Bay to pick up the Boston pilot from his schooner before coming to rest, under his guidance, in Boston Harbour. No sooner was the ship tied up than off came the hatches and the work of discharging the cargo began. When the discharging of the Boston cargo was completed on went the hatches and tarpaulins, in went the battens and the wedges and off went *Kasenga* to sea again, round Cape Cod and down past Block Island and Montauk point, along the southern shore of Long Island and past the Ambrose light vessel before making her way through the Verrezano narrows and into the East River to tie up to a pier in Brooklyn; not for her the fancy passenger piers in the Hudson River, but the workaday freight piers and warehouses of Brooklyn, where the last of the North American cargo was discharged. Again the ship swarming with stevedores, or longshoremen as they describe themselves in that part of the world. Again the clatter of hatchboards being removed or replaced and the clang of hatch beams being dumped on the deck or into their slots in the hatch coamings. The rattle of winches, the pinging of the derrick guys as the loads came on them and the shadows of cargo slings swinging across the decks. Noise and apparent confusion, strangers all over the ship, until the holds are empty and swept and cleaned, the hatches covered and the ship ready to move down to Baltimore, her first loading port for the East. Down past the low-lying New

Jersey coast, past Atlantic City to Cape May and across the mouth of Delaware Bay. Onwards to Cape Charles at the southern end of Chesapeake Bay and northwards up the Bay to Baltimore to load for India. The heavy products of the developed West for the developing sub-continent. Steel plates, railway iron and reinforcing rods. Fencing wire and oil lamps, tractors and glass and motor cars and all manner of smaller manufactured items. Then out again down the Bay and up the coast to New York, another visit to Brooklyn, more cargo work, more swarms of people.

In those days, when ships were much more numerous than they are today, and when so many of them carried four apprentices, all youngsters between the ages of sixteen and twenty-one, there was in New York, at the Hotel Chelsea at 222 West 23rd Street, a remarkable institution known as The British Apprentice Club. It was founded in December 1921 and issue No. 1 of Volume 1 of its magazine included a small pamphlet, setting out its aims, which is so relevant to the time when Jack Arnot first went to sea as to be worth reproducing in full.

'Americans who were in England during the war or in the winter after the Armistice remember with deepest gratitude the boundless hospitality, the true-hearted practical friendship lavished by the British of all conditions and classes upon our boys in uniform on their soil. That hospitality was from the heart. That friendship counted no cost. Both were given to the utmost limit of individual power. And why?

'Our own best beloved can never come home again. Let us think of American fathers and mothers and sisters, so far away, and take their boys into our boys' stead.

'And that they did – not in theory, but in loving, working, literal fact.

'The memory of it, precious as it is, imposes upon us of America a strong desire to show our answering mind.

'One means lies close at hand – an opportunity with the British Merchant Marine to whom our debt can never be paid. Forty-seven thousand of that gallant service were killed or wounded by submarine attack alone, in our common cause in the Great War. Over half of all our Expeditionary Force was carried by the British Merchant Marine to France. And that the A.E.F. after its arrival in France possessed means to live and do the work it came to do was again, to an overwhelming degree, due to the sleepless gallantry of British Merchant sailors. British merchant ships, in times of peace, lie in New York longer than in any other port in the world. Many of them carry cadet officers – "apprentices" – of whom, therefore, there are in normal times, always from 65 to 150 in our harbour. These are responsible, intelligent, well-taught, clean-cut, young Britons, from 14 to 20 years old, sons of clergy, professional men, sea captains, business men, tradesmen, many of whom have matriculated for Oxford or gone through a public school, before nautical training in school and at sea.

'Practically every British Merchant Marine officer has been an "apprentice". Sir Ernest Shackleton was such – Sir James Charles and Sir Herbert J. Haddock.

'Lying at our docks for weeks without personal friends, with no knowledge of the town, and by a wise provision without money to spend (since they are confronted as a rule by the worst and wickedest that the town has to show), they have sailed away at last – generations of them – glad to shake off the dust of an unlovely America.

'Therein lay the opportunity.

'Last December, in a suite of rooms in the Hotel Chelsea, 222 West 23rd Street, the British Apprentice Club was started – started just as a matter of experiment, by two American ladies whose eyes had seen the glory of our debt rolled up by English love and sorrow, on English soil, in the trail of the war. The plan of these two women was, to offer to British boys so many thousand miles from home, a little, cozy, homelike club, always open, as nearly as might be like their own mothers' sitting rooms – a place where they might meet and make friends, find relaxation, see their home papers, hear music or make it, take tea and supper and do or find, in short, whatever their individual tastes or needs from time to time might suggest.

'The British Apprentice Club, advertised by word of mouth from Calcutta to the White Sea, from Cape Town to Melbourne, has prospered with a strong and certain growth. Between May 1st and July 30th 1922, it received 1,171 visits for afternoon, evening, or all day, from cadet members – and in this slack shipping season. The life of the club has enriched in many directions. Mrs. Spaulding, the resident manager, finds an endless variety of service to render, from dealing with colds and toothaches or playing the piano for sing-songs to conducting parties to tennis or the zoo; from helping or getting help in troublesome private affairs to visiting hospitals, getting up dances or arranging weekend parties for visits to the country homes of new friends.

'A growing number of Americans are now actively participating in this enterprise, the nature of which is essentially one of spontaneous friendship. It is hoped, then, that the officials of the British Shipping Companies, one and all, will cooperate in two ways: first, by making the Club known to their Cadets as they enter port; and second, by making known to the Club management any way in which the Club might increase its usefulness.'

The B.A.C. was still going in the Second World War. During his time as an apprentice Jack Arnot used the club and derived great benefit from its existence. It is more than easy for a merchant seaman to spend a lifetime at sea and see little more than the docksides and 'the worst and wickedest' of the world. You could call the B.A.C. the brain child of do-gooders, but it worked and was appreciated by many thousands of apprentices. Items from the B.A.C. Review give indications of the club's activities. From *Notes on 1922*:

'March 26. Dame Clara Butt, giving a song recital in the largest auditorium in New York, the Hippodrome, sent the B.A.C. a present of twenty tickets, with her greetings. At the close of the concert, the cadets, who were all in uniform, stood up en masse and gave her three good cheers. Whereupon Dame Clara, who had been told of their desire, sang, specially for them, "Land of Hope and Glory" and "Annie Laurie". Fancy the effect of that big voice, in that big hall, before that big audience, focused on one point!

And 'Oct 31st. On the invitation of Miss Margaret Stevenson, Mrs Spaulding and cadets Barnard, Newcomb, Boulton, Ralph, Bell, Verney, Thomas, Horne, Harries, V.H. Vizer, Mugford, Darlington, Baker, Nicholas, Hanningan, Verall, Rigby, Barker, Chambers, Hall, Sprigg, Bowyer, Graville, Liddiard, Ewer, Rogers, Russel and Crisp attended a Hallowe'n dance given by the probationary nurses of the Presbyterian Hospital.

And in 1923

'July 4th. American Independence Day, celebrated by cadet parties visiting Sound beach and Bedford hills.'

The review indicates in the clearest possible way the degree to which the club was appreciated. From its foundation in June to the end of 1922 apprentices made 2,911 visits to it, and in 1923, the first full year, 5,345, or fifteen a day, by which time membership had reached 1,292.

April 1924, and time to renew the voyage with a twenty-one day passage across the Atlantic, into the Mediterranean and onwards to Port Said, where the ship was bunkered, a necessary but unpleasant job involving dirt and swarms of none too honest Egyptians all over the ship. Accommodation doors and portholes are sealed against the dust with brown paper and paste and the apprentices desert their half deck for the duration of the coaling exercise. The coal lighters come alongside and stages are rigged against the ship's side, those lower down projecting further from the side than those higher up so that they form a sort of staircase. Men stand on every step and the bags of coal are passed upward from stage to stage until they are dumped on deck and emptied into the bunkers. Hundreds of labourers are involved and the loading of hundreds of tons of coal into the bunkers is completed extraordinarily quickly. The labourers leave, taking with them whatever they have managed to steal, the stages are removed and the ship is washed down, though it will be many washings later that she is clean again. The brown paper is stripped off the doors and portholes of the accommodation, the coal dust which has managed to filter through the best-made barriers is cleaned away, and the ship hangs her searchlight over the bow and moves into the canal to, emerge at Suez some fifteen hours later and resume the voyage to Karachi.

Once more down the Red Sea, past Perim and Aden and Socotra and into the Arabian Sea with the south-west monsoon up her stern bustling the ship along on her last long passages before a spell of hard work on the Indian coast, during which passages range from three days to three hours, with hatches on and off at the end and beginning of each in the hot, damp atmosphere of the middle of the Indian summer. Two days after Karachi comes Bombay, then a day and a half to Mangalore, 388 miles further south on India's west coast. Then a day to Tillicherry followed by five hours to Calicut, then nine hours to Cochin, discharging cargo at every port of call. A day to Tuticorin and half a day across the Gulf of Manaar to Colombo, followed by a relatively long haul of 1,257 miles to Rangoon before striking northwards to Calcutta, the final discharging and first loading port. Final discharging port meant no rest or pause, more the opposite, for discharging and loading go on together until the ship takes her pilot down the Hooghly to Sandheads, bound for Rangoon for rice.

Off the southernmost point of the Irawaddy delta lies the Alguada reef and as *Kasenga* passed by the second mate, keeping the afternoon watch, noticed that the lighthouse's Red Ensign was flying upside down, which is one of the standard distress signals, and was also at half mast. All attempts to communicate with the lighthouse failed and so a radio message was sent to Rangoon, which message resulted in the despatch of a tug and a doctor to the lighthouse to discover that one of the keepers had fallen and broken a leg. No doubt he would have blessed Mr. King, the second mate, for having noticed the signal.

Rangoon for rice. A difficult cargo to load requiring constant supervision of the coolies in the holds if the airways are to be left free to channel air through the cargo. It is much easier to forget them, or build them carelessly so that the airflow is not clean, than to do the job properly, so the mates and apprentices are up and down the ladders into the holds times without number. Excellent exercise leading to sound slumber when the day's work is done, but not to the extent of entirely eliminating the desire for a run ashore from time to time, perhaps to see some of the 'worst and wickedest', for there is no B.A.C. in Rangoon! To look into an empty hold is to conclude that it is so cavernous as to be unfillable, but in due course Rangoon has filled its share of the space and *Kasenga* makes the three-and-a-half-day passage to Vizagapatam in the state of Orissa before working her way southwards by way of Cocanada, Madras, Pondicherry and Cudalore and, thence round Dondra Head and the Pointe de Galle to Colombo, the final loading port.

Tea and plumbago, cashews and desiccated coconuts. The rattle of winches and the pinging of runners and guys as the last of the homeward cargo comes aboard. Lighters delivered full to the ship by small steam tugs, and when empty taken back to the wharves for loading again. The harbour full of shipping, all lying to buoys and working cargo over both sides to and from lighters. A P. & O. passenger liner bound for Hong Kong making a brief stop, as is an Orient liner bound for Australia. Sunlight and heat and noise and purpose as the raw materials required by European and North American people and factories are put aboard the ships which will carry them home. Desperate, or seemingly desperate, arguments between foremen and hatchmen, between hatchmen and winch drivers, between hatchmen and coolies in the holds. Every conversation looks and sounds like the beginning of a blood feud but all end suddenly in peace. In the breaks for meals the lightermen prepare their food on the decks of their vessels and the coolies on board unwrap the provisions they have brought with them and squat in corners all over the ship to eat. When the cargo is in the lighters are towed away, the hatch beams and boards and tarpaulins go on and are battened down. The derricks come down and are securely lashed in their cradles for the long passage home. The pilot comes aboard, the ship is cast off from her buoy and moves through the crowded harbour and out between the breakwater ends to sea, dropping the pilot and, fully loaded, starts the true homeward passage.

At the strait of Bab el Mandeb at the southern end of the Red Sea lies the island of Perim, where *Kasenga* pauses to bunker before moving on to Port Sudan, intolerably hot at this time of year, the beginning of August, with air-conditioning barely thought of yet and certainly not provided in ships such as *Kasenga*. Northwards again, through the canal and the eastern Mediterranean, past Sicily and Sardinia and up to Marseilles to begin discharging the cargo. Not much is left there, most of the cargo being for British ports, but there is some for Dunkirk as well before *Kasenga* makes the last short 105 mile leg across the Channel to Tilbury where, seventeen months give or take a few days after she signed on her crew in Newcastle, she paid off all but those remaining with her round the British coast.

Seventeen months; 57,000 miles; fifty-eight ports and six passages of the Suez canal. The Jack Arnot who came home from his first voyage was a very much more experienced lad than he who set out in April 1923. Well set on the road to becoming a sailor, he had grown to his full six feet and had filled out to become a very solid young man, not bad looking to boot. The interest in engineering which he had developed in *Conway* and which had led to his winning an engineering prize there, had continued and, though he had not the quickest mind in the Merchant Service he had the important quality of 'stickability' in quantity.

Chapter 2

City of Harvard

The seventeen-month voyage in *Kasenga* earned twenty-one days of leave, including the days of signing off and signing on the next ship. The voyage had got Jack nearly half way in his quest for the thirty-six months of sea time needed before he could sit his second mate's ticket; nineteen months to go. He began chipping away at the deficit when he signed on *City of Harvard* in Birkenhead on 20th September 1924 at his current rate of pay of thirty shillings a month.

City of Harvard was another ex-German ship, formerly the *Giessen*, built by Bremer Vulkan in 1907. A shade smaller than *Kasenga* at 7,091 tons she none the less had good accommodation for some twenty passengers, a rather unusual number, for passenger accommodation on that scale would never have been built into a British ship where the requirement to carry a doctor when more than twelve passengers are carried would make such a number uneconomic. No doubt in the early postwar years the accommodation could be filled at prices which would pay for the doctor without too much trouble.

The voyage was almost a repeat of Jack's first voyage except that after the first visit to India she came back to European and U.K. ports before returning to India and then did the same again before crossing the Atlantic to New York, her only North American port. It was during this visit to New York that Jack's engineering bent got its first demonstration since he had won a prize of a brass candlestick for the subject in the *Conway*. He had, for some reason, always been interested in the gyroscope and its application as the basis of the gyro compass. He had corresponded with the Sperry Company and, during his stay in New York, was able to persuade Captain Ryder-Large to let him attend a two-week course, at Sperry, on the gyro compass, emerging on 27th August 1925 with their operator's certificate number 556. In 1925 gyro compasses were thin on the ground, to put it at its

17

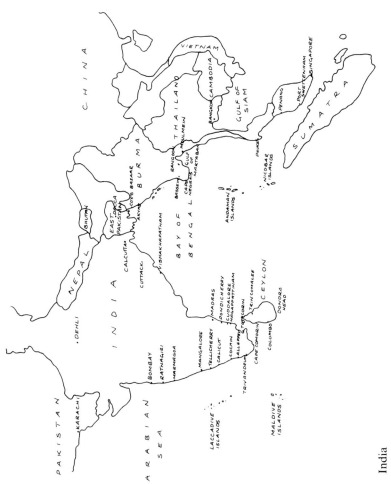

India

City of Harvard (National Maritime Museum)

City of Hong Kong (National Maritime Museum)

best, being seen only in the largest of passenger liners, and they were not entirely trusted. Seafarers are an ultra-conservative race. An eye for the future, for the first gyro that Jack was to encounter and use at sea was in *City of Lille*, seven years later.

City of Harvard must have been a ship with a reputation and regarded as of consequence by her owners, for her Master was a man of some distinction, Commander E. Ryder-Large, D.S.O. O.B.E. R.D. R.N.R., both in name and decorations a man more likely to be master of a passenger ship than a cargo liner. Apart from the distinction of her Master she carried four mates, which would relieve the mate himself of most of his watchkeeping duties and allow him to concentrate on keeping the ship right up to the mark. Perhaps she carried more than twenty passengers, for she ran to printed passenger lists in the form of a booklet with a picture of the ship on the front cover, with pages listing the senior officers, the passengers by destination, the approximate arrival dates and lists of the company's agents. The passenger list which Jack preserved covered the passage from Bombay to Colombo, Madras, Rangoon and Calcutta on her second 'circuit'. It advises that the S.S. *City of Harvard* will sail on 18th October 1925 for Colombo, arriving about 21st October, for Madras, arriving about 24th October, for Rangoon, arriving about 29th October and for Calcutta arriving about 3rd November, and that the agents are Forbes, Forbes, Campbell and Co. Ltd. of Forbes Building, Home Street, P.O. Box No 79, Fort, Bombay.

After listing the senior officers it goes on to list the Colombo passengers as follows:

> H.M. The King of Belgians
> H.M. The Queen of Belgians
> Captain Goffinet, A.D.C.
> Professor Nolf
> Valet to His Majesty
> Maid to Her Majesty
> Mrs. H. M. Bartram-Kiddell
> Mr. G S. Bassous
> Miss Harper
> Capt. C. W. McClellan
> Mrs. Nagarvalla
> Miss Nagarvalla
> Lady Robinson
> Miss Robinson

And for Calcutta: Mrs. J. W. Milne
And as a deck passenger to Colombo:
Mr. Johan Ahali.

City of Harvard, under the guidance of Captain Ryder-Large, with the assistance of his four mates, four apprentices, his surgeon, his Chief Engineer and assistant engineers, his Chief Steward and assistant stewards no doubt delivered his distinguished passengers safely to Colombo, for the ship continued her voyage to her listed ports and at the last of them, Calcutta, began loading for home, completing her cargo at Madras and Colombo before returning to Leith, where she arrived on 16th January 1926 after calling at Plymouth, London, Dunkirk and Antwerp. Another 56,798 miles, another sixteen months of sea time in the book, another string of lessons learned but still three months short of time for second mate.

But Ellermans were not, in common with all shipowners at that time, over generous with leave and eighteen days later, on 3rd February 1926, Jack signed on the *City of Hong Kong*, this time not as an apprentice but as Fifth Mate, an unusual appointment, for most cargo liners carried three or four mates, the fourth sometimes being described as extra third, but only the larger passenger liners customarily carried more than that. However, *City of Hong Kong* was more than a simple cargo liner, she was a cargo/passenger ship with accommodation for ninety-nine passengers and was a relatively new addition to the fleet. Jack's biggest ship yet, she was of 9,579 tons, built by Earle's of Hull in 1924, quite a change from turn of the century reparations tonnage and distinctly, sailing as uncertificated fifth mate, a feather in Jack's cap, recognition of his capability as a seaman and of the regard in which he had been held by his former Masters, whose reports on their apprentices at the end of each voyage must have included good ones for young Jack Arnot. And though they may have been ungenerous with leave, Ellerman and Bucknall were considerate of Jack's need to get back to the U.K. as soon as possible after he had his thirty-six months of sea time in so that he could sit for second mate, for they sent him off for what, after his two long voyages, must have seemed like a weekend jaunt round the Isle of Wight. More than that, it is true, 12,702 miles to the West Coast of India and back, three months and a day, and going no further east than Bombay, from Birkenhead and back to Liverpool, a short voyage by previous standards, but providing the essential time at sea to bring the total over three years. The apprenticeship was over and the way was clear to make the attempt on the first of the professional exams.

Because the voyages had each been so long the sea time was interrupted by only two leaves totalling thirty-nine days, including signing on and off days, so Jack had got in this three years of sea time in just over three years and one month, taking 126,519 miles, just short of six times round the world to achieve it. But owing to the services in which Ellerman and Bucknall were engaged he had not yet crossed either the equator or that other imaginary benchmark drawn across the face of the globe, the date line, though he had crossed the prime meridian rather more frequently than the fourteen times he had been through the Suez Canal, for each jaunt to Antwerp or Dunkirk, and the passage round the North of Scotland all involve a crossing, whilst the trip up to the London Docks and out to sea again scores twice. Tilbury, though, is east of the meridian so *Kasenga*'s closing passage from Dunkirk to Tilbury did not involve moving from East to West longitude and back again.

The entries in Jack's mother's 'book of family doings', a notebook recording significant, and insignificant, events and dates, are succinct.

> May 6th, Jack paid off *City of Hong Kong*. Came home.
> May 10th, Jack goes to school in Liverpool.

Truly the end of the beginning.

Chapter 3

Jack goes to school in Liverpool

Just the sort of thing that mothers would say of a nineteen-year-old son who, having completed a testing apprenticeship at sea and having got his time in for second mate, was going to Cleaver and Hutchinson's college to prepare himself for the exam. Hardly 'going to school'! The College was owned and run by two R.N.R. Extra Masters in an old Victorian house in Faulkiner Street, close by the Anglican Cathedral, and did not survive its founders.

Theoretically, if the shipowner had fulfilled his part of the bargain to teach the apprentice the business of a ship's officer a young man should be able, on the completion of his sea time, to come ashore and sit the exam without further ado. But even in those companies which set the highest standards, giving their apprentices 'school' work to do during their voyages, work based on the syllabus for the forthcoming examination, the demands of life in a working ship and the nature of teenage boys made such an unprepared attempt unlikely to succeed. Whilst the physical aspects of seamanship and cargo work were mostly well learned by experience under the hand of hard-driving mates and boatswains, the theoretical side would be less well taught. The routine business of watchkeeping, of steering, of the rules for the avoidance of collision, of taking soundings, and sights and working them up were well practised but the underlying theory less well understood.

Boys being boys the schoolwork, where it was set, was almost invariably left until the final passage home. Many are the exercises in trigonometrical identities, in astronomical navigation, in meteorology, which have been rushed through in bad weather in the Bay of Biscay in a flooded half deck in between watches. Many is the essay which has had its concluding paragraphs cut short of their proper glory by the arrival of the pilot at the Bar Lightship. It is something of a wonder that the work was done at all, and less of a wonder that the lads in ships whose owners set no school work completed their sea time unprepared for the exam.

So it was that in every port where the exams were held there were schools which ran courses for the preparation of men for the three main exams, Second and First Mate, and Master. In those days the exams were held in seven ports, Cardiff, Glasgow, Liverpool, London, Newcastle, Hull and Leith; fortnightly in the five major ports and monthly in Hull and Leith. The courses at the colleges were geared to this timetable and also had to provide for a continuous intake of students as their ships came home, sea time accumulated, and the ex-apprentices and serving mates came into the colleges for preparation. Quite a formidable educational task but with one fundamental advantage; all the students were eager to learn, and eager to complete the course and leave, qualified, at the earliest opportunity, and not just because of driving ambition. Only the men from the better companies would be being paid at all. The rest were living off their fat (?).

Attendance at the colleges had advantages beyond the underlying need to master the theory. On leaving the examination room the candidates would repair to the college with their papers, which would be analysed by the staff so that any patterns of questioning which an examiner might develop could be identified and used to help in preparing students. With exams at fortnightly intervals patterning would be hard to avoid. And whilst the written papers had times ranging from one and a half to three hours the final session, the 'oral' had no time limit. The syllabus was wide ranging with a catch-all item at the end. The syllabus for Second Mate, Oral, was as follows.

1. a. Rigging of ships. Strength of ropes, wire and hemp. Rigging purchases of various kinds and knowledge of power gained by various purchases. Knotting and splicing hemp and steel ropes with strict reference to current practice. Seizings, racking, chain stoppers, etc.
   b. Sending topmasts up and down.
   c. Bending, setting and taking in fore and aft sails. Management of boats under oars and sail and in heavy weather. Beaching or landing. Coming alongside.
   d. Helm orders. Conning the ship.

2. a. Marking and use of the ordinary lead line.
   b. Use and upkeep of mechanical logs and sounding machines.

c. Use and upkeep of engine room and other telegraphs.

d. Rocket and line-throwing apparatus.

3. a. Anchors and Cables. Use, upkeep and survey.

b. Knowledge of use and maintenance of deck appliances and steering gear.

c. Fire extinguishing apparatus – steam, chemical and other appliances.

4. a. Preparations and precautions for getting under way. Duties prior to proceeding to sea, making harbour or coming alongside, especially at the after end of the ship.

b. Keeping an anchor watch. Dragging anchor.

c. Duties of officer of watch. Use of compass to ascertain risk of collision.

5. a. A full knowledge of the content and application of the regulations for preventing collision at sea. (Candidates will not be placed in the position of handling a sailing ship, but will be expected to recognise a sailing ship's lights and to have knowledge of her possible manoeuvres according to the direction of the wind.)

b. Distress and pilot signals; penalties for misuse.

c. British uniform system of buoyage.

d. An intelligent use of 'Notices to Mariners'. (Candidates will not be required to commit these to memory.)

6. Signals.

To send and receive signals in:-

a. British semaphore up to eight words per minute.

b. Morse code by flash lamp up to six words per minute.

c. International code of signals.

7. Practical.

a. To read and understand a barometer, thermometer, hydrometer and hygrometer. (The instruments supplied by the Meterological Office will be taken as standard.)

b. To use an azimuth mirror, pelorus (bearing plate) or other instrument for taking bearings; to place these bearings on a chart, having corrected for given compass error.

c. To use a sextant for taking vertical and horizontal angles; to read a sextant both on and off the arc.

d. To correct a sextant into which has been introduced some or all of perpendicularity, side and index errors.

e. To find the index error of a given sextant.

f. To check chronometers by signal made by buzzer or other method; to compare two chronometers.

8. The examiner may ask the candidate questions arising out of the written work, if he deems it necessary on account of any weakness shown by the candidate. (This applies particularly to paper 5.)

(Paper five covered cargo work and elementary ship construction.)

That Oral, and six papers totalling fourteen and a half hours on Navigation and Chartwork, and 'Knowledge of Principles', through to English, comprised the target to be attacked with the aid of the appropriate school and its staff. Small wonder that a British certificate of competency was so prized a document.

Jack went to live in digs in Aigburth, a modest tram ride from the school. The days at the college were devoted to mastering the syllabus under the tutelage of the lecturers. At the bigger schools, such as the Liverpool Technical College, these were, for the most part, men with those qualifications which Jack now sought, who had 'swallowed the anchor' and gone into education. And a mixed bunch they were too. The dry as dust, with whom it was a struggle to stay awake, the tipplers, who were great in the morning but not so good in the afternoon and the entertainers whose lectures were peppered with anecdote stringing the essential facts together while keeping the class alert and interested. There was a wealth of experience in the lecturing staff ranging from that in very large passenger ships to those whose seafaring had been in the hungriest of tramps. One had spent time in cable ships and maintained through thick and thin that he was privy to the secret of the location of a bed of diamonds beneath the Atlantic. His tale was that, in grappling for a broken submarine telegraph cable, the grapnel had surfaced with diamond-bearing mud on its flukes. Whereupon the ship had dropped a marker buoy and spent the next two days not grappling for cable but taking sight after sight to fix the position of the diamonds with great accuracy, after which the buoy was recovered and normal operations resumed. With everyone sworn to secrecy the voyage was concluded, but there is no record of anyone going back to the spot and getting rich.

Others had been involved in actual collisions and other incidents, which lent drama to their lectures and a touch of reality to the business using of little wooden models, or green and red and white clusters of lights, to demonstrate how to avoid the collision situation. In the 'rule of the road' sessions that part of 5.a. of the Oral syllabus, which is in parentheses, became a frightening reality requiring mental agility of a high order which, if not achieved in the examination room would lead to certain failure.

The game, in which the examiners delighted, depended on the twin facts that the arc of visibility of each of a sailing ship's three lights was known, as was the fact that a square-rigged ship could sail no closer than six points off the wind. The examiner would sit at one side of a table, with the candidate the other, and would place a red, green or white bead on the table and make a statement, coupled with a question, in the following form:

Assume a green light.
> 'That bears North from you, the wind is East. How is she heading?' Allowing seconds only for the panic to subside the candidate's reasoning would take the following line:
> Green light. Shows from right ahead to two points abaft the beam on the starboard side, so she must be heading between South and East North East.
> But with the wind East she cannot point eastwards of South South East or North North East.
> So she can only be heading between South and South South East.

That reads simply enough but a string of them fired at a candidate weakened by fourteen and a half hours of written papers was an ideal way of finding out who could think on his feet and who could not. The bracketed part of Oral 5.a. probably sent more men back for a second attempt than any other part of the Oral exam, unless the sheer detailed knowledge of the regulations for the prevention of collision at sea demanded by the examiners did that. These rules were contained in thirty-one 'articles' covering fifteen pages of print and had to be known word for word. Learning them was a daunting task. Beyond that, because of the breadth of the syllabus there was almost unlimited ground for the examiner to plough. Jack nearly lost the battle on the buoyancy regulations for lifeboats. The indications were for a question on wooden boats, but the examiner opted for steel.

Even in preparation for the somewhat chancy Oral the college could offer great help, for again, after it the candidates repaired to the college and reported, as best they could, the questions they had been asked and by which examiner. Over the years a vast body of knowledge related to each examiner's pet questions had been built up which was of immense value in preparing for the Oral. It was indeed maintained that the somewhat elderly examiner, Captain X, was so set in his ways that he asked seventy-six questions, always in the same order, and that if you knew the answers to them you had nothing to fear, but if you got just one wrong it knocked him out of his stride and there was no knowing where he would go next, to the severe disadvantage of the candidate.

The days went by in serious study with just the occasional lapse when the beer and sandwich lunch accidentally went into extra time. Evenings, after an excellent high tea in the digs, were spent in further study with an occasional visit to the pictures or perhaps the Rialto ballroom. Being intelligent, hard working and well prepared, Jack sat the exam on 26th June, after six weeks of study. He failed, but history does not relate which paper. The rules required that the whole exam had to be passed in one attempt, with no re-sitting of failed papers or carrying forward of passes, so Jack took the next opportunity to sit again a fortnight later and, at that second attempt, passed. Family doings records:

June 29th. Jack failed in exam.
July 13th. Jack passed exam.

* * *

July 10th. Jack came home.
And then . . . August 25th. Jack sailed fourth mate *City of Cairo*.

The next chapter was to begin.

Chapter 4

'One and a half years as third of three watchkeeping officers'

After the second mate's ticket comes the first mate's ticket. The requirements are simple. Achieve the age of twenty-one and a half, serve eighteen months as third of three watchkeeping officers or better. And pass the exam. Jack's accumulation of the sea time began in the *City of Cairo* quite soon after he emerged from the examination room with the basic ticket. With his shiny new second mate's ticket making what he hoped was an obvious bulge in his pocket, Jack joined the *City of Cairo* on 3rd August 1926 as fourth mate. Despite his rank of fourth mate the time spent would count for his ticket as he was regarded as being in charge of the mate's four to eight watch, freeing the mate for other duties, for the mate, if the master is the managing director, is the general manager of the ship. For all the time from now until he achieved the position of master Jack's lot would be watchkeeping at sea and cargo work in port. Whilst fourth mate, or mate, he would keep the four to eight watch morning and evening. When elevated to third mate, the eight to twelve and as second mate the twelve to four. Whatever the watch the basic routine would be the same.

Called at 'one bell', fifteen minutes before the eight bells which would mark the change of watch, he would prepare and arrive on the bridge with a minute or two to spare. A visit to the chartroom to look at the log book and the chart and he would go out onto the bridge or into the wheelhouse where the departing mate of the watch would hand over, telling him the course being steered, the engine revolutions and speed, the compass error and any upcoming alterations of course or special instructions from the master. Weather forecasts, if any, would be discussed, the trim of the ventilators and the way the ship was steering reviewed. Vessels in sight would be pointed out and mention made of events of note during the past four hours.

City of Cairo (National Maritime Museum)

City of Dunedin (World Ship Society)

Land or lights in sight identified, the relieved mate would complete the writing of the log and go below.

That is the theory. Practice is sometimes different. Having gleaned all the basic information from the log, the chart and the Master's order book and checked the course on the wheelhouse blackboard, the relieving mate would meet with the man he was relieving and be told something like: 'She's heading straight between the anchors, keep the foremast right ahead. Goodnight!'

Alone on the bridge the watchkeeper paces back and forth, keeping a lookout, watching other shipping, ensuring that potential collision situations do not occur by making the necessary alterations of course to avoid them or just standing on if no risk exists. Only in extreme situations will the engines be moved from their set revolutions and by the time that becomes necessary the master will almost certainly be on the bridge, either having been called or having come up by instinct of necessity. Periodically on passing through the wheelhouse the mate checks the course being steered by looking at the compass, and leans on the quartermaster should the standard of steering not be good enough. At least once in each watch, cloud cover permitting, a compass bearing of a star or the sun will be used to check the error of the standard compass and, if it has changed, the course to steer will be altered to cope. In the middle of the watch the stand by man, on coming up to relieve the wheel, brings tea for the mate, and with luck, toast or biscuits.

If the ship is in sight of land half hourly bearings will be taken and plotted on the chart and appropriate course corrections made to keep the ship 'on the line'. Periodically the weather conditions and the barometer reading will be noted in the log, as will be all alterations of course and speed and significant fixes of position. When the man at the wheel is changed he hands over the course to the relief (it will be written on a blackboard anyway) and reports it to the mate before going down. The lookout calls lights and traffic as he sees it, reporting it, if he is on the fo'c's'le head by striking the ship's bell. Father may come up, to keep an eye on a new mate, such as Jack in his early days in the *City of Cairo*, or just for a chat. The ship moves onwards, rolling or not, pitching or not, taking spray or heavy water aboard, or not, but moving slowly but firmly towards her destination.

After four hours, more or less, according to whether or not the clock is being 'flogged' for changes of longitude during the watch, relief comes and after handing over the watch to his successor the mate can go below.

In the open ocean the position must be fixed periodically. The most accurate fix is by star sights at dawn or dusk so, more than likely, star sights

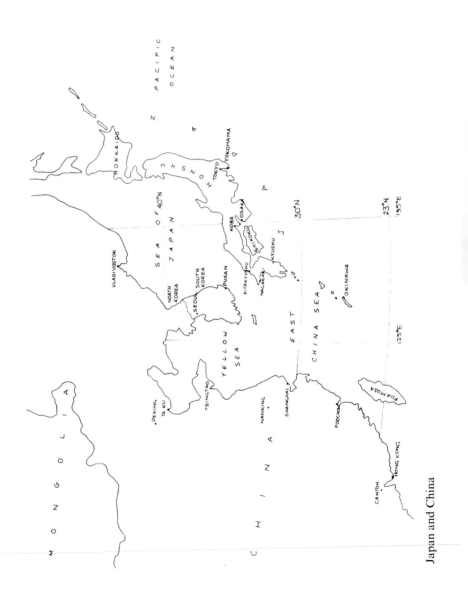

Japan and China

fall to the fourth mate, keeping the four to eight watch. The stars to use are, if cloud cover permits, selected in advance so that the position lines derived would cross each other at a broad angle, three stars and hence three position lines being the ideal, enclosing a triangle within which the ship must be; the smaller the triangle the better the position. At dawn the stars can be selected visually before they fade, but at dusk they can either be selected from the almanac for their relative bearings and altitudes, or from memory, so that in either case the position lines form a satisfactory triangle. Having seen the star fix the master might well alter course slightly, if necessary, to get the ship back on the line by the following noon.

By tradition the Noon position is the prime position of the day, the anchor point. Again it is achieved by crossing two position lines but this time both obtained by observation of the sun at different times. For longitude the sight was usually taken about breakfast time when the sun would be bearing nearly east to give a position line which ran north and south. This was 'Run up' to noon by transferring it along the ship's course at the ship's speed for the time between the sight and Noon. This was usually done by calculation, not by drawing. At Noon the sun's meridian altitude led quickly to the determination of the latitude at Noon and that, with the earlier sight for longitude, gave the Noon position.

It was customary for all the mates, and perhaps the senior apprentice, to take longitude sights at times of their own choosing and work them up to Noon. The second mate decided what time, ship's time, Noon would most likely be and informed the master and mates. A few minutes before noon the fourth mate, or perhaps the senior apprentice, would relieve the third mate as officer of the watch so that he, along with the master and the other mates could all take noon sights for latitude. By custom the altitudes were reported to the master who averaged them mentally and announced what meridian altitude was to be used for calculating latitude, whereupon the 'Noon Derby' began. All the mates calculated their noon positions, reported them to the master who again averaged them and announced the noon position. The averaging would seldom cover a spread of more than two or three miles, any result outside such a limit being discarded as a poor observation. Then the subsequent work was divided. The second mate calculated the course and distance to the next 'waypoint'. The mate calculated the course and distance run for the day from last noon, and the average speed, while the third mate calculated the amount of 'set' experienced over the past twenty-four hours. When all this was done and entered in the log everyone but the second mate, who had to remain on watch, could repair below for a noontide beer, or gin, or whatever. Five minutes past noon was regarded as being quite late enough for completion of the noon derby, for much of the calculation could be laid out in advance. By the use of the 'magic number', pre-calculated, the discovery of latitude was reduced to a single subtraction once the meridian altitude was known. The correction of the longitude for error of the latitude used in its determination at breakfast time could be reduced to a single mental multiplication sum. The format for the individual calculations of course and distance could be laid out in advance with many of the figures filled in. It all became a game, albeit a serious game, and woe betide the mate whose figures were not different enough to be nonsense but different enough to make the averaging difficult. The navigation was, in the main, extremely accurate.

The sixteen hours each day off watch were not entirely free. The mate had the job of keeping the ship physically in good shape, of keeping the official fair copy log, of seeing to all the cargo paper work, of managing and employing the hands, and completing numerous abstracts of information demanded by the owners. The second mate was responsible for the charts and chronometers. He had to get time signals at least once a day and to correct the charts from periodical notices to mariners, a time-consuming

Branksome Hall (World Ship Society)

task as a single correction might have to be made to two or more charts drawn to different scales. He had to see that the complement of charts was complete for the planned voyage and keep his registers up to date. Woe betide him if the master did not find the next chart required at the top to the heap! The third mate was responsible for lifeboats, their provisions, their water, their bungs. He was responsible for fire fighting equipment, for smoke helmets, for fire axes and sand buckets. For lifebuoys and rockets and flares. For keeping them in date and replacing them as their lives expired. The fourth mate was everybody's dogsbody.

Entering and leaving port the stations were different from what they are today. The master was, of course, on the bridge, as was the third mate, working the engine room telegraphs, supervising the man at the wheel and noting the times of the engine movements. The mate was on the fo'c's'le head, in charge of the anchors and the ropes at that end of the ship. The second mate was at the stern, seeing to the mooring or unmooring of that end of the ship, hence the reference to the after part of the ship in the syllabus for the oral part of the second mate's exam. The fourth mate was on the main deck, looking after the pilot ladder, the boat rope and the gangway.

In port, working cargo, the mate was in overall charge. For him the responsibility for loading the cargo so that the ship was trimmed properly and stable, neither too tender nor too stiff. For him the responsibility of seeing that tea was stowed nowhere near anything from which it could take taint, which is practically everything else. For him the responsibility of ensuring that cargo for Boston was not overstowed by cargo for a subsequent call at New York. For seeing that liquids were not stowed over absorbent solids, lest the containers should rupture. For seeing that the ship was filled, and that the agents had up-to-date information as to space remaining. The list is endless, and incorporates supervision of the cargo plan and the documentation of the cargo, manifests, bills of lading and the like. Life in port was hard for the mate.

The other mates spent their days on deck and in the holds, ensuring that the loading as planned by the mate actually followed the plan, and that the cargo was stowed suitably according to its nature. Airways in a bagged rice cargo. Dunnage and matting and talcum powder to prevent rubber sticking to itself or to the ship. Barrels stowed 'bung up and bilge free', and properly chocked. Camphor nowhere near tea. Bagged grain, or anything in sacks, loaded as close up to the deckhead as possible – the last tier is the one which causes all the sweat and the dockers would leave it out if they could get away with it. Everything properly lodged and secure so that the motion of the ship will not reduce a cased cargo to matchwood. The days, and nights if night work was the custom, spent climbing in and out of the holds to ensure that everything which had to went in, and that everything which went in would come out in good condition. Measuring the remaining space at the end of the day, marking up the cargo plan. Loading was hard work.

As was discharging. The right cargo for the port to come out, and nothing else. Pilferage to be discouraged by constant vigilance. Damaged cargo to be set aside for survey. If the holds were not completely open, the remaining hatch beams to be bolted in to prevent a snagged cargo hook lifting a beam out and depositing it, and hatchboards and possibly cargo, onto the heads of the men in the lower hold. The state of the cargo gear, the blocks, runners and guys to be kept under review. Watchmen to be sought for sensitive holds, those containing easily pilferable cargo, or highly desirable cargo, like beer or whisky. It takes no time at all for an insufficiently supervised and watched gang working whisky to become incapable of work and aggressive to boot. Hard and heavy work, long hours and limited time to go ashore for relaxation.

This, then, was Jack's life for the next few years. He was nineteen, and could not reasonably hope to be Master until he was past forty but none the less it was a life he enjoyed for itself, not just as a means to an end. In the *City of Cairo* he broke new ground, or rather ploughed new seas. After the opening visit to India she went by way of Singapore, to Hong Kong and Japan and southwards to Manila before going by way of Malaya and India back through the Red Sea and the Suez Canal to the United States. Though he had, at Singapore, been within sight of the equator Jack had not yet crossed it. No line crossing certificate for him just yet.

City of Cairo then went by way of Gibraltar to New York, Philadelphia, Baltimore and back to New York where, after five months in the ship, he transferred to the *City of Dunedin*, with promotion to third mate. Where the *City of Cairo* went subsequently is irrelevant, but the *City of Dunedin* went round the India–Burmah track, returned to the U.K. and the Continent and made another Indian voyage before Jack was paid off in Leith on the 9th December 1927. The joint voyages of the two ships totalled 49,305 miles and took sixteen months, leaving only two months of sea time to get for the next exam.

That voyage was worth fifteen days of leave and at the end of it, on 24th December 1927, Jack joined *Branksome Hall* in Middlesborough, as third mate. She was yet another reparations vessel, ex *Arensburg*, built by Swan Hunter in 1905 and the smallest so far at 4,261 tons. The voyage began unusually for, having left her last European loading port she went, not by way of the Suez Canal but round the Cape of Good Hope to Durban. So at last Jack had crossed the equator and became entitled to a line crossing certificate, which he did not get. From Durban *Branksome Hall* went by way of Lorenço Marques and Beira in East Africa to Colombo and the Indian coast before coming back to Europe by way of the canal. 20,288 miles, twenty ports, six and a half months and on 15th June 1928 Jack paid off in Liverpool with time in for mate.

Family doings records:

June 15th. Jack came home.
June 18th. Jack started school in Liverpool, first mate.

Jack Arnot had the required sea time, and to spare. He had the required years, twenty-one and a half, with ten days to spare. Back to Cleaver and Hutchinson.

Chapter 5

First Mate (Foreign-Going)

So back to the by now familiar Cleaver and Hutchinson, this time to study for the middle of the three exams. The syllabus was in many ways an extension of that for second mate but new subjects were imported. Again the exams opened with Practical Navigation 1 and 2, three hours and two hours respectively, but the work was more advanced. Whereas for second mate the astronomical navigation had all been solar, for mate it was stellar. Chart work went far beyond bearings and courses and what was for second mate a single paper, 'Cargo work and elementary ship construction', three hours, became 'Ship construction and stability', three hours, and 'Ship maintenance, routine and cargo work', three hours. The emphasis has moved from mere watchkeeping to ship management, reflecting the actual duties of second mates and mates, though to sail with the rank of one's certificate was, in those days, highly unusual! Meterology had a two-hour paper to itself and the written papers for mate totalled fifteen hours, with the Oral of unspecified length to follow. The syllabus for the oral demonstrates the forward movement and reflects the differences in the jobs of mates and second mates. It was as follows.

1. a. Shifting large spars and rigging sheers.
   b. The handling of heavy weights and special reference to strength of gear used.
   c. The use and maintenance of all deck and above deck appliances and fitting – winches, capstans, windlasses, emergency steering gear, and fittings used between anchor and cable locker. Hoisting in boats.
   d. Bending, setting and taking in fore and aft sails. Management and equipment of ship's lifeboats and numbers of persons who may be carried in each class of boat.

38

2. Anchors – different kinds. Advantages and disadvantages of
each. How to rig a sea anchor and what means to employ to
keep a vessel, disabled or unmanageable, out of the trough of
the sea and lessen her drift. Cables and their care. Preparations for anchoring. Operation of anchoring with single
anchor and use of second anchor. Clearing a foul anchor.
Mooring. Clearing a foul hawse. Anchoring in a tideway and
in a confined space. Dragging anchor. Anchor watch. Slipping a cable. To carry out an anchor with boats. Getting under
way.

3. a. Effect of propellers on the steering of a ship. Stopping,
going astern and manoeuvring. Turning circles. Effects of
current, wind, sea, shallows, draft.
b. Coming alongside a wharf, etc. Turning a steamship short
round, manoeuvring in rivers and harbours. Emergency
manoeuvres. Man overboard.
c. Management of steamships in stormy weather.
d. To get a cast of the deep sea lead.

4. a. Testing life buoys and life jackets; other life-saving gear.
b. Accidents, eg., collision, running aground, accidents to
hatches, leaks, fires and their treatment. Running repairs.
Handling a disabled ship.
c. A practical knowledge of the screening of ship's navigation
lights.
d. Preparation for dry-docking. Use of shores, bilge blocks
and bilge shores.

5. Regulations for prevention of collision at sea – as par 42,
section 5 (Oral) Second Mate.

6. Signals, As par 42, Section 6 (Oral), Second Mate.

7. The examiner may ask the candidate questions arising out of
the written work, if he deems it necessary on account of
weakness shown by the candidate.

This time Jack was, perhaps, a mite over confident, for he took the exam on
23rd July after a bare five weeks of work, and failed, probably rather

disastrously, for 'family doings' records that he came home on 26th July and stayed home, combining leave with study, until August 20th when he returned to Liverpool and Cleaver and Hutchinson. After three more weeks of study he took the exam again on 11th September, and passed. Another milestone. Another qualification, leaving only one to go, for Jack had no intention of going on for honours in the form of the 'Extra Master' qualification.

The sea time required for Master depended on the position held. Whereas for mate it was specified as being time spent as 'third of three watchkeeping officers' (or better), for Master the time required ranged from one and half years as First Mate, holding a Mate's certification to two and a half years as third of three watchkeepers, with time spent as second mate factored to bring it to a common figure. What Jack could really look forward to was a mix of time as third of three with, if he were fortunate, some time as second mate, with a resultant real time requirement of between two and two and a half years. Having told the company of his success he went home to wait for a call, which was not long in coming for, on 2nd October 1928, he set off by train for Marseilles.

At Marseilles he joined the *City of Nagpur*, one of the Hall Line's larger passenger ships, vintage 1914, 8,331 tons, built by Workman Clark in Belfast and carrying 222 first-class and 92 second-class passengers. She carried Jack to Port Said where, on 19th October 1928, he signed on as third mate of the *City of Salisbury*.

Chapter 6

City of Salisbury

When Jack climbed *City of Salisbury*'s gangway one bright autumn day in 1928 in Port Said to sign on as third mate he was not to know that he would complete the sea time he sought for Master in her without ever coming near the U.K. Indeed, having joined her in Port Said, he was to leave her there, two years and eight months later, for she was still not homeward bound, and he came home as a passenger in *City of Durban*. No doubt the homeward passage counted as leave!

City of Salisbury was relatively new and had a relatively short life. Built in 1924 at Sunderland by William Grey, she was a steamer of 5,924 tons. Her short life of fourteen years ended when she sank off Boston on 23rd April 1938, by which time Jack was long gone from her. In her lifetime she was footloose and fancy-free, wandering the world more extravagantly than the most travelled of the dedicated elderly cruisers who fill the *QE2*, the Cunard *Countess*, the *Canberra* and all the other vessels which include world cruises in their activities these days.

Thirty-two months, 137,904 miles, 139 ports. Eight transits of the Suez Canal and two of the Panama Canal. Eight crossings of the equator and two westbound crossings of the date line, losing two days out of his life! A voyage reminiscent of the Flying Dutchman, more appropriate to a tramp streamer than to a cargo liner and of a duration which would simply not be tolerated by today's seafarers, nor would it have to be with repatriation by air a cheap and common practice.

The voyage took Jack to a host of new places, to that far land where 'if you go any further from home you are on the way back'. The initial stages of the voyage were typical Ellerman. From Port Said to the East Coast of America, and back to India. Then back again to North America but then instead of returning to India, through the Panama Canal and across the vast Pacific to New Zealand and on to Sydney. Thence up to Celebes, Java and

Sumatra and Singapore and Malaya and on to India, whence westwards again to North America. Back this time, not to India but to Ceylon, Malaya and the Dutch East Indies and then back to North America. Down the East Coast and through the Panama Canal again and on to Australia before coming up through the East Indies again to Singapore. And on to Ceylon and the East Coast of America again then back to India. Back on the Ellerman track again *City of Salisbury* returned by way of Suez to America before heading East again for India. Before she got there Jack left her, relieved in Port Said on 16th June 1931.

After five and a half years on the Ellerman track between India and Burmah and the East Coast of the United States new vistas opened up and much more of the world and its ports came into Jack's ken, his horizons broadened and he felt as though he had broken out of a pen. The first new venture was his initial passage of the Panama Canal. Arriving off Colon at dawn, *City of Salisbury* came through the breakwater into Limon Bay, picked up her pilot and moved slowly though the bay and up the Gatun reach to the flight of three locks which lifted her twenty-six metres to the level of Gatun Lake. Everywhere else in the world the pilot is on board as an adviser, with the Master remaining in charge and responsible for the ship, but in the Panama Canal the pilot actually takes charge and assumes responsibility, a more than reasonable state of affairs in the special circumstances of the canal. Except in the locks the passage is through buoyed channels in the two lakes, Gatun and Miraflores, or in similarly marked channels in the 'cuts', or excavated parts of the canal, and presents no particular difficulties except when two vessels meet in the confined channel. But the locks are another matter. The ship is towed through by electric 'mules ' running on tracks each side of the locks and does not use her own power at all. Protection of the locks from damage by mishandled ships is one of the principal reasons for the transfer of responsibility.

Once out of the locks and into Gatun Lake, the *City of Salisbury* proceeded under her own power, through the channel in the lake and into the Gaillard and Culebra 'cuts', at the end of which she arrived at the single Pedro Miguel lock, which lowered her some nine metres into the Miraflores lake. Onwards through that to the flight of two locks at Miraflores which lowered her the remaining seventeen metres, give or take a little for tidal differences between the Caribbean and the Pacific, into the sea reach which led her into the Pacific at Balboa. After negotiating the forty-three and a half miles of the canal she emerged after a passage of eight or nine hours into the Pacific Ocean a few miles east, surprisingly, of the longitude at which she went in.

City of Nagpur (National Maritime Museum)

City of Salisbury (World Ship Society)

Next, the longest passage yet, 6,509 miles to Auckland in New Zealand; twenty-three days at sea with nothing but a smudge on the horizon to mark the Tuamotu Archipelago as *City of Salisbury* passed to the south of it after thirteen days at sea in clear south-east trade wind weather. Days of routine watchkeeping, of seeing to the lifeboats and safety gear. Of enjoying a beer with the mate after the noon derby had been run; of games of cribbage with the second mate before dinner and games of deck tennis with apprentices, engineers and mates on number two hatch over which an extra, well-worn tarpaulin had been placed to protect the working tarpaulins beneath. A hard game this, played with desperate competitiveness using a rope quoit encased in canvas and feeling something like a round brick. In the deck tennis season nail scissors were not needed for ordinary nail trimming, only for damage control! Reading occupied a lot of time, for listening to the radio occupied none, the transportable radio which could be used over long distances being, as yet, uninvented. Though it was early days yet Jack devoted some time to preliminary wrestling with the new subjects, untouched in the second and first mate's exams, which would feature in that for Master; Ship's business. The Magnetic Compass and Engineering Knowledge. Always with the depth of knowledge required becoming greater as the seniority of the exam increased. Plenty to learn, but the exam still a long time away.

Three days out *City of Salisbury* crossed the equator with no ceremony. The day before arrival in Auckland she crossed the 180th meridian and went from Monday straight to Wednesday. One day gone. Through the Colville channel into the Hauraki Gulf, thence into Waitemata harbour to tie up at a pier at the foot of Auckland's main street to work cargo, make friends and enjoy the hospitality of New Zealand, the green country where the inhabitants reckon that their prosperity stems wholly from green things. From forest products through to paper and from grass through to lamb, butter and wool. New cargoes to load; wool and sheep pelts in various forms. Animal products including tennis racquet string made from sheep's gut, not cat's; no fresh farm products, for *City of Salisbury* had no refrigerated capacity, being built for other trades.

From Auckland *City of Salisbury* went down to windy Wellington and then, leaving the North Island astern, on to Lyttleton, the port for Christchurch, that gem of an English town set, improbably, in forty-four degrees of south latitude. In 1929 the time ball at Port Lyttleton was still working, and remained so until 1934. These devices were common throughout the world in the period from the marine chronometer coming into common use in the nineteenth century until the routine use of wireless time signals made them redundant in 1930s. Perhaps fourteen of them still exist and function, though as historic artefacts rather than as working timekeepers. They are in places as diverse as Greenwich and Edinburgh and San Francisco, with no less than five, including Lyttleton, in the antipodes.

Navigation, in particular the knowledge of longitude, requires that a ship carries with her Greenwich Mean Time, which was, and is, the time maintained by the ship's chronometers. The clockwork chronometer as developed by Earnshaw and others is a very accurate timekeeper but changes in temperature and atmospheric pressure, the motion of the ship and the variable viscosity of clock oil over a long voyage cause them to wander from their rate, so periodical time checks are essential. The time balls which were one form of check before the radio time signal was invented were substantial spheres hoisted on masts and which, either by direct electrical contact with a regulator clock, or manually by a man watching that clock, were lowered at a known and published G.M.T. They were sited so as to be visible from as much as possible of a port or anchorage and were the shipmaster's main means of checking his chronometers in the pre-electronic age. And now the chronometers are quartz, and deadly accurate, making wireless time signals themselves almost redundant.

City of Durban (National Maritime Museum)

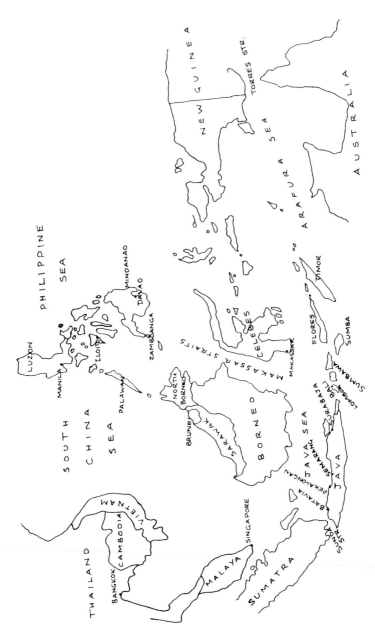

The East Indies

City of Salisbury moved down from Lyttleton to Dunedin, as Scottish as Christchurch is English, in forty-six degrees of South latitude, before coming back up the east coast of the South Island and through the Cook Strait, past Wellington on the one hand and Picton on the other and across the Tasman Sea to Sydney. Into the magnificent harbour of Port Jackson through the imposing Heads. Southwestwards past the exclusive suburbs of Watson's Bay and Rose Bay, turning westwards past the Zoo on the north shore and the Domain and Circular Quay on the south. Past where one day the controversial, futuristic Opera House would stand and into the commercial quays through the strait shortly to be the site of the Sydney Harbour bridge, built in 1932 and the first of the two great bridges of that decade. For all his wanderings, for all the hundreds of thousands of miles of his voyages, Jack was to see neither the Sydney Harbour nor the Golden Gate bridge. Nor, for that matter the Verrezano Narrows bridge at New York, the Humber bridge near Hull or the Severn Bridge. All his passages on the American coast between Boston and New York, between New York and Philadelphia and Baltimore, were Atlantic passages, though the short cuts of the Cape Cod canal, which eliminated the need to go round the cape, and the Chesapeake and Delaware canal, avoiding the long passage round the promontory guarding Chesapeake bay and terminating at its southern end at Cape Charles, had been in use for many years. Not only was Jack's working environment very different from today's but the physical face of the globe lacked a number of features which we now take for granted. Even the Suez Canal, a passage included in so many of his voyages, would hardly, in its form in 1930, be recognisable by today's users. It is wider, deeper, now has two northern channels and a 'lay by' at El Ballah and is an altogether bigger thing than the single, thirty-two-foot channel that it once was.

City of Salisbury's voyage continued its unusual track, wandering in the steaming heat and tropical lushness of the East Indies, around the coasts of the relatively freshly populated Antipodes and the ports of the 'New World', having no contact with the ancient civilisation of Europe and only the briefest, passing, contact with that ancient Egyptian culture. Only on the Indian coast were the world's roots apparent.

The departure from Sydney was the beginning of a passage seldom made, then or now, by British ships. *City of Salisbury*, bound for Makassar, sailed northwards up the Australian coast, past Brisbane and outside the Great Barrier Reef into the Coral Sea, whence through the Torres Strait, into the Arafura Sea, past Timor and into the Banda Sea before rounding the south-eastern point of Celebes, now Sulawesi, to arrive at Makassar, now Ujung Pandang. Later in the voyage the ship made what was to be the longest passage of Jack's seafaring life, probably as long as any passage routinely made by merchant ships if you discount V.L.C.C.'s slow steaming round the Cape to Europe. It is 7,657 miles from Panama to Brisbane; twenty-seven days at sea, a long time by any standards.

City of Salisbury did not visit South America, nor the West Coast of North America, nor Japan or China, nor South Africa, but she went nearly everywhere else. After her sixth visit to New York and its nearby ports she sailed again for India. Jack's sea time for Master was complete and at Port Said, where he had joined her, he was relieved to return home as a passenger in the City of Durban.

'Family doings,' 30th June 1930: 'Jack came home.'

Chapter 7

City of Lille

On 13th July 1931 Jack went off to Liverpool again to work for his Master's ticket, the objective of eight years of seafaring, of study, of success in two subordinate exams and of the accumulation of practical experience in the ports and on the oceans of the world. The depression cast a pall over shipping and Ellermans were working in a way which gave officers long breaks between voyages, off pay, rather than dispensing with their services altogether.

So this time, rather than risk failure and a re-sit and with little prospect of a ship in the immediate future, Jack settled down to three months of concentrated study, and emerged on 17th October with his certificate entitling him to be 'Master of a Foreign-Going Steam Ship', the certificate qualifying him for the job he really wanted when, after many more years of watchkeeping and gaining experience, it might be offered to him. He had five and a half months to wait before he took that ticket to sea and, though he did not know it, he was to make only two more voyages with Ellermans before moving to another company.

It was on 29th March 1932 that he joined *City of Lille* in Glasgow as third mate. She was a four-year-old motorship of 6,588 tons. By comparison with the ships in which Jack had served hitherto she was of strikingly modern appearance, having only one well deck, aft, which gave her, in her Ellerman colours, a long unbroken broad band of white, narrowed only in way of the well deck, over the grey hull. Though she retained the traditional straight stem she had a cruiser stern and a short, straight, motorship funnel.

The voyage was to be 'modified typical' Ellerman, serving the usual American, Indian, Burmese and East Indian ports but including two visits to the West Coast of the United States, two trans-Pacific passages from San Francisco to Manila and visits to the Chinese ports of Shanghai, Dairen, Taku Bar (Tientsin), 73,613 miles and fifteen months, paying off in London

49

on 4th July 1932. For the most part an ordinary voyage but including one very unusual incident to add to Jack's store of experience.

If the service were regarded as New York based she loaded homeward in Shanghai, Malaya, India and North Africa, filling her holds with the produce of the East, rubber, desiccated coconut, coconut fibre and derivative products, rattans, cashew nuts and plumbago, palm oil and a host of other odds and ends. As she cleared the Strait of Gibraltar she was down to her Winter North Atlantic marks.

Up until Monday 23rd January, Captain Hugh Parry, his Mate T. Mathias, Second and Third Mates Miller and Arnot and Chief Engineer Merriman, had experienced a perfectly normal Ellerman voyage. As that day dawned the ship was rolling and pitching easily in a light breeze, a slight sea and a long moderate swell, with an overcast sky and good visibility. At 10.45 the peace of the forenoon watch was disturbed by a wireless message sent out by *City of Delhi*, a 7,400-ton Ellerman steamer, telling all within range that she had shed her propeller in a position some 500 miles north of the *City of Lille*, in 44.15N 49.44W, on the western edge of the Grand Banks.

By 12.30 *Lille* had been ordered to go to the rescue and she set off northward in deteriorating weather, with the crew working away getting the tow ready. The *Lille* end of the tow comprised two 100-fathom five-inch wires and one four-and-a-half inch wire joined in a single line, which was to be attached to forty fathoms of *Delhi*'s anchor cable. Getting these wires onto the after well deck and flaking them ready to run was no light task and took until 21.30 the following day, the 24th, during which time the ship had, pitching into an exceptionally high swell, partly flooded the forepeak store and put some water down No. 1. hatch, open during the preparation of the tow.

Not under command lights were sighted at 00.30 on Wednesday, 25th January, and twenty-five minutes later *Lille* hove to, having identified *Delhi* and been told that she was not yet ready to receive a rocket. *Lille* remained hove to until 03.30 when *Delhi* declared herself ready and *Lille* moved into position on her port bow. The first rocket succeeded in putting a line across *Delhi*'s foredeck and, with Captain Parry keeping as close as possible to the other ship, lines, then light wires, then the tow were hauled across until by 04.25 *Delhi* had the end of the wire on board, and twenty minutes later all of the wire part of the tow was in the water. All this, of course, being achieved in pitch darkness.

The business of shackling the end of the wire to the end of *Delhi*'s anchor cable took until nine minutes past six, when the tow commenced. Throughout the business of passing and connecting the tow the long northerly swell, the darkness and frequent heavy snow squalls had made both manoeuvring and working extremely difficult. Slowly at first, gradually increasing the speed through 40 R.P.M. at 0630, 45 at 0735, until 63 R.P.M. were settled on as representing full speed at 1008. The log was streamed and the little convoy settled down to a long haul, for from the starting point Halifax was 584 miles away, almost directly due west.

Through the rest of the 26th January the weather was merely bad; a fresh to strong NW breeze, a rough sea and the relentless long, high swell, until by evening the wind fell light, the swell moderated and *Lille* was rolling and pitching easily, with the crew oiling the tow where it was made fast, and where it passed through fairleads, continuously. The weight of the tow was taken on four sets of bollards in a fore and aft line on the port quarter, with the bitter end lashed to the No. 4, port, samson post.

By 2130 the wind and sea had increased again sufficiently to call for a reduction to 55 R.P.M. It blew throughout the night, but by two the following afternoon, the 26th, 63 revs were again possible in improving weather. But not for long, for by midnight a strong easterly was helping them along. Throughout the middle and morning watches on the 27th the

City of Lille (National Maritime Museum)

wind, sea and swell increased but the tow went on without difficulty. By noon the gale had whipped up a sea described in the log as mountainous and *Lille* was shipping heavy water fore and aft. By 1600 the following sea was called precipitous, oil was being seeped through the hawse pipes to flatten it and she was shipping heavy water, not only in the after well deck but amidships as well until, at 2200, she was pooped, with substantial damage. The door to the crew's W.C. was stove in and a bulkhead demolished. Two ventilators lost their plugs, the gangway was smashed beyond repair, No. 2 lifeboat was washed out of its chocks. Two wire reels were smashed, the forward deep tank vents were flattened, the saloon door broken and the hawse pipe cover plates bent. The fo'c's'le head bell was found lying broken on deck. All this from a following sea.

And the tow parted at approximately 2200 on Friday 27th January. Fortunately the tow was trailing astern, foul of nothing, so Captain Parry motored on westwards keeping it so. Two ships without propellers would be more than twice as bad as one. Speaking to the Brooklyn *Daily Eagle* later the mate said, 'We were like a submarine', and the paper talked of a hurricane, though it was never logged worse than a strong gale. The storm continued all night with the ship moving westwards at 55 revs. At 0830 on the morning of the 28th she was pooped again, and sustained further damage, but the gale had by then begun to moderate and at 0915 Captain Parry began turning slowly to port to begin the return to, and search for, the *City of Delhi*.

Steering S65E the crew began the arduous task of recovering the tow. Too big to go round a winch drum the wire had to be recovered bit by bit. Stop a smaller wire to the tow at the fairlead, haul the tow on board till it reaches the winch; stop the tow, refasten the wire to the tow at the fairlead and winch the tow in. Time and time again until, at 1130, the broken end, a splice at the end of the second length, came aboard. The gale continued, and with the ship taking water fore and aft the crew set about repairing the tow and preparing it for further use. The snow had stopped, but continuous rain and mist added to the general discomfort, and to the difficulty of finding the tow. By midnight, twenty-six hours after losing the tow, there was thick fog.

Fifteen minutes into Sunday 29th Janury a vessel was sighted two points on the starboard bow, one mile distant, and she was soon identified as the *Delhi*. The breeze and sea were now moderate, but visibility poor and the towing gear not yet ready so *Lille* lay to on a southerly heading, rolling heavily in the murk. As the night wore on the wind increased again to gale force and the fog thickened. During the forenoon Captain Parry kept the bridge while everyone else worked on the towing gear. By 1330 it was ready

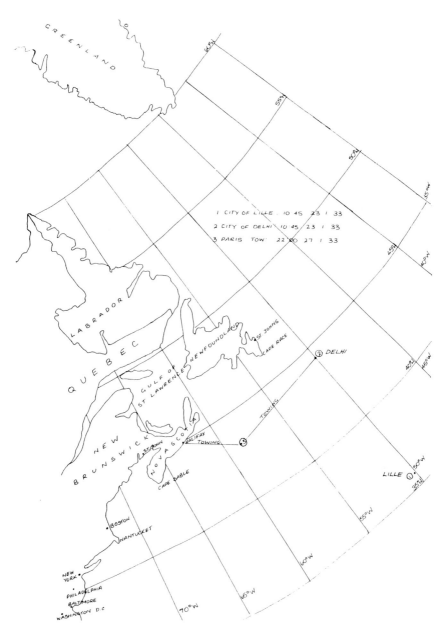

Grand Banks and Nova Scotia

and *Lille* approached *Delhi*. The first rocket fell short, blown black by the wind. So did the second, so *D elhi* sent a rocket, which carried, and contact was renewed at 1341. The wires and cables routine was once again followed through and by 1531 the tow was connected and ready. Slowly the weight of the *Delhi* was put on the tow, working up through forty to fifty revs, and the ships brought round to a course of due west, but not for long. Conditions were so bad, and the experience of losing the tow so recent, that by 1850 the two ships were hove to heading east south east, not the way they wanted to go at all. By 2300 *Lille* was down to 40 revs, the engines on standby, in a gale and thick fog. 'B.O.T. regulations strictly adhered to,' says the log. Bad enough today with radar, but a tow hove to in fog on a major shipping track on the Grand Banks was certainly no place to be without it.

An hour later, at midnight, the wind had dropped, the thick fog had become occasional fog banks, the ships were riding easily in sight of each other. By 0130 on the 30th January it was still thus, so *Lille* began a slow turn to port and increased to 55 revs until by 0200 they were settled on a course just south of west. As the dawn broke the wind freshened, the sea and swell got up and the course was altered to N57W to ease the motion and the strains on the tow. By breakfast time the convoy was heading nearly north, by noon they were round to N15W and down to 45 revs, with both ships rolling and pitching heavily and shipping water overall. In a strong westerly gale at 2135 they were round to N12E, in good order and with the tow well oiled.

The last observed position had been evening stars on the 26th. The search for the lost ship was done by dead reckoning and the discreet use of the d/f set. At 0412 on the 30th a position by wireless bearings was achieved which showed the ships to be further west than they had thought, so the gradual northward alterations forced by the weather were not too disadvantageous.

Tuesday 31st January arrived. Daylight revealed a forepeak flooded by water entering through the hawse pipe covers and a flooded forward contactor house, both of which had to be bailed out with buckets. Though the wind stayed fresh the shelter of the land reduced the sea to 'moderating rough', and the swell to short. Even so *Lille* was still rolling very heavily and shipping water overall, but the improving conditions allowed the revs to be increased though 50 to 60 by mid morning. By noon the breeze and swell were moderate and the sea slight. Half an hour later the Sambro light vessel was abeam and half an hour after that the convoy reduced speed in thick snow. At 1330 they sighted the fairway buoy at a distance of half a mile and hove to to keep it in sight before, in clearing weather, proceeding to Chebucto Head, where the tug *Foundation Franklin* made fast to the *City of*

Delhi. The *City of Lille* slipped the towing wire, leaving it to the other ship to get on board, and resumed her voyage to New York, where she arrived on 8th February.

The salvage, one of the longest tows by a motorship at the time, was reported in the Brooklyn *Daily Eagle*. After discharging in New York the *City of Lille* sailed on to the West Coast of the United States, then on to the Philippines, Shanghai, Dairen, Taku Bar, Shanghai, Hong Kong, the Philippines, Malaya, Colombo and North Europe before returning to the U.K. If not exactly all in the day's work, the salvage did not, in those days, warrant sending anyone home ahead of the normal end of the voyage.

Both ships survived the war. *City of Delhi*, built in 1925, was scrapped in May 1957. *City of Lille*, built in 1928, was sold to Monrovia in May 1957 and scrapped in 1963.

Chapter 8

City of Barcelona

When *City of Lille* came home to London on 4th July 1933 the depression in shipping was at its worst, and Jack's expectation was for a period of extended leave, without pay, awaiting his turn for another ship. He was to be pleasantly surprised, if going without leave at all between voyages is a pleasant surprise. Perhaps by sheer luck, perhaps in recognition of his part in the salvage of the *City of Delhi*, Jack was immediately transferred to the *City of Barcelona*, joining her the following day, 5th July 1933, with promotion to second mate. Being ambitious and unattached Jack had no quarrel with that, and was quite content with his one day at home on 22nd July while the ship was discharging in Liverpool. Somewhere between then and September 23rd when she sailed from London to Durban the ship was laid up for a few weeks, during which time Jack was the fortunate officer to be retained on full pay in charge of the ship, no small benefit in times like those.

City of Barcelona was a steamer of 5,787 tons, again a relatively new ship, built by Barclay Curle in Glasgow in 1930 and due to have a long life, sailing for Ellermans until she was scrapped at Antwerp in 1958. Unbeknownst to him at the time, she was to be Jack's last Ellerman ship, indeed his last conventional cargo liner. She was a good-looking ship with a heavy lift capability to add to the interest and difficulty of cargo work.

The voyage departed from the pattern to which Jack had become accustomed in that it opened with a passage from London to Durban, Lorenço Marques and Beira before crossing the Indian Ocean to Singapore. From Malaya and India she took the Suez route to North America whence she returned to South Africa, visiting Walvis Bay, Luderitz Bay, Cape Town, Port Elizabeth, East London, Durban, Lorenço Marques, Beira and Mombasa before crossing to Burmah. Another visit to North America, back to India and home to Manchester on 18th October, after 57,440 miles, completed the voyage. Part one of Jack Arnot's seafaring life had ended.

And, after the experience of the salvage in *City of Lille*, the voyage in *City of Barcelona* ended on a high note, with Jack's reputation in the eyes of the Masters under whom he had served of the best. It was necessary for Masters to issue certificates to their mates detailing their watchkeeping time and reporting on their characters. Jack's certificates were uniformly fulsome. Only that for the *City of Lille* is missing – perhaps because of the swift transfer from one ship to the other it was never written, for certification of sea time was not required by Jack for further exams. But that from the Master of the *City of Barcelona* is one to proud of. It misstates the length of the voyage and, for some reason, is signed at Bombay some six weeks before the voyage was completed. It reads as follows:

Ellerman Lines Ltd.

HALL LINE

S.S. *City of Barcelona*
at Bombay

28th August 1934

This is to certify that Mr. J. McK. Arnot has served in the above steamer as second officer for the past fifteen months. During our lay-ups he has been in sole charge of the vessel and responsible for her many shifts, etc. Last voyage he acted as Chief Officer for about three months in full charge owing to sickness of the Chief Officer.

He is also a gyro compass expert and holds high certificates from the Sperry Gyro Compass Company.

I am very pleased to be able to conscientiously recommend this young man to be able to fill ANY position on board a steamer. He is strictly sober and a thoroughly competent officer.

Illegible
Master

Sydney C. Garner
Marine Superintendent,
Ellerman Lines
Bombay.
28/8/34

City of Barcelona (National Maritime Museum)

City of Barcelona at Manchester – funnel top and topmasts struck (World Ship Society)

Jack's future with Ellermans was bright, but he was to choose to seize other opportunities and follow other paths. It is highly unlikely that, had he stayed with Ellermans, the event which changed his life in 1949 would have occurred; had that been the case the rest of this book might well have been a repetition, with minor variations and perhaps some wartime adventures, of what has gone before. But that was not to be.

This chapter, and the account of Jack's life with Ellermans, ends with a summary of his voyages which illustrates the wide-ranging nature of cargo liner operations in the twenties and thirties.

	Kas	Hvd	H.K.	Cro	Dun	Brk	Sal	Lle	Brc	Totl
Newcastle on Tyne	1									1
Hull	2							1		3
Oran	2						4			6
Port Said	6	6	2	2	4	1	10	4	4	39
Suez	6	6	2	2	4	1	8	4	4	37
Bombay	3	2	1		1		2	1	1	11
Karachi	3	1	1		1		2	1	1	10
Port Sudan	3	1	1		1		2	1		9
Marseilles	2	2		1				1		6
Dunkirk	2	2			2					6
Middlesbrough	1					1			1	3
Glasgow	1			1				1		3
Birkenhead	1	2	1	1	1			1	1	8
Naples	1									1
Calcutta	2	2			2		2			8
Madras	2	2			2		3			9
Colombo	3	4		2	2	1	8	2	2	24
Boston	1						6	1	1	9
New York	2	1		2	2		12	3	2	24
Baltimore	1			1			4		1	7
Mangalore	1					1		1		3
Tillicherry	1									1
Calicut	1					1	2		1	5
Cochin	1					2	1	1	1	6
Tuticorin	1									1
Rangoon	2	1			2				1	6
Visagapatam	1									1
Cocanada	1									1
Pondicherry	1									1
Cudalore	1									1
Perim	1			1						2
London	1	3	1		2	2		1	3	13
Plymouth		2	1							3
Le Havre		1							1	2
Antwerp		2	1	1		2		1	2	9

	Kas	Hvd	H.K.	Cro	Dun	Brk	Sal	Lle	Brc	Totl
Leith	2			1						3
Liverpool	1			1				1	2	5
Hook of Holland			1							1
Bremen			1							1
Hamburg			1		1				3	5
Southampton			1							1
Singapore			2				5	2	1	10
Hong Kong			2					3		5
Shanghai			1					3		4
Kobe			1							1
Yokohama			1							1
Karatsu			1							1
Manila			1				1	4		6
Aba			1							1
Zamboanga			1							1
Iloilo			1					2		3
Port Swettenham			1				2	2	1	6
Penang			1				4	2	1	8
Gibraltar			1							1
Philadelphia			1	1			6	1	1	10
Aden				2			2		1	5
Durban						1			2	3
Lorenço Marques						1			2	3
Beira						1			2	3
Marmagoa						1	1			2
Allepey						1		1	1	3
Portland, Maine							1			1
Norfolk Va.							2	2		4
Colon							2	2		4
Panama							2	2		4
Auckland							1			1
Wellington							1			1
Port Lyttleton							1			1
Dunedin							1			1
Sydney							2			2
Mackay							1			1
Makassar							3			3
Passaruan							3			3
Surabaya							4			4
Semarang							4			4
Telok Berang							2			2
Batavia							3			3
Belawan Deli							3			3
Newport News							3	2		6
Davao							1			1
Pamekasan							2			2
Pekalongan							2			2

	Kas	*Hvd*	*H.K.*	*Cro*	*Dun*	*Brk*	*Sal*	*Lle*	*Brc*	**Totl**
Brisbane							1			1
Newcastle, N.S.W.							1			1
Melbourne							1			1
Adelaide							1			1
Fremantle							1			1
Halifax Nova Scotia							1	1	1	3
St. Johns New Brwk.							1			1
Alexandria							1			1
Manchester								1	1	2
Almeria								1		1
Deep Water Point								1		1
Savannah								2		2
Los Angeles								2		2
San Francisco								2		2
Ceuta								1		1
Dairen								1		1
Taku Bar								1		1
Cebu								1		1
Port Lamon								1		1
Kalachel									1	1
Walvis Bay									1	1
Luderitz Bay									1	1
Cape Town									1	1
Port Elizabeth									1	1
East London									1	1
Mazanza									1	1
Nosi Bee									1	1
Mombasa									1	1
Moulmein									1	1
Barcelona									1	1
Total Ports, 112.	58	43	11	33	32	18	139	69	58	461

Voyages

Kasenga	19	months	57,019	miles	58 ports
City of Harvard	16	months	56,798	miles	43 ports
City of Hong Kong	3	months	12,702	miles	11 ports
City of Cairo	6½	months	12,261	miles	33 ports
City of Dunedin	9½	months	37,141	miles	32 ports
Branksome Hall	6	months	20,288	miles	18 ports
City of Salisbury	32	months	137,904	miles	139 ports
City of Lille	14½	months	73,613	miles	69 ports
City of Barcelona	15½	months	57,440	miles	58 ports
	122	months	465,166	miles	461 ports

Chapter 9

Pedrinbas

When Jack paid off from *City of Barcelona* on 18th December 1934 he faced the prospect of an extended spell at home, off pay. The depression of industry in which shipping suffered as much as any other occupation was still evident, with ships laid up in those creeks and harbours around the world where fees were lowest. Different shipowners resorted to different cost-saving practices, most of which involved seafarers going without pay. In tramp shipping, where coal out and grain home was the basis of operations, outward cargoes were hard to find, but the grain kept on growing. Owners without outward cargoes were known to send their ships out to Australia light, ahead of the harvest, and anchor them in obscure inlets, where fees were nil, to await the time to load for home. The crews lived in primitive conditions, away from all human habitation, on short commons and in many cases by the light of oil lamps as generators were shut down for economy. But at least they were being paid.

The Hall Line adopted a policy of not shedding its officers completely but established a 'rota'. When Jack paid off he could not expect to be offered another ship for three or four months, during which time he would not be paid, so it was small wonder that long voyages were popular, and the near year and a half in the *City of Barcelona* must have been very welcome to him. What pleasure the telegram which arrived at the Arnot house on December 31st 1934 must have brought with it.

> 'Are you free to accept two months' employment marine superintendent at Glasgow finishing new ship commencing Wednesday or Thursday.'
>
> Anglicus Arnot

Anglicus Arnot was Jack's uncle David, a naval architect employed by Wilson, Sons & Co. Ltd., a company with many interests in Brazil, among which were trading in and carrying coal and salt about the Brazilian coast. Their telegraphic code name worldwide was Anglicus and David Arnot was in Britain to see to the completion and despatch of their latest ship *Pedrinhas*, as well as to design, and place the contracts for, a tug and a brace of lighters for the company.

Pedrinhas, unnamed on 31st December, was a typical tramp design, a ship of 3,666 gross tons, 366 feet long and having a triple expansion steam engine of 1,500 horse power. She had been started as a speculative build, probably with Hogarth's Baron Line in mind, in the worst of the depression of the early thirties, and had lain uncompleted on the stocks in Lithgow's Kingston yard at Port Glasgow for the last two years. Wilsons had bought her on the stocks and to be completed for £50,000. Not surprisingly Jack accepted the job at the princely salary of £6 per week. And it was princely, for second mates were at that time paid £10.35 per month and masters £35. He was better off than as second mate of the *City of Barcelona*, except that he had to find for himself instead of living, at sea, 'all found'.

The next two months were filled with activities not normally undertaken by second mates with relatively new Master's tickets. The ship had to be inspected from stem to stern and the extent of the ravages of the weather during two years of neglect assessed. They turned out to be minor, but none the less their repair, followed by minor modifications, cleaning and cement washing the double bottom tanks, painting the ship and generally getting her ready for launching had all to be seen to, all under a constant bombardment of letters from David Arnot in London. The whole of the exchange of letters throughout the superintendentship was, by today's standards, incredibly stilted, with the letter being responded to frequently referred to as 'your favour of', the correspondent as 'your good self' and with Uncle David referring to himself throughout as 'we'.

The subjects of the letters are mainly technical, concerned with the upper deck fittings on the air pipes to the double bottom tanks, the translation of signs on cabin doors and the like throughout the ship into Portuguese, and include instances of David Arnot hoping that inactivity will get a better specification out of the builder than could reasonably be expected!

The hiatus in the building of the ship had coincided with the universal changeover in the system of helm orders. From time immemorial 'Port your helm' had meant shove the tiller to port, sending the ship's head to starboard. While *Pedrinhas* was lying unnamed, unwanted and deserted, the system was changed by international agreement, so that the use of the wheel instead of the tiller was recognised, and 'Port your helm' meant turn the wheel to port, moving the ship's head to port also.

Wheel steering had been the norm for many a year, but helm indicators on the wheel pedestal reflected the old practice and indicated the tiller position, not the rudder position. This was the subject of some correspondence, for the wheel had been fitted before the change, and the indicator had to be modified to work backwards.

And from time to time the Naval Architect and the seaman got at cross purposes, as when Jack's use of the term 'fife rail' confused Uncle David, who thought of it as a 'sheer pole'.

Day by day the ship came nearer to completion, day by day came the letters from London, and day by day the replies flowed back. The lists grew, lists of boatswain's stores, of paints and oils and shackles and marline spikes and ropes and cordage and flags and charts and dividers and parallel rulers. And lists of medical supplies and timber and food and drink and books and of all the things which a ship needs at sea. The problem was compounded and the lists made longer because, not only was she a new ship, but she was going to a less developed country, and was expected to provide for herself for her first year. Everything had to be thought of, not just the routine events in a ship's life, but what could only be guessed at in the way of what might be required by a ship operating far from home in a literally corrosive trade, the carriage of salt, and working in the main in and out of lighters, without the benefit of quay walls and the convenience of cranes.

Launching day, 17th January 1935. The report of the launching is brief and does no justice to the romance of the occasion. The ship, whose construction had been at a standstill for two years, had found a buyer at last, and was being launched into the world's greatest shipbuilding river to make her way half across the world never to come home. The report read,

Length of Standing Ways	386 ft.
End of Ways from Stern	30 ft. 6 in
Length of Check Wires	415 ft.
Fore end of Ways to After Drag	33 ft.
Keel above ways, Fore Poppet	1 ft.
Keel above ways, After Poppet	2 ft.
Distance between Ways	16 ft. 8 in.
Bearing Surface	2 ft.
Length of Sliding Ways	306 ft. 6 in.
Area of Sliding Ways	1226 sq.ft.
Launching Weight	1850 tons

Pressure per sq ft.	1.51 tons
Declivity of Ways	15/32″ per ft.
Declivity of Keel	7/16″ per ft.

Commencement of launch, 11.00 a.m. 17th January 1935 from Messrs Lithgows Kingston Yard, Port Glasgow.
Vessel took the water at 11.34 a.m. and was brought up by her checks (four bundles of chain, 35 tons each) in 27 feet. The draught on launching was 5 ft. 0 in. forward, 6 ft. 1 in. aft, a mean of 5 ft. 6 in.

After launching *Pedrinhas* was towed to and moored in Port Glasgow harbour, and the next day was towed up the Clyde and moored at Finnieston Quay to have her engines installed.

All young mates aspire to command and naturally wish to have it sooner rather than later, and not only for the money, which was considerable. The Master of *Pedrinhas* was paid £35 per month, which was eighty-five percent more than the Mate and nearly two and a half times the pay of the second mate. But more than that, it is for command that young men go to sea on deck, and nearly new Master's tickets burning holes in the pockets of second mate's uniforms lead to opportunity diagnosis and seizure, or did in the case of Jack Arnot. He must have been weighing up the ways and means of grasping the opportunity which had so miraculously presented itself from the moment the telegram offering him a two month's superintendent's job arrived for, on 10th January, even before the launch, he sent this letter to David Arnot.

Dear Sir,

I wish to formally apply for the position of Master of your S.S. *Pedrinhas*.

My qualifications being already known to you I will omit them here, but enclose copies of references for your information.

As regards Officers for the vessel I could obtain good and reliable men. The crew could be engaged through the usual channels and there should be no difficulty is selecting good men owing to the large number unemployed.

I respectfully trust that this application will receive your favourable consideration

I remain,

Yours obediently,

J. McK. Arnot

This letter was acknowledged the following day and within the fortnight came the letter for which Jack had been hoping.

Dear Mr. Arnot,

S.S. *Pedrinhas*

With further reference to your application of the 10th inst. we are prepared to put you in command of the above vessel for the voyage to Brazil. You will understand that it can only be for the voyage to Brazil, as when trading on the Coast according to Brazilian Law the ship must have a Brazilian Master.

Also we do not wish in any way to prejudice you as regards your employment with the Ellerman Hall Line, and we take it that you would wish to communicate with them in order to obtain their permission to take on this work.

The salary would be at the rate of £35 per month and you would, of course, require to engage your own Officers and Crew, all of whom would be repatriated by us, the Officers being found 2nd class passages and the Crew 3rd class or steerage home and 3rd class rail to the port at which they signed on. The undersigned hopes to be in Glasgow on Tuesday next and it would be as well to do nothing about the Officers until he has had an opportunity of discussing the matter with you.

So far as the Engineers go, we are inclined to think that as she is a new ship it would be advisable to arrange with Messrs. Rowans at least to provide a Chief Engineer for the run out – a man whom they know and can trust to do the right thing by the machinery, and doubtless if this arrangement comes about he may also want to engage his own juniors. This, however, can be discussed with Messrs. Rowans next week.

Please also get your passport up to date.

Yours faithfully,
For CIA CABOTAGEM DE PERNAMBUCO

D. Arnot,
Agent

Those two very British, stilted, formal letters hide almost to the extent of burying it the sense of fulfilment that Jack Arnot must, on 23rd January 1935, have felt. Ten years and three months after joining *Kasenga* as a first voyage apprentice, four years and two months after leaving the examination room in Liverpool qualified to take it he had, in the depths of the thirties recession and with just a little bit of help from his friends, achieved a command. Albeit for a voyage which would only last a month, but command none the less; experience which would be invaluable in the years to come and, regrettably, an eminence which he would not attain again for many years.

Nor do they tell the story. The first verbal response to Jack's letter was quite different from the final acceptance. In David Arnot's view young lads just a week over twenty-eight years old were quite unsuitable material for command, even of a small tramp steamer, especially a brand new one. The application was really quite out of order and did Mr. Arnot really put himself forward seriously, to which Jack's response was 'yes, certainly'. Was it not one of the normal functions of a marine superintendent to find the crew for a delivery voyage? In his view it most certainly was. He was fully qualified, had been well trained in a good shipping company and had been in charge of a watch at sea for eight years and had, forby, taken part in a famous salvage when the *City of Lille*, in which he was third mate, had towed the *City of Delhi* to safety through a week of the foulest of North Atlantic weather.

In the end David Arnot allowed himself to be convinced, but not before he had done an elaborate calculation setting the costs of getting a Brazilian crew to Glasgow to take the ship out against the costs of using a British crew and repatriating them. Against total delivery costs of £1,300 the use of a British crew showed a saving of £42.12s.8d. Perhaps that was justification enough. For Jack Arnot's part the offer to find good Officers for the voyage was a euphemism for 'lots of my friends and colleagues in the Hall Line are unemployed, so I'll round up three of them', which he did. The mate was to be M. E. Miller, lately second mate of *City of Lille*. The second mate was one J. F. Lindell, of whom nothing more is known. The third mate's job was taken by Harry Rome, who went on to command in the Shaw Saville Line, and then to be their Marine Superintendent. A fairly distinguished bunch of young men for a tiny collier.

So now the pressure was really on. Any deficiencies in Jack's performance as Superintendent would fall on his own shoulders as Master. The tempo of list writing increased, the engines were installed, a chronometer valued for insurance at £25 was hired for the voyage at £1.5s.0d per month from Christie and Wilson, of the Broomielaw, Glasgow. The ship being Brazilian registered, the formalities involving the Brazilian Consul were formidable, and the volume of paperwork immense, but as time went by the Superintendent kept on top of the job, the stores and supplies arrived and were stowed and the ship began to approach readiness for sea. She had not yet run her trials, for they were to be run in a loaded condition and would be done in the Firth of Clyde after the passage down the river. There was no point in going down the river for trials and then returning to load.

Jack arranged for the three Mates to join the ship on 25th February, though they would not sign on till sailing day, and loading began. The cargo was, guess what, coal, a cargo to be, according to the Charter Party, 'not exceeding 5,500 tons or less then 5,000 tons, and not exceeding what she can reasonably stow and carry, over and above her tackle, apparel, provisions and furniture; and being so loaded shall therewith proceed with all possible despatch to SANTOS.'

On that day Jack Arnot stood on his own bridge for the first time for the move to Rothesay Dock, where the coal cargo was to be loaded. But not as Master, for signing on would not be till sailing day, the mates and others attending the ship at this time being paid a daily rate but not being, technically, holders of the ranks they would hold after signing on. Quite what his legal position was on that day is obscure, but he and the pilot took the ship the six miles down the river, six miles of Scottish shipbuilding history. Past the Queen's and Prince's docks, past the Govan yards where Fairfields then built passenger and high class cargo liners for the great shipping companies of the world; Then on past Alexander Stephen's Linthouse yard, also the birthplace of many a great liner between 1870 and the late 1960s. Past Charles Connel's Scotstoun yard, chiefly known for the quality of their cargo liners and particularly for their long series of very handsome ships for the Ben Line of Leith, opposite which lay the King

Pedrinhas (Cia De Cabotagem de Pernambuco)

Pedrinhas (Cia De Cabotagem de Pernambuco)

George V dock where the bigger ocean going cargo ships berthed. Past
Harland and Wolff's engine works and Barclay Curle's two dry docks at
Elderslie and, on the other bank, Lobnitz's yard, famous for its dredgers,
and so to the Rothesay dock on the North bank, opposite the river Cart and
just short of John Brown's famous Clydebank shipyard.

The following day, 26th February, the Chief Officer's log book begins,
'Day opens with light westerly airs, fine, clear and frosty.' The next entry is
'Builders workmen attending to various tasks.' And the next, timed at
10.30 a.m., 'commenced loading'. Loading coal. The mate's thoughts on
having his shiny new ship subjected to the filthy task of loading a full cargo
of coal almost before the paint was dry can be imagined, for no matter what
precautions are taken, sealing doors and portholes with brown paper and
paste, blocking ventilators with rags and abandoning the accommodation as
far as possible whilst coal is being loaded, the dust gets everywhere and the
subsequent clean-up is a daunting task.

Left to Right: H. M. Rome, 3rd Mate, J. F. Lindell, 2nd Mate,
Captain J. McK. Arnot, M. E. C. Miller, Mate, J. W. Close, Wireless Officer *(Cia
De Cabotagem De Pernambuco)*

Thursday, 27th February, opened much the same, except that it was snowing, and loading began again at eight in the morning. By two-thirty, when the crew signed on, the snow had stopped and by the time loading was completed at ten at night the sky was overcast and the weather fine. Friday the 28th, sailing day, dawned overcast and dull, with light variable airs.

So now the ship prepares to depart the Clyde, never to return. Handsome she looks as, loaded to her marks and drawing 21 ft. 6 in. forward and 21 ft. 8 in. aft, she makes fast the tugs Flying Kite and Flying Cormorant and Pilot McMillan climbs to the bridge. She positively sparkles in her grey paint, with her white and varnished upperworks topped by her plain black funnel, plain, that is, but for the letters 'CP', entwined, in white, below the hounds band. At three minutes past eight *Pedrinhas* cast off and by eight sixteen was clear of the dock and ready for the passage down river. To starboard, in John Brown's fitting out basin, towers the vast bulk of *Queen Mary*, launched by Her Majesty a bare five months earlier after a period of idleness on the stocks similar to that of *Pedrinhas*. The ship gathers way and the landmarks on either bank slide by. The shipbreaking and sewage works at Dalmuir, the Erskine ferry, followed by the entrance to the Forth and Clyde canal, Bowling Harbour and the tanks of the Dunglass oil terminal.

The river begins to open out and soon great Dumbarton Rock, concealing the yards of ferry specialists Denny of Dumbarton, is abeam. The channel is well marked, for it is narrow and bounded by shallows which turn to mudflats at low water, and soon swings to the southern bank past Port Glasgow, with the old East shipyards where the historic *Comet* was built by John Wood (junior) for Henry Bell and then, shortly, past Lithgow's Kingston yard from which *Pedrinhas* had been launched six weeks earlier; 9.45 a.m. saw her off Greenock and the Scott shipyards, casting off her tugs.

On her own for the first time she rounded Cloch point at 10.25 a.m. and after a brief glimpse of the open waters of the Firth returned to Kempock point at 10.50 a.m. to embark 'officials', for the trials, from the tug *Flying Scotsman*. Then down Firth again for speed trials over the Skelmorlie measured mile and back for anchor trials and compass adjustment at the Tail of the Bank, where countless ships have done the same over the years, from great liners to tiny coasters.

That night she embarked an extra pilot and made off southbound for a twelve-hour fuel consumption trial, passing by the Cumbraes and Ailsa Craig and Corsewall point before turning off Loch Ryan in the early hours to retrace her track to anchor at the Tail of the Bank again at 2.15 p.m. Half an hour later all the officials, observers and pilots had left the ship, and she shortly began to get her anchor in, so that at 3.05 p.m. on Friday, 1st March 1935, the log reads:

> 'S.S. *Pedrinhas* from Tail of the Bank and Trials towards Santos, Slight sea, wind SW force 2, full ahead, courses various to Master's orders.'

She was on her way.

The early hours of Saturday morning found her in fog in the North Channel, with an anxious Master seeking wireless bearings of Port Patrick and Liverpool, for *Pedrinhas* had no radio direction-finding equipment, and taking soundings with the deep-sea sounding machine, for she had no echo sounder. The bearings proved useless, and with her engines at slow and the syren sounding every two minutes she crept southwards into the Irish Sea, taking soundings at intervals until at six in the morning the fog lifted, the Chicken Rock light at the southern end of the Isle of Man was sighted, and full speed resumed. Mid-morning saw her off the South Stack, and early afternoon off Bardsey Island and the Lleyn peninsula, their last daylight view of Britain, with only the Bishop's and Small's lights left as contact with the land and the ship's course set for the next landfall at Madeira.

As the days went by *Pedrinhas* steamed southwestwards at a shade under eight knots and burned eighteen tons of coal a day. On Monday, 4th March, the temperature began to rise out of the low forties into the mid-fifties, though the wind remained strong and the ship rolled and pitched and shipped water in her well decks until, by Wednesday the 6th, she was rolling and pitching heavily in a full gale when, at five in the evening, the telemotor steering gear failed. After an hour of steering with the emergency wheel on the poop the rudder jammed hard to port, the engines were stopped and the rudder secured. It was not until half an hour after midnight that the fault was found, but by 4.00 a.m. full speed was resumed, though the telemotor gear was still defective and she had still to be steered from the poop from then till 11.00 a.m., by which time the fault had been found and rectified. Whilst stopped she rolled heavily, making things uncomfortable for all on board and difficult and dangerous for the engineers wrestling with the heavy steering engine and rudder quadrant. Neptune had had his dues, and thereafter the wind fell light, the temperature rose into the sixties and the sea calmed, though a long, heavy swell kept the *Pedrinhas* rolling heavily.

A week into the voyage, on Saturday, 9th March, 1,500 miles from the Tail of the Bank, Pargo Point in Madeira came abeam and the course was altered for San Antonio, the westernmost of the Cape Verde Islands, a thousand miles away. An hour and a half's flying time in a 747, but five days of steaming time in *Pedrinhas*, plodding along at her stately eight knots, rolling easily in the moderate sea kicked up by the north-east trade winds. The temperature rose into the seventies and the crew worked about the decks and rigging, making beam slings, greasing the topping lifts and doing the hundred and one jobs which have to be done to keep even a small ship in being as a going concern.

Wednesday, 13th March, brought a crisis. The chief engineer reported that, having measured up the coal remaining in the bunkers, he believed that the ship had been burning 21.8 tons per day rather than the estimated 18. Re-measurement reduced the figure to 20 but with only 319 tons remaining in the bunkers and sixteen days to go to Santos things looked a little tight, so Jack ordered that the coal fed to the boilers for the next twenty-four hours be weighed, and reduced the revolutions from 52 to 49. The log does not report the results of the experiment, but in the succeeding days the speed fell marginally but the coal consumption is reported at $14\frac{1}{2}$ tons a day, which is supported by the bunkers on arrival at Santos having 74 tons in them.

The forenoon of the following day brought the ship to San Antonio and the course was altered five degrees to the south for Fernando Noronha, a small group of islands which are home to a cable station and a penal settlement, just off the easternmost point of South America some three degrees south of the Equator, 1,300 miles away. The trade wind weather held up and the ship went peacefully on her way. The engine feed water, relied on as a reserve of domestic water, was found to be unfit to drink and what was left of the good water was transferred into a separate tank for drinking and cooking only. The steering gear failed briefly again when a pin dropped out of the steering engine for want of a split pin, but this was quickly diagnosed and repaired. Day by day the Equator drew nearer and at 5.00 p.m. on Tuesday, 19th March, in fine clear weather *Pedrinhas* crossed the line. The log reports 'Crossed Equator, King Neptune hailed and boarded, greeted all newcomers into the southern hemisphere and permitted the ship to proceed.' He no doubt found *Pedrinhas* a shade small compared with the cruise and passenger liners which he usually visited, and the swimming pool in which the newcomers were bathed after shaving and treatment, made from a tarpaulin slung from battens between number two hatch and the rail, likewise a trifle cramped. For Neptune to visit so small a ship was quite unusual, for he does not usually bother with small tramp steamers, even new ones on their maiden voyages. The following day

Pegasus came by in the guise of a German flying boat, which passed very close and very low a few hours before the ship reached Fernando Noronha, whence various courses were set until the following day the Abrolhos rocks, 800 miles down the coast of Brazil, could be laid on S21W.

On the 24th the engine revolutions were increased to fifty-two to achieve nine knots for arrival at Santos on the 28th March. At the beginning of the forenoon watch on Wednesday 27th Cape Frio was close abeam and in the afternoon Rio came abeam, though out of sight, and at two minutes past three the following afternoon *Pedrinhas* stopped her engines off Limoes Point to pick up her Santos pilot. A few minutes later she was under way again and, after a brief spell at anchor whilst customs and health authorities paid their visits and filled in their forms, she weighed again and by 6.40 in the evening was fast alongside the quay in No. 10 berth. Captain Arnot sat down to his typewriter and reported the voyage to his uncle, the Agent, David Arnot in London.

s.s. *Pedrinhas*,
Berth No. 10,
Santos,
Brazil.

Dear Sir

I have pleasure in reporting the safe arrival of the above vessel at Santos yesterday at 3.00 p.m.

With the exception of a few hours' fog and a ten-hour stoppage with steering gear trouble the voyage was uneventful.

After a week at sea we had some trouble with the telemotor glands; this was soon corrected. Later the control valve of the steering engine jammed in the open position which put the rudder hard over on the stops and it was necessary to move the engine back and overhaul the valve which had stuck in the gland. The engine was then run over to the normal hard over position and re-engaged with the quadrant. The rudder controller proved very useful in this case. No further trouble was experienced with the steering gear.

Being deeply laden the decks were awash for the first week of the passage but as we made southing the weather improved.

I dressed ship on arrival at Santos and was greeted with a salvo from the whistles of the *Neptuno* and *Emperor* to which I replied. The Doctor, Police and Customs got away from the ship about 6.00 p.m. and Wilson's men came aboard and got the necessary documents. We berthed in No. 10 berth at 7.00 p.m.

Mr. Howard came aboard this morning and Mr. Pullen and Mr. Coutts came aboard this afternoon. They were very pleased with the general appearance of the ship and remarked on her cleanliness.

The crew will live ashore from the 1st March and sail for London on the 8th March.

I enclose herewith the abstract for the voyage and the Chief Engineer's abstract will follow under separate cover.

I remain
Yours obediently,
J. McK. Arnot.
Master.

In twenty-six days, sixteen hours and six minutes *Pedrinhas* had steamed 5,439 miles at an average speed of 8.49 knots using 455 tons of coal to drive her at 11.9 miles per ton. Her mean draught lessened by 1 ft. 3 in. during the passage and she was delivered without damage to herself or her cargo. So ended Jack Arnot's first voyage in command.

There only remained repatriation, a pleasant voyage home as a passenger, first class, in the Royal Mail Line's *Highland Monarch*. A busman's holiday which Jack enjoyed to the full and especially memorable for his welcome on board. As he settled into his cabin the telephone rang. 'Captain Arnot?' 'Yes.' 'This is the Captain. Your third engineer has just come aboard drunk. Do something about it. And drinks in my room at six, if you will.' Whereupon the telephone was hung up.

Chapter 10

Burmah Oil

'Family doings' records that on 30th April 1935 Jack came home from Santos. No longer, for the present, a shipmaster nor even a ship's officer, just one of hundreds of qualified men on the Ellerman rota with little prospect of another voyage for months, nor of any income for months. A daunting prospect. Not one which the Jack Arnots of this world would relish, or be likely to accept with no attempt at avoiding action.

Jack was nothing if not a thinking man. His experience included a voyage in a motorship, and he came to the conclusion that, whilst motorships might not displace steamships, the trend must be to fuel oil rather than coal. The Royal Navy had already made the change and, though coal-fired merchant ships were still being built during the 1939–1945 war, oil firing has almost entirely replaced coal firing in the subsequent years. When the British 'Empire' merchant ship design was adopted by the United States in 1941 as the basis of the 'Liberty' ship, the largest class of ship ever built (2,710 identical vessels), the principal modifications included the change from coal to oil firing. And if the cleanliness and ease of handling of oil as compared with coal made it advantageous for use at sea, the same would certainly be true of many industrial applications as well. The logic, followed through, led, in Jack's mind, to the conclusion that, even if world trade in dry cargoes remained static, there would inevitably be a shift of emphasis from colliers to tankers as the years went by. But, forward thinking though he was, Jack could not have foreseen the tankers which would be developed to accommodate this accelerating trend in the sixties and onwards. In 1935 a big tanker was 7,000 tons, and the smaller ocean going ships ranged down to 2,000 tons.

No doubt others came to the same conclusions for, when Jack began to enquire around the U.K. based tanker companies, Shell, British Petroleum, Jacobs and the like, he found the employment situation to be as tough as, if

Highland Monarch (National Maritime Museum)

Masimpur (Jack Arnot)

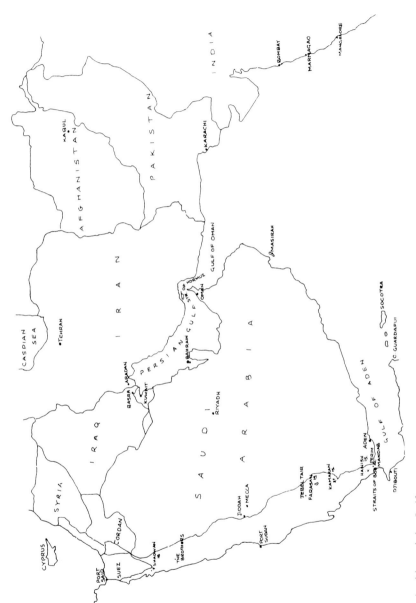

Arabia and the Gulf

not tougher than, that in cargo liners. But because of his personal situation he was able to look beyond the U.K.

He was single, and unattached. During his time on the North American routes he had come very close to losing that status when he nearly became engaged to a New York girl. Of wealthy parents, who not only approved of Jack, but whose family enterprise could provide Jack with executive employment, she was keen to have Jack marry her and settle to the good life in the States. It looked, on the face of it, like a marriage made in heaven, but not through Jack's eyes. Having got this far entirely as a result of his own efforts he was not inclined to become 'dependent' now; he doubted his capacity to become an industrial executive, a fear which would almost certainly have proved groundless, and he was unsure about quitting Britain for ever for the United States. So the marriage did not take place though almost to the day of her death Jack's mother exchanged letters at Christmas time with the rejected would-be bride.

Perhaps this explains why Jack, for the rest of his life, refused to go to weddings!

So, being so completely unattached, Jack was able to consider what amounted to voluntary exile in ships which traded entirely in oceans away from the British Isles and which, once delivered by their builders, never saw British waters again, not even during the war. The company to which he applied was the Burmah Oil Company, and on June 3rd 1935 he was interviewed and accepted by them.

Burmah, in the thirties, was still a company whose principal interest was the extraction of oil from the oilfields of Burmah, the major fields being Yenangyaung and Singu, and its refinement and sale, chiefly to India. For transporting the product out of Rangoon they had four tankers of 5–6,000 tons apiece which ran a shuttle service to the principal Indian ports of Calcutta, Karachi, Madras and Bombay, with occasional visits to lesser ports. The ships were named after the oilfields and, being built for the purpose of trading in the Indian Ocean and nowhere else, were suitable for the climate and very comfortable for their day. The tours of duty were long, three years, and leave minimal. At the end of his three years in Masimpur Jack was away from Burmah for six months, including the passage home and back out. No place for married men, but, for those content to be away from home, or to make ships their home, a pleasant enough environment and way of life. The tanker fleet was in many ways a little, rather democratic, self-contained social club as well as being efficient and hard working on the operational side. The atmosphere, and some of the practices, were largely governed by the fact that with a small fleet even six months' leave each three years meant that even within a ship third mates might sail as second mates and vice versa, second mates as mates, and vice versa. The days when every ship under the British flag virtually has two crews so that 104 Saturdays and Sundays, a dozen so Bank Holidays, and five or six weeks of leave per annum can be accommodated were then far away.

This need for rotation achieved its ultimate formalisation in 1939, when a pay structure which must be unique was advised to the sea-going staff. Effectively it related the pay of all officers holding Master's or Chief Engineer's certificates to length of service, and the length of service rate was paid no matter what rank an officer currently held, other than Master or Chief Engineer. Such an arrangement would hardly be acceptable today, but was eminently suitable for the conditions which then prevailed in the fleet. Whether this had anything to do with the deep and lasting friendships which developed in the fleet I do not know, but the spirit of fellowship in the fleet led to many such friendships which survived both the war and the transformation of the fleet to that which brought to company to its knees in 1974.

On 30th June, laden down with books on tanker construction and operation, Jack sailed in Paddy Henderson's S.S. *Sagaing* for Rangoon, calling at Gibraltar, Palma, Marseilles, Port Said, Suez, Port Sudan and Perim on the way. On the 7th August 1935 he joined S.S. *Masimpur* as third mate. With the fo'c's'les of merchant ships carrying their quota of men with Master's certificates sailing as A.B.s Jack was glad to be there, though it was not quite the same as being Master of *Pedrinhas*.

So began Jack's longest association with one employer in his whole life, just three months short of fifteen years, during which the world turned upside down and the Burmah ships sailed seas which they had never expected to see, carrying cargoes outside their normal experience.

Masimpur was a steamship, oil fired, of 5,586 tons, Sunderland built and commanded, when Jack joined her, by Captain D. B. Gower. Jack left her two years and ten months, and 166,496 miles later, in Bombay, after a typical series of Burmah voyages. Variety, indecent variety, characterised the first few. Rangoon–Calcutta was followed by Rangoon–Karachi and then by Rangoon–Madras before *Masimpur* did no less than five Rangoon–Karachis before Calcutta appeared again. After about a year in this settled life came the excitement of a Rangoon–Cochin, and a few months later a Rangoon–Marmagoa but when, after another year, Coconada joined the list of *Masimpur*'s ports it was complete. Altogether in Jack's first tour, in *Masimpur*, he visited Bombay 5 times, Karachi 16 times,

Calcutta 14 times, Madras 9 times, Cochin 7 times, Coconada 3 times, Marmagoa once and Rangoon 55 times, a total of 110 ports, one every $9\frac{1}{2}$ days or 1,514 miles.

It was time for leave, and Jack sailed from Bombay in P. & O.'s *Cathay*, arriving home, according to 'Family doings', on July 3rd 1938.

Chapter 11

Burmah Oil, second tour

Home on leave for five months Jack spent the first three weeks visiting relations in the North of England and Scotland, his travels ranging from Bury to Wilmslow and up to Dunblane and Ayr, for the family were numerous. Showing the flag round the family and at home in Bury he kept to himself his major plan for this leave until, in late July, he departed for London and Southampton.

Though the famous meeting between Hitler and Chamberlain which purported to guarantee 'Peace in our time' had not yet taken place the tension in Europe was apparent, and the fear of war widespread. The vital contribution which the Merchant Shipping Industry was to make to the Allied cause, and the reservation of employment in that service, were not yet as plain as they later became and Jack, at the age of 31, was concerned about the part which he would be required to play in any future war. Disinclined to remain in tankers, prime torpedo targets, and not a member of the R.N.R., he decided to kill two birds with one stone. He had a long-standing hankering to learn to fly and conceived the idea that with that qualification, added to his existing nautical and navigational qualifications, he would be just the sort of man that the Fleet Air Arm would require should war break out.

So off he went to Hamble to learn to fly, a venture which took him longer than he expected, longer than the average student, convincing him that he had probably not the aptitude for the extremely difficult job of flying onto and off carriers. He did emerge from the course on 22nd October with a private pilot's licence, but it was never used for the purpose for which it was obtained and was relegated to a few private flights from the aero clubs of Rangoon and Bombay. None the less it gave the leave a purpose and filled an old ambition.

A month later, on 20th November 1938, Jack embarked in P. & O.'s *Comorin*, a sister ship of *Cathay*, later lost to an engine-room fire during the war, for the passage back to work. Leaving *Comorin* in Bombay he took passage in the B.I. steamer *Egra* to Karachi where he joined S.S. *Badarpur*, an 8,000-ton tanker built by Hawthorn Leslie in 1922, as third mate. Though he was not to know it then, he was to remain in that ship for five years and four months, to visit ports which he had never expected a Burmah tanker to enter and to carry cargoes which he would not have expected to be within Burmah Oil's experience. In Badarpur he added 223,194 miles to his tally.

The first half of this mileage, almost exactly, was accumulated in the company's traditional trade, carrying oil from the fields in Burmah around the Bay of Bengal and the Arabian Sea. Sixteen visits to Bombay, eight to Karachi, eight to Cochin, three each to Calcutta and Madras and one each to Colombo and Cocanada when, after a 111,000 miles a new port, a new source of oil, Abadan, at the head of the Persian gulf, came into the schedule. Thirteen thousand miles later Badarpur made the last of twenty-two calls at Rangoon before it was closed by the Japanese invasion of Burmah. It was to be many a year before either Jack or *Badarpur* were to return to Rangoon, and then to a country recovering from the Japanese occupation and preparing for independence.

The work went on. Whether the crude came from the Burmese or Persian oilfields the ship had to arrive, load, make passages and discharge before returning to the loading port to repeat the cycle. Tanks had to be cleaned and prepared for new cargoes, frequently of different grades of oil. Crude, almost like soft tarmac; petrol, with its volatility and danger and a variety of semi-refined products in between. Constant vigilance lest familiarity lull someone, be it crew member or visitor from shore, into smoking outside the accommodation. At sea in those waters the hazard of unlit dhows at night, of south-west monsoon weather and, when Abadan joined the schedule, the fog and haze of the straits of Hormuz and the Gulf. Continuous hard work, but performed with skilled and dedicated colleagues in ships purpose built for tropical conditions. No air conditioning as yet, but large windows with sliding louvred shutters and large effective fans. Good food, with heavy emphasis on curries and dishes appropriate to the climate, served by cheery Burmese stewards. The companionship of shipmates which develops when voyages are long, as this one certainly was, but all against the background of developing war forcing changes of trading patterns.

With the fall of Burmah and the loss of the Burmese fields the whole tenor of *Badarpur*'s life changed. Abadan took the place of Rangoon as the loading port, Aden and Mombasa replaced Bombay and the other Indian ports as destinations, and the ship settled into a new routine involving longer passages and more time at sea. Abadan to Mombasa is 2,900 miles, compared with 2,300 for Rangoon to Bombay, and Abadan to Aden 2,000 whilst Rangoon to Cochin was a mere 1,600. The magnificent harbour at Mombasa replaced the difficult Hooghly at Calcutta and relatively straight-forward Abadan, Rangoon. Aden had little to commend it, but *Badarpur* had broken out of the confines of the Bay of Bengal and the coasts of Burmah and India. The weather was generally more congenial and life was better than for most people at that time of the war, though submarines and commerce raiders were an ever present hazard in the Indian Ocean. This revised circuit, north and south across the equator, east and west between the Persian Gulf and the Gulf of Aden did not last for long for after 70,000 miles, in mid-1943 when the battle for North Africa was in full swing and the invasion of Italy in prospect, *Badarpur* made her way from Aden, through the Gates of Hell and up the Red Sea to Port Sudan, Tor, Abu Zanema and Suez, thence through the canal to Port Said and onwards to Haifa to take up an entirely new trade.

Badarpur (J. V. Bartlett)

Badarpur became a latter day *Gunga Din*, a water carrier for the forces, loading water at Haifa and distributing it to the troops and warships in the Mediterranean theatre. To begin with the circuit was a closed one, Haifa, Port Said, sometimes Suez, Alexandria and back to Haifa; very short passages and, by the nature of her trade, a lot of time in port. *Badarpur*'s Mediterranean war represented her idlest time ever, with miles per month at an all time low, and time spent in port at an all time high: Thirty passages yielded a mere 6,273 miles, 209 miles each, in this period, before she broke out with a 1,000-mile passage to Malta, and thereafter the circuit embraced, at various times, Tripoli in Tunisia, Bizerta, Palermo in Sicily and, as the war progressed, the Italian ports of Brindisi and Taranto and Augusta in Sicily. Time at sea increased, and time in port fell, for the passage back to Haifa for another load of water was over 1,000 miles, out of sight of land. By this time Jack was second mate of the ship and his navigational skills came back into play after the spell on the Haifa–Alexandria beach-crawling route.

It was in Palermo, tied up alongside and watering an American destroyer that Jack, the epitome of conservative British seafaring tradition, heard over the destroyer's loudspeaker system the call: 'Liberty guys fall in abaft the after smokestack.' And cringed.

During that spell I was an apprentice in Alfred Holt's *Teucer*, which called at Alexandria in January 1944 and lay in the adjacent berth to *Badarpur*. My Uncle Jack took all the four apprentices from *Teucer* ashore one afternoon for a strawberry and cream tea, the like of which none of us had ever seen, nor have I since. Later, when the lights were lit, he took two of us ashore to a very sedate night club and introduced us to John Collins, all very exciting for wartime second and third voyage apprentices.

The war rolled on and *Badarpur* was near enough to home for it to be possible to send men home for leave in homeward-bound convoys so, on 20th April 1944 Jack joined Harrison's S.S. *Geologist* as a passenger, homeward bound in convoy for Loch Ewe, and onwards alone to Leith. There is no record of the date of his arrival there for 'Family Doings' is sparse, almost non-existent, during the years 1942 to 1952. Jack's father had died in 1940, his sister had to move house and live with her mother, and it was not until 1952 that the journal comes to life again.

So Jack's second tour of duty with Burmah Oil was of extended length and embraced unusual activities. The political upheavals in the East, the war drawing to a close, and the destabilisation of the area which was to follow it were to ensure that he was never to return to the prewar established routes and trades.

Chapter 12

Burmah Oil, third tour

What Jack did with his wartime leave is a mystery. A small ration of petrol would give him some freedom, but not enough to do any large-scale touring. No doubt he visited his family, using the spartan train services operating at the time. Perhaps he was glad that, even after five and a half years away, he only had four and a bit months of leave. In September 1944 he joined British India's S.S. *Umtata* to go back to work.

The Mediterranean was, of course, open, so *Umtata* went very directly: in convoy from Birkenhead to the straits of Gibraltar, then unescorted through the Mediterranean, through the Suez Canal and then onwards with a refuelling stop at Aden, by way of Colombo to Trincomalee on the East coast of Ceylon where, on 1st October Jack joined S.S. *Singu* as second mate.

Singu was a lovely little ship of 4,900 tons, built in 1931 by Swan Hunter on the Tyne. She was a typical Burmah Oil tanker of the penultimate generation with a solid block of accommodation set aft of a longish foredeck and surmounted by a bridge and wheelhouse well awninged against the sun. The officer's accommodation was spacious and cool, though not air conditioned, really a very comfortable place to live for the whole of Jack's third tour of duty with the company.

The dying war, and its aftermath, were to shift the pattern of trade and the movements of the company's tankers permanently away from Rangoon, to Abadan and the Indian ports, and the shortage of ship's officers resulting from the war was to bring into full play the flexibility of manning envisaged by B.O.C.'s single pay rate policy. Jack's stint in *Singu* began with no less than nine 779-mile round trips from Trincomalee to Colombo and back as second mate. Then there followed a long stint as mate with the ship plying between Abadan and a mixture of Indian ports, Bombay, Madras, Calcutta Marmagoa and Chittagong, with only two visits to Rangoon, after the

86

Japanese had left. Despite the change of loading port the job remained typical of the B.O.C. tanker routine and culminated in Jack's return to command on 7th May 1947 starting with a voyage from Abadan to Cochin. The first entry for twelve years in his Night Order Book, which he took from ship to ship, reads:

> From Abadan towards Cochin.
> 7th day of March 1947.
> The course to steer by Standard Compass is S51E to make S46E true.
> 'Take ½ hourly soundings from 0300 onwards. Let me know if you find less than 20 fathoms. Call me when you get an A.M. star position or at 0630 whichever is first.'

These orders were signed in turn by the watchkeeping officers among whom was Jim Fulleylove, 'Fulley', of whom more later.

From then until mid-July of 1947 Jack remained in *Singu*, sometimes as Master, sometimes as mate and, though he was not yet to know it, these were almost his last days of leading a traditional Burmah Oil tanker life in the conventional Burmah Oil tanker trades. In the latter part of July 1947 he flew home to a longer than usual spell of leave.

April of 1948 saw him embarked in P. & O.'s *Strathmore* for the passage back east to Bombay, where he transferred to the *Ethiopia*, which took him to Rangoon, from which port he made one voyage as mate of *Singu* to Abadan and Calcutta before flying back to Rangoon to join the little M.V. *Beme*, a war-built coastal tanker, first as mate then, very soon, as Master, shuttling up and down the Burmese coast from Akyab in the North to Mergui in the South, with frequent (twenty-one) calls at Rangoon. This was a very hard life, incessant cargo work, short passages, only one mate, indeed only one other Briton to talk to, all up and down the hot and steamy Burmese coast, always within twenty degrees of the Equator and with only one port of call which had any pretensions to being a city, Rangoon. But hard though it was it is probably in this ship that Jack developed the liking for very small ships which was to be the salient feature of the last twenty years of his seafaring life.

The frequent visits to Rangoon qualified Jack to attempt the Rangoon pilot's licence exam, which he passed, enabling him to take *Beme* in and out of the port without the aid of a pilot. The Rangoon River is not an easy one, so this represented a considerable achievement and demonstration of Jack's faith in himself.

Singu *(J. V. Bartlett)*

Beme *(Jack Arnot)*

The Rangoon river is not an easy one. As good a description of its difficulties as any is to be found in Frank C. Hendry's story *The Epic of the T.S.S. Alesia*, part of which reads as follows:

'Many years before the Great War Lord Roberts, when C. in C. India, visited Rangoon on a tour of inspection and reported that its principal defence was its dangerous river. It is, indeed, one of the most dangerous in Asia. Seen at high water it is a noble-looking river, a mile and a half wide at its mouth, flowing in a stream which is unbroken from bank to bank. At low water, however, it presents a different aspect; the hidden dangers, which high tide has treacherously concealed, become visible. Some of the navigable channels contract to less than a quarter of a mile, and through them a brown muddy current sweeps at a force which reaches eight knots. Swirling eddies will sometimes throw a large vessel athwart the river even against the pressure of her rudder.

'During spring tides the water will rise and fall as much as twenty-one feet and a vessel which strands at the top of high water, unless she can be got off promptly, has little chance of surviving through the following ebb tide. With one part of her suspended on a mud bank and the water rapidly receding and scouring the mud from under the other part, it is almost a certainty that she will break her back. To add to the natural dangers, during the south-west monsoon blinding rain squalls will suddenly blot out the banks of the river, concealing leading marks, beacons, buoys and lights. To cope with all these dangers a highly trained, highly paid, European pilot service is maintained and pilotage is, of course, compulsory.

'Rangoon is twenty miles up the river and has a dangerous bar, the Hastings Shoal, immediately below it. At Elephant Point on the right bank at the entrance to the river there is a signal station, and the pilotage extends a further eighteen miles seaward from there. A spit runs for about three miles below the point and parallel with it there is a deep reach called the Spit Channel which is full of eddies and nasty cross currents. The end of it is marked by a red lightship marking a right angled turn to starboard which leads down to the outer bar. On the bar the depths are constantly varying, as the silt from the river is either deposited, or scoured away by the strong tides. The trim white painted pilot brig, which usually lay at anchor about six miles off the low palm fringed coast, and eighteen miles from Elephant Point, was a familiar and welcome sight to eastern traders right up until 1922.'

Jack Arnot prepared notes for himself prior to the exam which also illustrate the difficulty of the river. They begin with 'Tidal Notes and Information'.

'The tidal stream is strongest on the night of the second day after Full or New Moon. It then runs in the channels at the rate of seven knots and there are only a few minutes of slack water. After Neaps the stream gradually increases in strength and continues to run strong until the moon quarters when it suddenly drops in strength. On the second and third days after the Moon's quartering there is slack water on the flood for one and a half hours and on the ebb for one hour. The flood tide at Springs makes suddenly and rises six feet in the first hour, but the ebb stream still continues running in mid channel and it is not slack water until one hour after the water has started to rise. The tidal stream turns earlier inshore than in mid channel.

'Caution. At the outer bar the first of the flood sets to the northeast taking the direction of the channel but after the banks are covered about two and a half hours after low water the flood sets strongly onto the Spit Sands over which it turns direct from Elephant Point, the average strength of the tide being five to seven knots. The freshets during July, August and September are highest on the second day after the Moon quarters.

'March to September, Northern Sun, the day tides are highest. October to February, Southern Sun, the night tides are highest.'

And if the river itself was not enough to contend with some of the notes deal with traffic. The International rule of the Road requires that vessels keep to the starboard side of a channel but;

'When to keep to the Port side of the channel:
1. In the Manby Point channel vessel outward bound keeps over to PORT so as to enable inward bound vessel to swing to port having rounded U.M.P. buoy.

2. Inward bound vessels when able to do so keep over to port in order to go over Hastings Tracks.
3. In Liffey Reach, coming up and deep ship coming down let deep ship have better water by keeping over to port.
4. When Using Chakey Tracks.

And just to make life that little bit more difficult there are the Eddies.

'Eddy Points
1. Vicinity of Elephant Point.
2. Middle Bank Buoys.
3. North De Silva point and lower Chakey Buoy.
4. Chaky Point.
5. Hastings Buoy First Spring Flood.
6. Between LMP and UMP Buoys especially on Ebb.
7. Between Sempaphan and Manby Points.'

After ten months of this hard graft Jack must have established the reputation of being a go-anywhere, take-anything anywhere man, for they found him an even smaller ship for his next voyage.

Chapter 13

M.V. *Sabari*

In February of 1949 the Burmah Shell Oil Storage and Distributing Co. of India Ltd., a mouthful of a name which was designed to ensure that both shareholders and the host country were acknowledged, wanted to move their motor barge *Sabari*, from Calcutta to Cochin, and Burmah offered the services of their little-ship expert, Jack Arnot, to do the job. He didn't volunteer, but it wasn't in his nature to refuse an out of the ordinary venture such as this. A voyage of 1,361 miles with an unsuitable crew in a vessel designed and built for river work. No epic, but no simple task either.

The account of the voyage is mostly gleaned from notes which Jack compiled for the benefit of anyone having to do a similar job. These notes not only detail the ship and her voyage, but included hints for successors.

Sabari was a motor barge a 120 feet long, with a beam of 18 ft. and a depth of 7 ft. Gross tonnage was 154 and she was powered by a five cylinder Gardner diesel developing 120 brake horsepower which was alleged to yield eight knots. She had been built in Calcutta in 1935. To accommodate a European Master a wooden cabin, 15 × 7 ft., was built on deck forward of the bridge, and forward of that a steel breakwater was built to protect it. Divided into two parts to form a sleeping cabin and a bathroom it was supposed to be watertight, but it wasn't. Besides a camp bed it held a table and chair, a primus stove and a shelf for the radio. The primus was needed because capacity limitations ruled out the employment of a cook for the sole European.

Charts and almanacs and tide tables were provided, but Jack took his own parallel rulers, dividers, Nories tables and barometer. No chronometer was available so Jack's watch had to suffice. The navigation lights were oil lights, and the ship's bell a length of iron rail, hit with a hammer. The dry card compass was borrowed from the British India company. The crew, excluding the Master, was eleven strong, enough for a good-sized modern containership; a bosun, three quartermasters, three sailors, two 'drivers' and two greasers. All the men were on a single voyage contract with repatriation from Cochin to Calcutta.

The start of the voyage was delayed, for surveying the ship, and turning the survey into permission from the Port Officer to begin the voyage, took three weeks. During that hiatus the ship was bunkered and ballasted with river water to a draft of 3 ft. 8 in. forward and 5 ft. 1 in. aft. Provisions for ten days were taken on board.

It wasn't long after sailing that the shortcomings of the crew showed themselves. Jack's notes on this subject say it all:

'CREW.

The crew consisted of river men a few of whom had at one time or another done a deep sea voyage. They were most unsatisfactory for the following reasons.

a. Having spent their lives in river craft under the orders of a Serang who, as often as not, was probably a relation they were quite undisciplined.

b. They had no idea of time, or of keeping any fixed period at the wheel. Each man steered until he was tired and then howled for a relief. If one left orders to be called at a certain time like as not they would call you an hour or more late.

c. Their steering by compass was so careless that I spent most nights in a deck chair alongside the wheel.

d. Few of them had trousers with the result that when there was a job of work to do one hand was used to hold up their lungi and the other for the job.

e. Their Hindustani was very limited and most parts of the ship had only a Chittagonian name. This was, of course, due to the fact that they had worked together all their lives and had no need to learn the Hindustani for such things.

f. I think they were the laziest crew I ever set eyes upon.

g. Nearly all were seasick.

h. The No. 1. Driver considered that half speed on his engine was as fast as it should go. Whenever I speeded it up it was slowed down again as soon as I went to sleep with some foolish excuse when taxed for a reason. As the crew were anxious to go to Madras the engine broke down just off the Madras breakwater and the driver declared that it would not restart. Fortunately I happened to know just what had been done to stop it.'

Sabari (Jack Arnot)

There are other interesting notes on the voyage:

'NAVIGATION.

Navigation by watch and radio time signal proved quite accurate enough for this job. A cocked hat of five miles diameter by Marq St. Hilaire was not unusual.

It has to be borne in mind that a two-knot current in a five-knot ship is similar to a five-knot current in a twelve-knot ship. Current effect was rather alarming until one got used to it. With a high following sea there is a great danger of pooping in a small slow vessel of this type.

NEVER SAIL WITHOUT AN ALARM CLOCK.

Had I had an alarm clock I could have had twice the amount of sleep that I did, owing to the fact that I could not trust the crew to call me at any set time.

WATCHES.

During the day the man at the wheel had a whistle which he blew (or was supposed to) if he sighted anything. At night there was a man at the wheel and either the Serang or the Lascar who kept watch and watch during the hours of darkness with orders to call me if they sighted anything. There was always a driver on watch in the engine room. The No. 1. driver sat on the engine skylight all in the way and howled abuse at the driver below almost all the time except for a few short spells for sleep.

FOOD.

The food shown on the list for cabin use was more than ample for two weeks. There should be an uptake to take away the soot and fumes from the stoves.

If possible only English, Australian and American tinned foods should be used. Indian tinned foods should be avoided. The plastic cups provided were useless. Filled with hot liquid they split.

RADIO ACCUMULATORS

I did not get a chance to test these to see if they were fully charged before we sailed. The result was that the first accumulator was exhausted in about two hours. I therefore had to use the second one for time signals only in case it was not fully charged. NEVER TAKE ANYTHING ON TRUST ON A VOYAGE OF THIS KIND.

The voyage began at 11.30 a.m. on 18th February and ended with arrival at Cochin at 6.30 p.m. on March 3rd which meant an average speed at sea of 4.44 knots. The original passage plan called for a first and only stop at Madras, but that was before the designed speed of 8 knots was found to be unattainable by a factor of 50 percent. On 22nd February the log notes that 'owing to slow progress and the fact that I will now be four days overdue in Madras I have decided to call at Visagapatam to report and store, and then proceed to Cochin direct.'

Leaving Visagapatam the engine failed to start astern when approaching the fuel jetty, and *Sabari* struck it, bending her port forward davit. The weather on the passage was mainly pretty good, but the least sea caused this very small, low vessel to be wet and uncomfortable.

Rather than go round the outside of Ceylon Jack took the ship through the Palk Strait and the Pamban Pass between that Island and the southern tip of India. (Shown on most maps as Adam's Bridge.) Arriving at the pass the pilot came aboard, speaking only Tamil, a language unknown either to Jack or to his crew. He was without credentials of any sort, and demanded that Jack go ashore, four miles in a canoe, to pay the pilotage dues. By this time, after a hard couple of days and nights, Jack was too exhausted to contemplate this, quite apart from the fact that it would mean leaving the ship in an unsafe position in charge of the bosun. So he refused and wrote a letter to the harbourmaster at Pamban, enclosed an estimated fee of fourteen rupees, and sacked the pilot. The passage of the strait was made without incident.

Without a doubt Jack Arnot was glad to ring Finished with Engines at Cochin at the end of the thirteen-day voyage, looking forward to a return to the main fleet, to a short spell as mate of *Badarpur*, then on to a permanent Master's job in *Yenangyaung*.

Chapter 14

Badarpur and *Yenangyaung*

Leaving *Sabari* at the Shell depot in Cochin, Jack checked into an hotel and settled down to await the arrival of *Badarpur*. His last duty in connection with the little ship was to see the crew off on their repatriation trip to Calcutta. Filling in his time after that was no great problem, for he was an enthusiastic correspondent. Writing letters, and resting after his strenuous thirteen-day adventure, kept him occupied.

Badarpur, Jack's home throughout the war, arrived and he signed on as mate. After part discharging at Cochin she sailed to Karachi where she left the rest of her cargo. Thence she steamed northeast into the Persian Gulf and up to Abadan in the Shatt al Arab river to load a full cargo for Karachi. In the next four and a half months she was to do the Abadan-Karachi round trip three times before rounding Ceylon to visit Chittagong and Rangoon. To conclude Jack's time in her she wound up with a passage from Abadan to Bombay.

There Jack transferred to *Yenangyaung* as Master, with appointment within the company as a permanent Master. He had been with Burmah Oil fourteen years by then and was 42 years old. In all those fourteen years he had not served in *Yenangyaung* before.

She was a 5,447 ton motorship, built by Swan Hunter in 1937, relatively new by Burmah Oil standards. Like all the others she was built for the tropics and, though tiny by today's standards, was entirely suited to her work. Jack remained in her until the end of March 1950 with the ship's voyages all loading at Abadan and discharging on both the west and east coasts of India, ranging as far as Chittagong and Calcutta.

The work was arduous, particularly for the Master, for the idea that three-year tours away from the U.K. were a good thing had gone out of fashion. Qualified officers were in short supply. As a result of this the ship sailed on many of her voyages short handed, with only two mates instead of

97

the normal three, inevitably involving the Master in a certain amount of watchkeeping. Apart from the fact that this was something which Jack had worked twenty-six years to get out of it was in addition to all his other duties and responsibilities. Even when there was a full complement of officers they were not always up to proper Burmah standards.

The same comment on staff quality applied to all departments. Though *Yenangyaung* had an early radar set it was unreliable and did not always work. The same was true of the ship's radio equipment which, in those days, was a morse code installation, not a telephonic system. It could be said that it was to the vagaries of the radio gear that Jack owed the momentous change which was to occur in his life.

A fellow Master, an Irishman, had, in response to a letter from Jack while he was hanging about in Cochin, bought him a ticket in the Irish Sweep. He actually bought four, two for himself and two for Jack, marked them as to ownership and lodged them in the bank. The letter was not acknowledged and Jack forgot all about it. In due course the sweep was drawn and one of Jack's tickets drew a horse which, apart from being worth a prize anyway, makes the ticket a very valuable piece of paper.

Yenangyaung (Burmah Oil Co. Ltd.)

The bookies take no time at all to discover the names of the owners of tickets which have drawn horses, and they set about finding Jack, with a view to buying his ticket from him before the race. He later acknowledged that, had they found him, he would have sold half of it for £100, or the whole for a good offer; but fate intervened.

The bookies discovered his name, and his address c/o the Burmah Oil Company. They wheedled out of the B.O.C. the name of his ship and set about sending him offers by wireless for the whole or part of the ticket, but were disappointed to get no response. On that October day in 1949 *Yenangyang* was bound from Abadan towards Bombay with her wireless out of commission. The messages were only received after the race had been run, Jack's horse had won and the £25,000 prize had become his.

Jack remained Master of *Yenangyaung* until the end of March 1950, when he resigned to take advantage of his good fortune, to go on to make a private voyage across the two greatest oceans of the world.

*   *   *

The following chapters, which deal with Jack's last days with Burmah Oil and the voyage to New Zealand which followed his resignation, are his own work, edited very little and then mainly to eliminate his wondrous spelling errors. A fine navigator, a first class seaman, member of the Institute of Naval Architects he might be, but he could not spell to save his life. He always agreed that he made a 'pritty' poor fist of it.

Chapter 15

The chance presents itself

My ship, the Burmah Oil Company's tanker *Yenangyaung*, bound from Abadan to Madras with a cargo of petrol, kerosene and aviation spirit for the cars, lamps and aircraft of India was making a steady twelve knots southbound out of the Persian Gulf. She had dropped the Quoins lighthouse which guards the entrance a couple of hours earlier and was moving along with nothing in sight in a circle of sea. The hilly, desert waste of the Marakan coast to the east was lost in a shimmering heat haze, the sand and the flies and the heat and stink of the refinery were behind us and we could expect to keep our little circle of sea to ourselves, bar the passing ship or dhow, for the next five days.

At about eleven o'clock in the forenoon of that October day in 1949 I was working on the ship's accounts in my office. Rials, Rupees and Pounds Sterling were chasing each other round my brain, weary of this most unshipmasterlike task and weary, too, after the passage down the Gulf and out through the Strait of Hormuz. So, ruminating on the probable ultimate fate of shipowners and accountants in the less favourable part of the hereafter, I stepped out on deck for a breath of air.

As I paced to and fro in the shade of the bridge above the duty seacunnie approached me and, saluting, handed me a radiogram which, being certain in my own mind that it would contain changes of orders to make my already complicated life even more so, I tore open somewhat ill temperedly. How wrong can you be; the message read 'Hearty congratulations. Your ticket wins £25,000. I missed it by one. Pearson.' I read it again, and again, and feared that I was perhaps asleep and dreaming but I looked in through my bedroom porthole as I passed it and saw that both beds were empty, so I must be awake. After a turn or two more across the deck I looked at it again and, bemused to say the least, put it in my pocket.

The chain of events leading to this message was a long one, beginning some months earlier when I was stranded in Cochin awaiting the arrival of an overdue *Yenangyaung* for me to take command of her. The south-west monsoon was at its height and it rained from morning to night and from night to morning and to fill in the weary days of waiting I caught up on the backlog of my correspondence, which included my writing a letter to another of the company's Masters, Captain Pearson, then at home in Dublin on leave. After finishing the letter, but before sealing the envelope I remembered that I had, before the war, had tickets in the Irish Sweep so I added a postscript saying 'If they still run the Irish Sweep please buy me a couple of tickets', and I enclosed a cheque for one pound. I did not expect an answer, for Captain Pearson would, before long, be returning to the fleet, and I then forgot all about it.

On receiving my letter Captain Pearson got hold of a book of tickets and, being a perfect gentleman, wrote the first two in my name, followed by some for himself and it must have been my second that was the lucky one if his 'missed it by one'. On such a slender chance does the future course of one's life hang.

Pearson is a man with a well developed sense of humour so it crossed my mind that the cable might be a leg pull but, knowing him also to be not an unkind man, I soon discarded that idea and looked again at the message to reassure myself and when eight bells sounded at noon, the end of the forenoon watch, I made my way to the bridge to oversee the fixing of the noon position and the setting of the course to take us down to Cape Comorin, some five days away. That customary duty done I returned to my own deck and sent my boy for Mr. Caldwell, the Chief Officer, known throughout the fleet as 'The impeccable Mr. Caldwell'. When he joined me I showed him the cable and asked him what HE thought it might mean and, after reading it carefully a couple of times his imperturbability crumbled and he almost gibbered 'Good God, Good God, sir, congratulations, sir, you've won the Irish Sweep', which helped to confirm that I could still read and understand.

Later, when the Chief Engineer, a canny Scot, came to my room for our daily meeting about fuel consumption and associated engineering matters I showed it to him too. Putting on his specs he read it carefully and merely asked me how many tickets I had bought and, when I told him two, just grunted and said, 'My word, you might have saved ten bob.' We went on from there to discuss the possible total or partial confiscation of the take should it find its way to the United Kingdom, then governed by a Labour Government desperately scratching round for funds to lose in ventures like the Ground Nuts scheme, and I decided that prudence dictated that it be left where it was, in Eire, and I sent a radio message to Pearson asking him to lodge it in a Dublin bank.

But it wasn't as simple as that, there was paperwork to be mastered. Pearson sent out to me the ticket and the claim form, which, as we were a working tanker spending little time in port and a lot of time at sea, took a while to meet up with me. It found me in Madras, where I took it to the British consul who witnessed my signatures on the forms so that they were fit for presentation to the Irish Sweep. Then I had to devise the best and safest way to get them to Dublin and I decided that as our voyage was to take us next to Chittagong, thence to Abadan where the company had an office, I would keep it till the latter port and send it to London with the company's mail for onward transmission by registered post to Dublin, which I did, and which worked.

By now the news of my good fortune was all round the fleet, the company and the eastern world of oil and shipping, the total population of which seemed to think that life should now be one long party with me signing the chits. Whilst I am all for a party I thought this was a bit much with the documents flitting about in frail, fallible, aeroplanes so I settled for a statement to the effect that yes, there would be parties, but only when the money was safely in a Dublin bank. In due course Pearson advised me of the name of the bank and a short while later the manager cabled me that the cash had been safely deposited. So at last I knew it was really true and our ports of call were the scenes of many a happy shindig.

Burmah's tankers were designed for the Indian Ocean, their trade was all in and around that Ocean and none of them, not even during the war, had ever been home. Before the war life in these ships, for those who did not mind exile, with home leave only every three years, was very pleasant. Not so now, for we were constantly short of staff and many of the people we did have were inexperienced. Officers were hard to come by and engineers even more so with many an engine room staffed by any scallywags that could be found. Crews which had, prewar, been willing and pleasant became troublesome under the guidance of corrupt unions riddled with bribery. Constant nagging by London about the cost of feeding the ships caused mountains of correspondence and the ships themselves were old and falling into bad repair with resultant damage to cargo and all the paperwork that that entailed. Life as Master of one of these tankers was, in the postwar era, not the life I had sweated twenty years to achieve and with my new security I began to think of alternatives.

Years ago someone had given me a book called *Deep Water and Shoal*, by a man called Robinson, which recounted a voyage round the world in a small yacht. The story had caught my imagination and ever since reading it I had dreamed of making a similar voyage which would take me to the little visited islands of the Pacific Ocean. The more I thought about it the more I liked it and the more I liked it the more I contrasted it with the hard life of a tanker Captain at the present time, and the very real danger of the breakdown of my health if I kept going in the job. Even if I didn't crack, by the time I reached pension age in seven years time at fifty I might find that I was past such a voyage, so one day early in March I decided that there was no time like the present and wrote my letter of resignation. In the fullness of time I was relieved in Karachi and left the Burmah Oil Company with a considerable streak of regret, for I had many good friends in the firm and I had attained the goal of all who have struggled through the Board of Trade exams, command of my own ship. I now set out to get myself home.

Easier said than done. It was Holy Year and most of the westbound planes on the Cairo–Rome–London route were full, at least as far as Rome and the best I could do was book a flight nine days hence. I put up at the Officers Club in Karachi to wait out the nine days and one evening I slipped badly in the bath and in falling dislocated my right shoulder, laying myself out. I lay on the bathroom floor, unconscious, for some time before I was found and a doctor sent for who strapped me up with sticking plaster for the night and then, the next day, decided that I would have to live in a plaster cast from neck to waist for the next six weeks. With my arm stuck out in front of me like some Indian Fakir I was in no state to occupy an aeroplane seat so I used the longest six weeks of my life to plan my voyage in some detail. Day after day I planned, and watched the camels, with their jangling bells and supercilious expressions, trundling past the club pulling ridiculously small carts. And I watched the sun setting a little more to the north each day as summer came nearer.

In the middle of this enforced idleness one of the company's ships under the command of my old friend Captain Fulleylove, M.B.E., arrived in port which, though he was to be only a day or two in Karachi, cheered me up no end. Contact made we planned dinner at the Carlton that night. Fulley arrived at about seven in the evening and, after a few preliminary snifters, we hailed a taxi to take us to the Carlton where our conversation was somewhat one tracked. Fulley and I had often talked of my dream voyage but neither of us could quite see how it could be managed until we retired and even then the infirmity of age, or lack of cash, might well make it impossible. So now I outlined to Fulley my plan to go home, find a suitable yacht and sail her out to New Zealand by way of Panama and the Pacific islands. The prospect of my voyage, and the bottle of Liebfraumilch with which we washed our dinner down, were all too much for Fulley and before we parted he had decided to take part of his next long leave in the Pacific, and said that he would meet me in Papeete, Tahiti, in October 1951.

Fulley went back to his ship and I went back to my club to sit out the hot, uncomfortable days until the plaster could come off and I could make my way home. By the time that day arrived the plaster felt like a strait jacket; but the day did come, and a New Zealand doctor assisted by a New Zealand nurse attacked the plaster with an enormous pair of shears, close relations to those used for trimming hedges. The doctor wielded the shears and the nurse the insecticide pump and after a few minutes of hacking and chopping I was free. Three days later I was told I could travel and I was soon on my way in a plane seventy per cent of whose passengers were priests bound for Rome. Sitting next to me was an elderly Korean priest with a long white beard which I had to untangle from his seat belt each time we took off or landed.

We left Karachi at 9.30 one very hot night and landed at Bahrain for fuel at half past midnight. Sunrise found us not far from the Suez canal and we landed at Cairo at 6.30 for breakfast. At 9.00 we were off again across the Mediterranean sea and over the island of Capri to land in Rome, where most of our passengers left us, in time for lunch. Onwards to London where we landed with a couple of heavy bounces at 5.00 in the evening, twenty hours plus five hours of longitude, from Karachi.

The B.O.A.C. bus took us into London where I found an hotel which, for an extortionate fee, would tolerate my presence for one night only. The change of climate and scenery in so short a space of time was rather startling, and I noticed that London buses and taxis move faster than camels, making one apt to misjudge things when crossing the street.

Chapter 16

In search of a vessel

The next morning, after a very poor breakfast, I left my hotel, put my bags in the left luggage office at St. Pancras and went to the company's office and thence to lunch at the Cock in Fleet Street with a friend, the one who had passed the ticket and claim form on to Dublin. Then, as always when in London, I had a walk on the embankment and a look at *Discovery* and then along the Strand, where I bought a fifteen and a sixpenny shirt for two pounds ten, before going to the station to catch the train to Manchester. The station seemed to me to be even dirtier than when I last saw it three years ago.

When I reached home in Bury that evening in unexpectedly fine weather my Mother asked what I intended to do next, for she knew that I had left Burmah Oil. I told her at some length of my plan for a voyage to New Zealand and, though her only adverse comment took the form of the question, 'If you want to go to New Zealand why don't you go in a passenger ship? You can afford it,' I could see that she disapproved of the whole venture. Mother knew how to make her waves of disapproval felt! The rest of my relations said little but I could see that, with the exception of my sister Annie, they thought that I was a little bit cracked.

Ever since reading *Deep Water and Shoal* away back in the thirties I had spent many a happy hour scanning the advertisements in *Yachting Monthly* and other yachting magazines to see what was on offer, and formulating ideas on the type of yacht which I would choose for the voyage, should I ever make it. She had not only to be capable of making the voyage, but also be one that I could not only afford to buy, but also afford to run. So now, armed with the latest editions and financially more capable than I had ever expected to be, I started writing to yacht brokers telling them what I was looking for and asking them what they had on offer.

Though I have spent nearly thirty years at sea I have very little experience of yachts and almost none of ocean-going boats, so at this time I was not entirely sure of what I wanted. Though I had toyed with the idea of a single-handed voyage I had ruled that out as being basically unwise and also undesirable for the storm of protest which it would bring forth from the family. I came to the conclusion that I should make it a two-man expedition, and began thinking in terms of a stout vessel of about forty feet, Bermudan ketch rigged for easy handling of the canvas, and copper sheathed against worm in tropical waters. She would have to have a small engine, preferably diesel rather than petrol, to get us in and out of port in calms or contrary winds.

Before long specifications began to arrive in shoals but none of them seemed to be what I wanted, though I recognised that no one ever gets exactly what he wants in a secondhand yacht, or even in a new one for that matter. Some filled all the requirements but one, and that was most often the copper sheathing, and even if copper had been obtainable I thought it would be unwise to sheath an iron fastened hull, of which there were many. The few that were copper sheathed all had the wrong rig and I felt that as a very amateur potential yachtsman I had not the knowledge to consider changing a rig, never mind the expense. Eventually the post brought details of a Burmudan ketch of forty feet, for sale at what seemed rather a high figure but which seemed to fill most of the requirements. She was lying at Bangor in North Wales, which is not to far from Bury, where I was, so I drove down one day to have a look at her.

I found her shored up in Dickie's yard with her masts unshipped but her first appearance pleased me. She had a sea-kindly hull with a nice sheer, a handsome flare to her bow, a deep keel, good freeboard and a canoe stern. On board she had a rather large and clumsy twenty horsepower diesel engine which took up a lot of space but she was, for her size, pretty roomy with full six feet headroom, which is important to me if I am not to have a permanently scarred bald pate. Sadly the standard of her internal fittings was poor, but none the less I liked the shape of her hull, and I liked her name *Simba*, which is *Lion* in one of the African languages.

Not being inclined to buy the first suitable boat I saw I next went down to Bristol to visit my brother Donald and see what might be on offer around there, with a vague idea that there might be a Bristol Channel pilot cutter, a fine seaworthy type of boat, available. But the working days of those boats are long past and the few remaining boats left of the type are old and are not in the best of condition, and anyway the rig is really too heavy for what I had in mind.

From Bristol I motored across lovely Wiltshire and Hampshire to

Southampton, where I spent a week looking round the most yacht populated part of Britain and inspecting every likely boat that was for sale that I could get access to, but found nothing remotely like what I was looking for. The taverns on the various harbours and waterfronts were perfect places for gathering information and I found that with pint in hand and an ear cocked to windward I heard a great deal about boats which interested me, but in following up such leads the end result was usually disappointment. Indeed, once I might be said to have been led up the garden path. One night I was in a pub called the Goatherd, I can't remember where, though it was situated a long way from the waterfront, and I met the father of a boy who had been a cadet in *Conway*, the training ship that I was in. One way and another he led me through a chain of acquaintances and pubs which culminated after midnight in me sitting somewhere near Portsmouth, with a flat battery, in the pouring rain, waiting for a break-down van to haul me back to Southampton.

A run down to Falmouth, as much for old times sake as anything, turned up nothing but two suitable yachts which were not for sale. At home there was a letter awaiting me telling of a boat, which seemed possible, lying at Birdham in Sussex, so I set off southbound yet again to find her lying in the non-tidal basin at Birdham Pool, a lovely spot on the upper reaches of Chichester harbour not far from Itchenor. Arriving at about three on a beautiful, hot summer's afternoon to find the family living aboard, but the owner away on business, I was guided round by his wife and arranged to return in the evening when he came back.

She was about fifty feet in length, heavily built and of, to my eye, rather clumsy appearance with a large steering wheel aft which worked the rudder through a screw mechanism covered by a wooden case which looked for all the world like a coffin. So after my first inspection I went looking for a pub to stay in, which was not too easy with a race meeting going on at Goodwood, and I settled for a local guest house, the Snipe, which I had noticed earlier, where I met a Captain Power, retired from the British India Shipping Company. Thus established with a bed for the night I walked to the Birdham Hotel where my cocked weather ear let me down and gleaned nothing about boats in general nor the one I was interested in in particular.

The owner was on board when I returned to the pool and I had another look around and a long yarn with him. He had never had her out under full sail, motoring wherever he went, and so had no real idea of her sailing qualities, and in the end I decided that she would be too big and heavy to be handled comfortably by two people under all conditions. I went ashore after telling the owner that was what I thought, but that I would let him know for sure in a day or two. At the Birdham Yacht Club, to which Captain Power took me that evening, the gleanings of my cocked weather ear led me to believe that the boat I had inspected was not all that she appeared to be, and a conversation with the surveyor who had last surveyed her added to my impression that all was not well though, of course, he would say nothing specific. Who knows, I might have asked him to survey her for me! So I turned her down and she was sold about a year later for about half the price I was asked, and I believe there was quite a lot of dry rot found in her.

Simba was, after weeks of writing and searching, still the only, or perhaps the best, possibly suitable boat which I had encountered, so I contacted the agents who were selling her to learn that she was then cruising in Irish waters. So I asked them to find out where she was and set off for Holyhead, pausing for the night at Hereford whence I rang the agent, who had found the yacht, which was lying at Howth, near Dublin. I caught the night ferry to Dunlaoghaire and arrived there after a somewhat sleepness night on account of having met an old shipmate among the passengers, and chartered a taxi to take me to Howth a few miles to the north. I found an hotel, booked in, had a couple of hours' sleep and breakfast and went out looking for Simba before she sailed away and there she was, lying at a mooring in the harbour. I got the local boatman to take me out to her only to find that there was nobody on board but gleaned from him the owner's name, Churchill, and had his house by the quay wall overlooking the harbour pointed out to me as I was rowed back ashore.

Weary as I was after a long drive and a sleepless night as a result of which I was not feeling as bright as I should have done, I walked round to the house, knocked at the door and asked for Mr. Chamberlain! The man who answered the door assured me that nobody of that name lived around there and that, regrettably, he was not the owner of *Simba*, and perhaps the corner shop might be able to help; so there I went and asked if they could tell me where Mr. Chamberlain lived, only to be told that no one of that name lived locally but that a Mr. Churchill lived just up the road!

I went to Mr. Churchill's house to find that he was out, and was told by his wife that she didn't know whether he would be back for lunch or not, so I did the best thing I could think of and said that I would go back to the hotel and that I would be there at noon. No message came at noon but later I was told that Mr. Churchill would be at home at 2.00, or that is what I thought I was told, for going there at that time I found that he had gone to the hotel to meet me at 2.00. I really must go to bed at night. We had crossed between the house and the hotel, but I waited and he duly came home. After a brief chat we went off in his dinghy to *Simba* and I had a good look around her before we started the engine and took her out of the harbour for a look at the sea and to get the feel of her, and then returned to the mooring. There and then I made up my mind that, even if *Simba* was not exactly what I wanted, she was certainly capable of the voyage to New Zealand and I agreed to buy her, provided that she surveyed satisfactorily and we could agree a price. Mr. Churchill agreed to bring her over to Bangor for survey.

After dinner I was at a loose end and the hotel receptionist and I went for a walk round the harbour in the lovely summer evening, stopping at one of the local pubs for a drink. To my great amusement this particular pub (they may all do the same for all I know) closed at 10.00 and opened again at five past, a proper Irish arrangement. In conversation my companion tried to sell me a ticket in the Irish Sweep, that being one of her hotel functions, and when I declined she wanted to know if I had ever known a winner, adding, before I could think up a suitable white lie, that she had sold three winning tickets, and that two of the three winners had already drunk themselves to death. We had more to talk about than that, for she came from Valentia and knew a famous ocean yachtsman, Connor O'Brien, who made a long voyage in his *Saoirse* and who had retired to Valentia.

I had been at home about ten days when a wire came from Mr. Churchill telling me that *Simba* would be in Conway in a couple of days' time, so I wound up the old Ford and bolted down to Bangor to arrange for Dickie's yard to slip the boat for survey, and to find a surveyor. One B. L. Dunphy was recommended to me so I went and found him at his home in Deganwy. Fixing up the survey took longer than I had expected for the 'small world' syndrome came into play. We soon discovered that a cousin of his had been at Cleaver and Hutchinson's cramming for one of the B.O.T. certificates at the same time as me, and was now in command of a large merchant ship. Mr. Dunphy surmised that the cousin would not be all that interested in long ocean passages in small sailing boats, having made a longish one in a lifeboat during the war. I fixed myself up at the Garth Hotel in Bangor, the best and most reasonable small hotel I have stayed in since the war: and I have tried a few! And waited.

Simba eventually arrived and I went and joined the owner on board one Sunday evening. We sat in the cockpit enjoying a nightcap and admiring the summer evening scene, with the fine old bridge picked out in fairy lights and the massive, daunting castle floodlit in the background. After a comfortable night and a hearty breakfast we sailed for Bangor at eight in the morning so as to cross the bar at Conway at high water. There was a fresh westerly wind so we decided to motor the short passage and, even though it was high summer, it was very cold and it even managed to rain. Arriving at Bangor on schedule we made fast to the wall at Dickie's yard to wait for the next day's high water to put her on the slip, shifting ballast and the anchor chains to the inshore side of the boat, and rigging preventer tackles to the masthead, to ensure that when she dried out she would not fall over.

At high water the next day she was floated onto a cradle and hauled up the slip into the yard and Mr. Dunphy, looking very grim and purposeful, set about his survey and, after two or three days of tapping and probing, reported *Simba* to be in reasonable condition. Only the weight of the anchors and the lengths of the cables came in for criticism, so I agreed a price with Mr. Churchill and bought her. The landlord of the Garth witnessed the signatures on all the paperwork and in a few hours she was mine. The chance had been taken and the Search completed.

Chapter 17

Getting to know her

I thought that I would take *Simba* round the Lleyn Peninsula to Pwllheli to get used to her, and to make plans for fitting her out for the long voyage to New Zealand, visiting a friend of mine who was on holiday at Abersoch, a few miles away, at the same time. Mr. Churchill, who had only sold *Simba* because he had recently moved from the south of England to Dublin to live, and found the weather so uncertain as to give him only a week or two's sailing each year, seemed loath to leave her, so I asked him if he would like to come round to Pwllheli with me. He jumped at the idea, even though he was supposed to be back in Dublin.

The tides for the next day or two were too small to float *Simba* off her cradle so we took a run down to Pwllheli to look at the place and see if the harbour held any problems. It rained most of the way there, and Pwllheli did not impress me too much, a holiday resort in decline, having had its day. Drab and post war dreary, with a long sea front backed by shabby boarding houses with a few people sitting at doors and windows, looking at the rain and the grey sea breaking on the stony beach across the front. We went down to the harbour, which is small and affords a certain amount of shelter, to discover that with *Simba*'s draft of 5 ft. 9 in. she could only enter an hour or so each side of high water. The harbour at Pwllheli was, in times gone by, used for shipping stone for paving roads, most of which was quarried from a prominent rock known as Careg-yr-Imbill, which guards and marks the harbour entrance and which, as a result of all that quarrying is but a shadow of its former self. Odd name for a rock; I believe it translates roughly to 'Bob's your Uncle'. Even though it was Sunday afternoon Mr. Jones, the manager of Western Marine Craft, assured me that he would find a berth for us when we arrived and, having failed to find anywhere providing afternoon tea, we took the car to a garage and left it to

111

await our arrival in *Simba*, and caught the bus back to Caernarvon where there was food, and another to Bangor.

We were stuck in Bangor for another couple of days because a combination of an unusually high barometer and an odd wind direction caused the tide to fail to reach its predicted height; but eventually one evening she floated off her cradle, we embarked a local Menai Straits pilot and set course for Caernarvon under power. As we passed westwards through the strait we passed the training ship in which I had prepared for my seafaring career, H.M.S. *Conway*, one of England's old 'wooden walls', a ship of ninety-six guns. Barring my first term I spent two very happy years in her and, as we passed, we dipped our red ensign to her but got no response, for, it being midsummer, all the boys were away on holiday and no watch was being kept on deck. The run to Bangor took about an hour and a half and at about 10.00 we moored to a dredger in the tidal dock, disembarked the pilot and turned in in anticipation of a 5.00 a.m. start to catch the tide on the bar.

The next day dawned gloomy, damp and miserable, and after a hearty breakfast of bacon and eggs, fried bread and coffee we cast off from the dredger and set sail. The passage nearly ended there, for though it was high water we only just managed to plough through the mud on the bar and get out into the western end of the Menai Strait and turn left for Caernarvon bay. In that dreary weather we decided to motor round to Pwllheli, setting only the mizzen as a steadying sail. The two-cylinder Pelapon twenty-horsepower diesel gave us about five knots as we chugged along the rain swept north coast of the Lleyn peninsula, through Bardsey sound, past Hell's Mouth and Abersoch where, being early for the tide at our destination, we anchored for lunch and fished unsuccessfully for our supper. At four-ish we hove up and motored eastwards for Careg-yr-Imbill and, rounding it into the entrance to Pwllheli harbour we were met by Mr. Jones's boat, which led us in and helped us to moor to two buoys alongside a yacht called *Red Witch*. An altogether uneventful passage, and I had still not had *Simba* under sail.

I went ashore to get my car from the garage while the still reluctant to leave Mr. Churchill got his things together and, at about 6.00 p.m., we set off for the graceful suspension bridge across the Menai Strait and onwards along the dull, straight road across Anglesey to Holyhead where, after we had had dinner together for the last time, Mr. Churchill boarded the night Ferry for Dun Laoghaire and I climbed back into the car and set off back to Pwllheli, arriving at about eleven thirty. I dragged the dinghy down the beach, rowed out to the *Simba* and was asleep within minutes of turning in.

A dull, overcast morning with a moderate southwesterly breeze greeted me when I awoke at 7.00 the next morning and my sleep demolishing swim round the ship was short and sharp, for the water was bitterly cold, and I wasted no time putting on my clothes. After bailing out the dinghy I rowed out to the point and, using silver paper for bait, I soon had two fine mackerel for my breakfast, and before the harbour was properly awake they were sizzling in the pan and coffee and toast were nearly ready for the table. In rationed Britain providing meals for oneself on one ration book was something of a problem, and catching fish a matter of importance. Bacon and egg could only be managed once a week, so if the fishing failed it was porridge again. Even the provision of fat for frying wasn't easy and I had to resort to the less tasty grilled mackerel from time to time. Several females offered their services as cook for the voyage, but none got the job, especially not the one who came aboard one day and volunteered to cook lunch and, after messing about for an interminable length of time, asked me how to cook the potatoes!

After breakfast I washed up, and formulated rule number one. All washing up to be done immediately after the meal. That morning I had a most pleasant feeling of possession. Here I was in my own little ship with no one but myself to consider for the time being. It was the first time in my life that I had been in that position, and I liked it.

My own little ship was 40 ft. 6 in. overall, 38 ft. 6 in on the waterline with a beam of 10 ft. 3 in. and a draft aft of 5 ft. 9 in. She was built in Lyme Regis by A. A. Hall in 1926 of Douglas Fir, with oak stem and stern posts and keel, from which was hung two and a half tons of lead, which, with the help of three quarters of a ton of internal pig iron ballast, ensured her stability. Her spars were of pine, the mainmast being some 50 ft. in height and the mizzen mast 30 ft., both being supported by galvanised iron wire shrouds made fast to bronze chainplates, and each sporting one set of crosstrees. The mainmast is stepped on the keelson in the bedroom just abaft the forepeak, and the mizzen in the cockpit just abaft the main cabin bulkhead. The mainsail has roller reefing and the mizzen is reefed conventionally with reef points and cringles. The main is sheeted to a horse on the cabin top forward of the doghouse and the mizzen to the afterdeck, the boom overhanging the stern by about 3 ft. There are guard rails round the deck from the after end of the cockpit to the mainmast shrouds.

The sails, when I bought her, comprised a jib, a staysail, the mainsail and the mizzen, both Bermudan, all in good condition and totalling 700 square feet. I added other specialist sails later.

The accommodation, starting from forward, comprised the following. A chain locker in the eyes of the ship. Then the forepeak with one bunk on the port side with drawers under it. I never used the forepeak for anything but the storage of sails, anchors, wires, mooring ropes, the dinghy's outboard motor and the hundred and one other odds and ends required to keep the ship going on a long voyage. A bulkhead and door separated the forepeak from the bedroom with two bunks with vi-spring mattresses one above the other on the port side, and to starboard two wardrobes separated by a dressing table and washbasin with cupboards above and drawers below. The aftermost wardrobe was fitted out with shelves as a food locker. There is 6 ft. 1 in. of headroom below the coachroof.

Aft of the bedroom is the main cabin, with the galley at its forward end to starboard and the W.C. compartment to port. The galley has a sink and a two-ring calor gas cooker with the locker for the gas bottle below it, along with drawers for cooking pots and cutlery, and a fresh water pump services the sink. Aft of all this is a 6 ft. bunk to port and a settee to starboard, with a swinging table in between. Abaft the table is the engine in a large wooden box, over which the cabin coachroof rises into a roomy doghouse, in which is another bunk which overlaps the one in the main cabin to some extent. The fuel tank and the semi-rotary bilge pump are on the starboard side of the doghouse, and under the two steps up from the cabin floor to the doghouse deck are two twenty-five gallon water tanks and a block of Nife batteries.

A door and sliding hatch lead from the doghouse to the 5 ft. square self-draining cockpit where both wheel and tiller steering are accommodated, with lockers under the seats on either side of the cockpit. Abaft the cockpit is a roomy afterpeak, about 4 ft. in length, which houses the rudder quadrant. The decks throughout are of teak. Such was the yacht which was to be my home for the next two years.

After breakfast I rowed ashore and, after checking that there was no mail for me at the Western Marine Craft office, I went into Pwllheli to stock up with food as best I could and then drove to Abersoch, where my friend Beresford Battersby was to take his holiday, some seven miles distant. I found it to be a pleasant little village, a vast improvement on Pwllheli, with fine cliffs and sandy beaches and a good, though somewhat exposed, anchorage for yachts; an ideal place for children on holiday, and there were plenty of them about. But the weather was no better than it was in Pwllheli. Back on board I spent the next few days overhauling everything and making lists of things required for the great voyage. Most mornings I went for a swim and then went fishing for my breakfast, as often as not dressed in an oilskin, for the weather that summer was awful and it rained and blew day after day. In the whole month that I was there it only failed to rain on two days and, as I was not keen on taking out my still strange vessel until I had fair weather, I just waited and waited.

One day I ran out of fresh water and had to go alongside the jetty to fill the tanks. As there was only sufficient depth for about an hour each side of high water there wasn't much time to waste, and at about high water I cast off from *Red Witch* and then cast off from my after buoy before starting the engine and going forward to cast off from the forward buoy. Then I came quickly aft and was steering toward the jetty when it all began to go wrong. The engine started to slow down, so I gave it more and more throttle but it went slower and slower and finally stopped. The wind and tide were swiftly driving me ashore so I ran forward and let go an anchor, which brought her up still afloat. Back in the cockpit I was opening up the engine box to find the cause of the stoppage when I noticed one of the mooring ropes leading over the side and found it to be nicely wound round the propeller; how it got there I just don't know but by fiddling with the clutch and hauling on the rope I managed to get it clear, got the engine started again and went forward to get the anchor up. When the cable came up and down the anchor refused to leave the bottom, clearly foul of some obstruction, so I decided to slip it and buoy it and come back for it later. When the cable was out to the bitter end I went down to the chain locker armed with a spanner and a marlinespike only to find that the shackle securing the end of the chain was rusted solid.

By this time the boatyard had noticed that all was not going to plan, to put it at its best, and someone rowed out to give me a hand, his first task being to row back ashore for a hacksaw, with which we cut the cable, and I was at last able to get alongside for my water. The tide was falling fast so I had to be quick, but I filled the tanks and got back to the mooring without further incident.

At low water my anchor was plain to see, lying with its cable in the mud with one fluke firmly hooked under a large ship's anchor chain which lay across the bottom of the harbour. There was nothing for it but to don my swimming trunks, row as near as possible to the anchor and then wade through the noisome mud. I was nearly up to my waist in the slimy stuff before I got to the anchor. It was no easy matter to disentangle it but eventually I got it and its chain into the dinghy and, covered from head to foot in mud and smelling like a midden, I rowed back to the ship to clean myself and the anchor and chain, make fast the end with a well greased shackle, and get the chain back in the locker and the anchor back on deck before going ashore to buy a hacksaw.

When Beresford and his wife, and their daughter Beverley, arrived we managed to get out on the first reasonably fine day for a cruise round Tremadoc Bay. The tide was right for a 9.00 a.m. departure and we motored out into the bay and fished without any luck. The weather didn't hold fine for long and by lunchtime we were back in Abersoch roads, anchored in quite a lop which did nothing for our lunch, but we had few options as, with *Simba*'s draft, we couldn't get back into Pwllheli until about 7.00 p.m. This was the first half decent day I had had in the fortnight I had been here, and for the next few days I was harbour bound by the tail end of a south-westerly gale. By then I was on a swinging mooring and at each change of tide I swung and fouled the mooring cable of a large motor launch which was moored close by, but because it was blowing so hard there was nothing we could do about it. When a lull came her owner took her up the harbour and put her on a mud bank, and I found that her chain had taken a bit of my paint off but had not, as I had feared, damaged my copper sheathing.

By this time I had come to the conclusion that this was no place to spend the winter fitting out, which had been my original intention. What I required was a harbour where I could moor *Simba* safely, preferably alongside, and leave her for a week at a time, with a good shipyard at hand to tackle the jobs which I couldn't do myself, and an adjacent chandlery. I thought back to my travels whilst searching for the boat and concluded that Birdham Pool on Chichester Harbour would be ideal. The pool is locked off from the river with little or no rise and fall, is sheltered and you can moor bow or stern on to the jetty, with dolphins to which to make fast your offshore ropes. And there is a good shipyard and local shop, and the Birdham Hotel and Yacht Club is handy. Perhaps too handy.

So now it was a matter of waiting for suitable weather for the passage round Strumble Head and Land's End and up the Channel to Birdham. During the wait my nephew Ian, now having left the sea for a business career, and his wife Joan, came down for a couple of days, during which we managed a day out round St. Tudwal's Island before worsening weather drove us to anchor at Abersoch to await the tide at Pwllheli. They went home, and I stored the ship for the trip round the land and bought a Valor stove, for it was getting very cold in the evenings, and settled down to wait for a fine spell for the voyage to Birdham. I had no radio at the time so I had to rely on fishermen and newspapers for weather forecasts. It was not until 15th September 1951 that what appeared to be a settled spell of weather arrived and I decided to go.

A friend from a neighbouring boat helped me get the dinghy aboard and, at about 7.00 p.m., in a light south-westerly breeze with a clear sky dappled with light cloud I prepared to sail. I trimmed and lit the navigation lights, secured everything on deck, had a good meal, started and warmed up the engine and at 8.30 in the gathering dusk I cast off and, having cleared the harbour entrance, set my course for the St. Patrick's Causeway Buoy in the middle of Cardigan Bay, and thence to Strumble Head, with the intention of making Milford Haven my first port of call.

It was a lovely summer's night and with little wind I continued under power, not feeling sure of myself under sail, having seen how quickly the weather could change in these parts. Every now and then I nipped below to make a cup of coffee, leaving *Simba* steering herself, which she would do for a few minutes in good weather once well settled on her course. Clouds came up with the dawn and the wind freshened, and continued to freshen as the morning drew on. I passed Strumble Head at about 10.30 p.m.; there was a big swell coming up and the sky was completely overcast and I was concerned about the weather. By 11.30 p.m. there was clearly a gale brewing, and after consulting the chart I decided to run for shelter in Fishguard harbour, where I arrived at 1.30 that afternoon. I anchored in the middle of the harbour in the part marked on the chart as being for small vessels, gave her a good scope of chain and went below for a well-earned sleep.

Chapter 18

Trouble

The harbour of Fishguard is not a natural one, having been made in the lee of Strumble Head with a view to attracting the trans-Atlantic liners which then used Liverpool and Cobh as their terminals. By no means big enough to accommodate today's liners it failed to achieve its aim even in the days of smaller ships, and became the terminal for the Rosslare ferries which were, first of all, passenger ferries connecting with the trains, and now carry cars as well.

The harbour is formed by two breakwaters, each half a mile long, partly enclosing a small bay with a maximum depth of seven fathoms in the shelter of the northern breakwater, and shallowing to nothing in the south-eastern part of the bay inside the east breakwater before ending at the embankment carrying the road from Godwick, where the harbour is, though it is called Fishguard harbour, to Fishguard itself, where there is a drying creek and the Yacht Club. The whole is surrounded by low hills and in fine weather is very appealing. The anchorage for small boats is in the south-eastern part of the bay, just within the shelter of the eastern breakwater but exposed to winds from the north-east. The most significant feature of the two towns seemed to me to be the enormous number of pubs supported by a labour force chiefly employed on the ferries and in their port, in fishing and in farming.

The drying creek has on its bank the village of Lower Fishguard, has one long quay on the northern side and a short breakwater at the entrance; it is only useful for shallow draft vessels and fishing boats which are content to dry out alongside the wall at low water. The new Yacht Club is at the seaward end of the quay and it and the sea cadets keep the creek in use.

I awoke at about 4.00 p.m. and went into the cockpit to have a look at the weather. As I passed through the doghouse I noticed that the barometer had fallen about a tenth of an inch in the last four hours, and on reaching the deck I found a moderate south-westerly gale blowing and quite a chop in the harbour. *Simba* was straining at her cable, but even though anchor bearings showed that she had not dragged I felt uneasy about my position, even in the harbour, with the wind blowing so hard and showing every sign of increasing. I went below to have a look at the chart, which showed a sand and mud bottom and I thought that the anchor should be well dug in by now but there was always the chance that one of the fierce jerks which were coming on the cable would part it. I got out the second anchor and bent onto it two of my four-inch mooring ropes tied together, made the inboard end fast round the mainmast at deck level and then hove in half of the chain on the anchor to which I was lying. Starting the engine I went ahead and gave her a sheer before going forward to drop the second anchor, slacking away the rope till I was at its full scope, and paying out about three quarters of the chain so that the weight of the ship was evenly taken by both anchors. After this I felt much more secure.

At about 6.00 p.m. I made myself a good hot dinner and then, after observing rule number one, I filled, trimmed and lit the anchor light and, as it was getting cold, lit the Valor stove as well and prepared for a nervous night. As the engine had shown itself to be rather hard to start from cold I ran it for a few minutes every hour, for if kept warm it would start first swing. Every hour I went on deck to see that all was as it should be, to check the anchor bearings and watch the weather, and as time went on the sea seemed to get up even though the wind remained steady. Though I had been looking forward to a long night in my bunk after the passage from Pwllheli I decided that in these conditions I must look at things every hour until the storm abated, meanwhile settling down to write a few letters and read a little. By 9.00 p.m. I was feeling sleepy so I took a look at the weather, which seemed much the same, dressed in flannel trousers, a sweater and slippers, set the alarm to go off at 10.00 p.m. and turned in on the doghouse settee. I had been reading by the light of a hurricane lamp to save my batteries and I left this lit, hanging in the main cabin, should I need a light on deck at any time.

Experienced seafarers have a sixth sense and at 9.50 p.m., with no prompting from the alarm, I awoke feeling that all was not as it should be. Everything was quieter and the motion of the boat was different and, like a flash, it occurred to me that the cables had parted and that I was drifting and I was out on deck in a second. To my horror I saw the northern breakwater, with seas breaking over its jagged concrete blocks, within a few feet of my stern, so close that the bulk of the breakwater blotted out the sky. It was blowing a full gale by now, the sky was overcast and with the wind blowing the tops off the seas it was hard to see very far. One bound took me into the cabin and I cranked the engine for my very life and it responded by starting first time. Back on deck in an instant I rammed the throttle to full ahead and clawed my way off the breakwater, having come within twenty feet of it at its closest. Had I woken half a minute later I doubt that I would be writing this at all.

Slowly, ever so painfully slowly, *Simba* moved ahead and away from the breakwater towards the middle of the harbour. The wind was still gathering force but I found that, provided I kept her head dead into it we could make slow progress to windward, but if I let her head fall off at all not only did I lose ground but I had the devil's own job to get her head to wind again. During a lull I ran forward to see what had happened to the anchors and could just see both the rope and the chain hanging up and down, pure lack of speed preventing the broken rope streaming astern into the propeller, thank heaven, for there was no time to recover it. So there were two good anchors, and an unknown quantity of rope and chain, adorning the bottom of the harbour.

I was back at the wheel before the next squall struck. The squalls were increasing in force and I reckoned that they were in excess of force twelve on the Beaufort scale, that is a wind of over sixty-five knots, hurricane force, and the comment in the scale at this point is 'No sail can stand, even running'. By midnight the squalls and rain became so heavy that even with the engine at maximum revs I was losing ground and getting dangerously close to the breakwater again, and it seemed to me that if the squalls lasted any longer than they had been doing, or if it blew any harder, I could not fail to finish up a total wreck on the jagged concrete.

When the rain eased a little I could see the passenger jetty, with the mailboat alongside, all brilliantly lit, no more than half a mile away, and I could not help but contrast my lot, soaked to the skin, desperately cold and fighting for my life, with that of the passengers tucked up in their nice warm bunks or downing their nightcaps in the bar. Years in the tropics had thinned my blood, and poor *Simba* was not even insured! The cat and mouse game between the ship, the wind and the breakwater had been going on a long time and the strength was draining from me. I feared for my endurance. At the back of my mind was the nagging fear that the engine might stop, either by accident or because of fuel shortage, for I could not take the time either to dip the tank nor to switch from one tank to the other.

Sometime about 1.30 a.m. a stronger squall even than usual struck the ship on the starboard bow, forcing her head round till the wind was four points or so on the bow and, with the enormous force of the wind in her masts and rigging she heeled over just as if she were being over driven under sail on the starboard tack. With the helm hard a starboard and the engine going full ahead she hung in this position, drifting to leeward towards the dreaded breakwater for what seemed to be an age. Very, very slowly she struggled back head to wind with the concrete only a matter of feet from our stern and I had to conclude that, unless I could get assistance soon, I would finish up as scrap timber on the breakwater and, though I was loath to do so, I thought there was nothing for it but to send a signal for help. I couldn't remember, and couldn't go below to find out, where the coast guard station was situated so I used my very powerful torch to send the S.O.S. signal in the general direction of the quay. After about an hour of intermittent signalling my light was seen by someone who had the wit to phone the coastguard station, and at about 2.30 a.m. I saw the maroons calling out the lifeboat crew go up. This gave me the little extra strength that I needed, now that I knew help was on its way.

Half an hour later an exceptionally heavy squall swept across the harbour, reducing visibility to nil and drenching me yet again and laying poor *Simba* nearly on her beam ends. As she recovered I struggled to get her head to wind again, watching the dreaded mole getting nearer and nearer and, just as I got her back under command, I smelt burning paraffin and gave a mental cheer for the lifeboat whose exhaust that smell must surely be. But peering to windward through the rain and wind I could see no sign of her and as I scanned from starboard to port I happened to notice that the slits in the ventilator in the cabin door were red, not dark as they should have been. The ship was on fire and I was caught between the devil and the not so deep and certainly not blue sea. If I left the helm for more than ten seconds she would fall off and blow swiftly down onto the breakwater, and if I did not she would burn and sink.

A quick look inside told me the worst. The last squall had caused the Valor stove to fall over and flames from the spilt, burning paraffin were leaping up from the floorboards in half a dozen places, and the only serviceable fire extinguisher was in the forepeak. There was nothing for it but to throw the bed and bedding from the doghouse settee onto the flames and hope that it would smother the fire, which, by the grace of God, it did, and the fire went out.

Another look round found the lifeboat approaching and it crossed my mind that lifeboats are, as their name implies, for saving life, not property, and that I might have to abandon *Simba*. I was so weary by this time that I hardly cared. The lifeboat, a fine, big, powerful modern vessel, came within hearing distance and the coxwain shouted, 'You will have to leave her, jump as I run under your lee.' To my good fortune he came past under my lee, but too far away for me to jump, and when, after making a big sweep round he came close again he managed to get a line to me. I took its end, and crawling on all fours along the deck managed to make it fast to the mainmast, foul of the rigging, but that could not be helped: the rope tautened, and *Simba* was in tow.

The coxwain had not intended to take me in tow, but now that he had achieved it he didn't know where to take me for the best, and after wandering about the harbour for some time he took me to the main harbour quay which was, by this time, a little bit sheltered, the wind having veered a bit towards the north-west. As we approached the quay the lifeboat shortened the tow and put one of her men aboard me to help me get lines to the quay and moor my boat. There was a big sea running, and *Simba* took a few hard knocks that night, but everyone was very helpful with ropes and fenders and we eventually got her safely tied up. I was so tired I could hardly stand.

The man put on board *Simba* was Ken Norris, a Customs Officer standing in for a regular member of the crew who was not available that night, and when we were finally secured and the lifeboat had departed for her station we had a stiff peg to warm us up. I was still dressed as I had been when I went on deck, in flannel trousers, a sweater and slippers, soaking wet and cold to my bones. I simply dropped these sodden rags to the deck, wrapped myself in a couple of blankets and turned in at five in the morning, with the gale abating. The mail boat had sailed, late, and I understand that it was only the third time in eighty years that the mail had failed to sail for stress of weather. The anemometer at Strumble Head had gone off the scale!

The local paper reported the rescue in detail and gave details of another yacht which had, during the night, sunk at her mooring. It also reported the delays to the mail steamer and to two other ships;

STEAMERS DELAYED

'The M.V. *Innisfallen*, due to leave Fishguard Harbour for Cork at midnight, was unable to cast off until 4.30 a.m. on Sunday morning. She had over 500 passengers on board.

Carrying nearly 200 passengers and due to leave Waterford for Fishguard on Saturday night the S.S. *Great Western* (Capt. B. Mendus) was unable to leave the quay owing to the wind of hurricane force. The S.S. *St. Andrew* (Capt. L. Davis) with over

1,000 passengers on the Rosslare–Fishguard route also failed to leave the quayside.

As the gale abated on Sunday morning both vessels were able to leave their berths and, after a rough passage, arrived at Fishguard during the afternoon. The first passengers from the *St. Andrew* were ashore by 3.00 p.m. and due to the excellent co-operation which exists between station staff, customs, immigration and special officers the tired passengers were dealt with in record time. The first special train was on its way to London within an hour of the boat's arrival. The second special followed soon after.'

The harbour wall against which I was now lying was, though not too bad a berth in normal weather, was not for yachts, being needed for coasters loading and discharging cargo. The harbourmaster came down to see me later in the morning and expressed concern that he could not think of a safe berth for me, so we decided to meet again the next day, Monday, and decide where I should go, and, fortunately, before I saw him I met Ken Norris, who suggested that I move into the creek at Lower Fishguard and lie alongside the wall opposite the Yacht Club. This seemed like a good idea, as anything would be better than the harbour wall where I was banging and crashing about, and it suited the harbourmaster for he would be rid of me. With my future berth sorted out I made my way to the house of the secretary of the Lifeboat to thank him for the boat's efforts the night before, and found him to be a sprightly, interesting man in his eighties who had held the post for thirty years. He was full of tales of the sea, and shipwrecks and disasters on the Welsh coast, and I could have stayed yarning with him much longer than I was able to.

Leaving him I went to the Lifeboat house to thank the Coxwain and leave a present for the crew for saving my dream from disaster and extinction, let alone saving my life, and when I got back on board Ken Norris joined me to pilot me across to the Yacht Club, where we tied up more or less at the front door. I couldn't rig masthead tackles, for that would have blocked the quay, but I shifted some ballast inboard so that she would not fall over. Well fendered from the rough stone wall she took the ground on a hard flat bottom and sat there very snug. The Yacht Club members were very friendly and helpful, giving me full use of the facilities, and I spent a few happy evenings there.

Before I could move again I had to acquire some anchors and chain. The harbourmaster kindly dragged the harbour bed for mine without success and a subsequent search by Ken Norris and another enthusiast from the Yacht Club fared no better so, hearing of a man who had a couple of secondhand anchors and some chain for sale I arranged to meet him in the Commercial Hotel. Whilst waiting for him I sneezed rather violently and a raucous voice shouted 'pardon', and, turning round quickly, surprised, I found that I had been excused by a grey parrot! My man arrived and he turned out to have an anchor of about the right weight and I bought it, and some chain to go with it. Ken Norris was keen to come round the coast with me if he could find the time and I arranged with him that we would sail the next morning for Penzance, or Milford Haven if the weather did not permit that, and, as I was to pick him up at the main harbour quay at six on Saturday morning, I had a farewell drink with my friends at the Yacht Club and turned in early with the alarm set for 5.00 a.m.

It went off on schedule with its usual shattering clamour and I turned out into the pre-dawn chill, made myself a hasty breakfast and by 5.30 a.m. had the engine running and cast off from the wall. Dawn was just breaking when I arrived at the main quay and promptly at six Ken came aboard, and a few minutes later we cleared the breakwater and set a course for the Bishop's lighthouse, to pass two miles off Strumble Head. It was not a bad morning for that awful summer. There was a lot of cloud but the sun broke through from time to time to warm and cheer us; as the wind was dead on the nose and as were in a hurry we set no sail and motored on. With a head wind a steadying sail does not steady, it merely makes a lot of noise and does itself no good at all, so we didn't set one.

There was quite a swell coming from the west but we managed to make about five knots with the help of the ebb and sighted the Bishop's at 9.00 a.m., with the wind freshening from the southwest and the sky clouding over. By 10.00 a.m. it was all getting worse, but I still had hopes of making Milford Haven that evening though I had abandoned the Penzance option. Before long we could see the rocks below the lighthouse which, with the tide racing over them and the moderate sea breaking among them, looked for all the world like a half drowned cemetery, which they would become for any vessel caught among them. By now we had a moderate gale blowing in our faces and were making little progress and the options narrowed down to one. Return to Fishguard. Just as we were about to turn, setting a jib, and a reefed main and mizzen as we did so, to sail back to Fishguard the engine stopped, our decision was confirmed, and we sailed slowly away from the graveyard.

The stoppage turned out to be caused by a fuel line blockage which I was unable to clear, so we simply sailed on, overtaken from time to time by trawlers running for shelter, and arrived off the breakwater as dusk fell. We made tack after tack against the tide, struggling to get into the harbour but it was not until 8.00 p.m. that we crept past the end of the North Breakwater and promptly lost the wind. How I hated the sight of that pile of concrete but, uncomfortably close to it as we were, there was nothing for it but to anchor; just as we were doing that a trawler came by and, in response to our hail, passed us a line and towed us in. We spent the night moored astern of him. Sunday morning saw us returning to Lower Fishguard under an engine fed with fuel from a bucket hung from the cabin roof.

Chapter 19

More trouble

I didn't seem to be able to shake myself loose from Fishguard. I was beginning to think that the fates were conspiring against me. September already, fitting out not even started and a date with Fulley in Tahiti a mere thirteen months hence. I reckoned that I must begin the long voyage to the Pacific no later than March if I was to keep my appointment and must get to Birdham as soon as possible; there were sails to order and make, the rigging to be checked from top to bottom, stores to buy and stow, the engine to overhaul and a thousand and one things to do to prepare *Simba* for her trip half round the world. Meanwhile day of foul weather followed day of foul weather. When the rain stopped it blew a gale which pushed a large swell into the harbour so that *Simba* bumped heavily for a while when taking the ground on the ebb, and again on the flood. Everyone rallied round with fenders and ropes, and I had several offers of a bed for the night, and was given a loan of the Yacht Club key; but I felt that I could not leave the boat in these conditions. Even after the gale had abated we bumped and banged for a while on several tides and I could only hope that no real damage had been done.

I got the fuel pipe cleared, so the engine was available should the weather let me sail, but I conclude that a rather more professional approach to the voyage round Land's End to Birdham would be a good thing, so I responded to an advertisement in *Yachting World* which claimed 'Anything which floats delivered anywhere'. (What price the Gobi Desert?) I asked for a quotation for moving *Simba* from Fishguard to Birdham and they replied very quickly, quoting what I thought to be a very reasonable £30. So I accepted the offer and insured the boat for the passage. They said that they would start on Friday, within the week, and I was relieved to think that I would at last escape from the Fishguard trap.

By Thursday the swell had abated and, being weary and dirty after a

126

string of disturbed nights, I checked into the local hotel and after a thorough bathing and sprucing up spent the evening in the Yacht Club before retiring for the best night's sleep for ages.

By ten in the evening of Friday there was no sign of Hoskins, the contractor, so I settled for another night in the hotel after I had checked *Simba*'s moorings. Walking back to Lower Fishguard the following morning I could see, as I rounded a bend, a large motor launch moored ahead of my boat and, as I had already assumed that *Simba* would be towed round, I thought that must be the tug. When I got aboard I found a large young man who introduced himself at John Hoskins and apologised for the delay. He had set off by train with his mechanic who had, unfortunately, fallen ill and had to return home, and was now trying to find another mechanic. The launch was nothing to do with him, for he proposed to sail and motor the boat round to Birdham. The lack of a mechanic did not matter too much for the present, for the voyage could not have been begun in the foul weather which prevailed. My daily call to Strumble Head lighthouse produced no weather optimism, so I decided to go and rescue my car from Pwllheli.

That in itself turned out to be no mean adventure. The first bus left Fishguard at 8.30 a.m. but the Hotel were not geared to starting breakfast before then, so I had to set off hungry. The first bus took me along the coast road to Cardigan. After that a succession of buses took me through the pouring rain on a tour of mid and north Wales. Aberayron, Aberystwyth, Machnyllwth, Dolgelly, Ffestiniog, finally reaching Pwllheli at 9.00 p.m.

The Tower Hotel found me a room with a very comfortable bed and I was soon asleep. Next morning I went to the garage and collected my car which, even though I had disconnected it, had a flat battery, but after a bit of charge it started the engine and got me moving. Western Marine Craft had no mail for me so, after a yarn with old acquaintances, I set sail southwards through the lonely, wet hills of North Wales and reached Aberystwyth in good time to stop for the night. The first hotel I tried would only let me have a double room, at double-room rates, so I looked further and settled for a single room in an hotel with a capacity of hundreds but only about twenty guests, all of whom, but for me, were elderly people sitting about playing bridge and waiting to die. Large hotels, empty of all but a handful of people such as these, are a mite depressing so I wasted no time next morning in getting away, and made Fishguard by 3.00 p.m.

John Hoskins still had no mechanic. The weather news was no better than usual, so, after two more days of hanging about in these conditions I decided that John and I would take the boat round and on Thursday, 5th

October, I rang Strumble Head to learn that, whilst there was no gale at present, the next was not far away. So we parked the car, got in some stores and when *Simba* floated we sailed for Land's End and points east. As usual the wind was dead on the nose so we motored, with the Ebb tide helping us on our way. The Bishop's, with its graveyard, was astern by sunset and by 2.00 a.m. we were past the Smalls and on course for Land's End, allowing a lot for the Bristol Channel tide and the south-westerly wind. By dawn on Friday the glass was falling and the weather looking unpromising but we were well on our way, with plenty of sea room, so we would just have to take what came. Working four hours watch and watch nobody got much sleep for, even wedged in a bunk, the motion of the boat made sleep nigh impossible. We crossed the main shipping lane in poor visibility with rain squalls and, not making much headway in the conditions, dusk found us in sight of Hartland Point, set far, far to the East by the wind and tide despite the large allowance which I had made. Altering course more to the westward we rounded Land's End in among a lot of shipping at 5.00 a.m. What a relief to be in the Channel at last, where the south-westerlies which had held me up for so long would now help us on our way.

Tired after two days and nights at sea, and with fuel running low, we ran into Newlyn harbour to restore both ourselves and the tank. The customs men descended on us as soon as we tied up, for Newlyn is the base for a large fishing fleet, but on learning that we were making a coastwise passage they left us in peace. We refuelled, lunched, rested and went walking over to Penzance for the few stores which we needed, being surprised to hear a great deal of French being spoken. French trawlers frequent the harbour and it behoves the locals to comprehend the language. The weather was not so hot but Newlyn and Penzance seemed somehow more cheery than Fishguard and the other Welsh ports I had been stuck in. Perhaps the 'stuck in' is why, for I now felt free, able to continue the passage to Birdham without being locked into port by unfavourable winds.

Next day, a splendid day quite unlike those we were used to, with a fresh south-west wind blowing, we breakfasted, made the boat shipshape and motored out of the harbour at 9.00 a.m., stopping the engine and making all plain sail when we were clear. Once out of the lee of the land the wind turned out not to be fresh, but a moderate gale which pushed us along at a cheerful seven knots. What a joy, to be sailing in decent weather instead of motoring in bad conditions or stormbound. I felt, at last, that this was what it was all about and saw the day and the future through a rosy glow.

Lulled, I was!

On this lovely day we both spent the morning in the cockpit enjoying the fine weather and the excellent sailing and, by noon, we were hungry and thinking about lunch. When I went down into the cabin to see to it I got the shock of my life or, after Fishguard, another shock of my life. There was a great deal of noise in the cabin and it didn't take me long to realise that it was bilge water sloshing about that was making it, so we had a quick bite and I started pumping, but I didn't seem to be making much impression and at 2.00 p.m. when I relieved John at the helm he took over the pump and it soon became obvious that the water was coming in faster than we could pump it out even without the frequent clogging of the pump, which required its dismantling and re-assembly before pumping could go on. By about 4.00 p.m. the water was floating the floorboards and pushing up the lino and we decided to make for Fowey, the nearest harbour, some twenty-two miles to the north-north-west. With the wind about west it was too close a fetch, so we took in our sails and started the engine and went on with one steering and the other pumping. We searched for the leak as best we could without success and soon the water reached the flywheel which, fortunately, was enclosed in the engine box or there would have been water everywhere. The engine itself had a bilge pump, designed by the devil himself, for it never in all its life worked for more than a few minutes at a time.

As darkness fell the sky clouded over and the outlook was not very bright. By about 7.00 p.m. we sighted Fowey lighthouse at the harbour entrance and hove sighs of relief, for by now the water was up to the level of the lower bunks and doing heavens knows what damage, never mind the risk of sinking. Fowey is a very useful little port, the only one of much use between Falmouth and Looe, with at least twenty feet of water in the cable wide channel; but I had never been there before. Nor had John. So I sent John forward to keep a lookout and steered into the channel with some trepidation, for the chart made it look more difficult than it really is, especially to the eye of one used to thinking in terms of somewhat bigger ships than *Simba*. The harbour is deep and I really had no idea where best to bring up so when, as we crept in, I spotted an enormous mooring buoy, just about as big as *Simba* herself, we made for it and tied up to it. Unfortunately it had a mate so close that if we swung we might foul it so we had to put an anchor out over the stern to prevent that danger. While all this was going on the dear old customs turned up again, but soon went away satisfied and we turned to with buckets and tried to bail the water out, which didn't seem to make much difference, so we made a hot meal and watched the water level. Sitting in a yacht's cabin with your feet in the water worrying about the leak and sinking and things like that is not yachting at its best, but as the water level seemed steady we turned in and slept after a long hard day.

I was woken next morning by a combination of an almighty splash and an ear splitting shriek from John, who had woken up and, from the upper bunk in which he had slept, could see the bedroom washbasin, full, overflowing and adding to the water already in the cabin. He was convinced that this meant that we would sink in a matter of minutes and he leapt out of the bunk into about three feet of cold and dirty water; hence the shriek. Shutting the washbasin stopcock stopped this extra unwanted leak immediately. We both got dressed and John rowed ashore to get help and very soon, with the aid of a most helpful young lady in the telephone exchange, made contact with the Harbour Board's repair shop who hurried to our aid. Very soon they were alongside with a motor-driven pump and suitable hoses and after an hour's pumping *Simba* was dry, or rather empty. We searched thoroughly for the leak but couldn't find it, so the pump was left on board and our angels of mercy arranged to come back in about four hours' time to see how much water we made in the interim. McGonagle's law prevailed and she didn't leak a drop. We were talking the situation over when the Harbour Master arrived to tell us that we must move, 'for he couldn't have yachts sinking at buoys which were needed for big ships', and it was while this order was being discussed that we noticed that water was beginning to show again in the bilge. A clue at last. With so many people on board the hole, or whatever, must have become submerged, and as we were all aft, in the cockpit, the leak was more likely to be aft than forward, so there we looked.

Under the cockpit floor is a copper pipe which carried water overboard from the exhaust silencer and cooler and which normally discharges above the waterline, but with all the extra weight on board its outlet was submerged. It was dripping none too gently into the bilge and we found that the underside of it was severely corroded along the length of its lowest part and so, when coming up the Channel with a heavy following sea, the outlet had frequently been submerged allowing water into the boat. Running the engine made things worse, for we were then pumping water into the boat, and the load of cheery chaps in the cockpit simply made the leak permanent. If we all sat on the foredeck she would stay dry!

At high water that afternoon we went alongside the Harbour Board's well-sheltered, but drying, jetty at Polruan, across the harbour from Fowey. The Board workshop made and fitted a new pipe, this time with a stopcock at the outboard end which would isolate the pipe when the engine was not running. Meanwhile John had persuaded the caretaker of the Mission of Seamen at Fowey to let us use his heating boiler to dry out our wet gear. Neither of us had a camera, more's the pity, for John, rowing our little pram dinghy, loaded with bedding till she had almost no freeboard and looking for all the world like a floating raft of discarded mattresses, was a sight worthy of record. Having by evening got the wet stuff across to Fowey we went ashore on the Polruan side and blundered about the cliff paths until, finding a friendly tavern, we joined the locals in sorting out the world's problems and forgot our own. Friendship and bonhomie reigned and, for our return journey along and down the cliff path we should, in wisdom, have been roped together, but we scrambled home and turned into the upper bunks which still had dry (?) bedding.

Next morning we sorted out the terrible mess left by the flooding and got our dried wet stuff back from Fowey. We got the outboard going and took a run up the superb, picturesque, harbour which, for all its rural beauty, is the most important export port for china clay. I was almost seduced into staying there and fitting out for the voyage at Polruan but, weighing the advantages of Birdham against the beauty of Fowey, decided to stick to the original plan. On returning to Polruan we found that the repair had been completed and that, with the bills and harbour dues paid, there was nothing to keep us so, when we floated on the following morning's tide, we moved out to a buoy and had breakfast. After that I rowed ashore, paid the bills and bought a couple of loaves of bread and a stock of Cornish pasties. By 10.30 a.m. we had the dinghy on board and everything lashed down for the final leg of the passage.

We sailed out into a fresh Channel breeze and a bright and cloudy sky with more bad weather forecast, so we plugged on under engine with just the mizzen set as a steadying sail. Nightfall found us with Start Point abeam with the evening cloudy, fine and clear. Through the Portland Race during the night we were close by the Needles at dawn. Breakfast on a fine, bracing autumn morning both smelt and tasted good and, as we made our way through the crowded shipping in the Solent and entered Spithead, we met the *Queen Mary*, inward bound. From little *Simba* she looked gigantic. We made the bar at Hayling Island with plenty of water under us, and motoring up Chichester Harbour in the shelter of the land and were at last able to shed our sweaters. Arriving off Birdham an hour from the bar we were soon locked in and fast in a berth on the river wall, bows in with the stern secured to two dolphins.

It was Thursday, 12th October 1951. But a year from now I was due to meet Fulley in faraway Tahiti. Time to set to and prepare for the voyage.

Chapter 20

Fitting out

In the fitting out berth at long last I had a few days less than six months to prepare the boat for the long-planned voyage. It looks like a long time written down like that, but, with a wooden boat which had so recently been half full of water to prepare, it was none too long. But long enough to allow me to take time off for recreation and I began by joining the Yacht Club, which was so handy to the pool.

The recovery of my car from Fishguard was my excuse for going there to enjoy the Club's laying up supper, which was a thoroughly good party, with lots of food and drink and good company and a bed for the night with a Fishguard friend. For a new club it had established itself very solidly and the evening, with all the numerous club trophies raced for through the summer being presented to their new owners, or represented to their old owners, was a great success, worth the trying journey which I made to get there. A long, slow train journey with a couple of changes and finishing in a steam railcar which dumped me in Goodwick, leaving me to walk to Fishguard. The return journey by road was longer than I had imaged. After the party the night before breakfast wasn't too early so it was after 9.00 a.m. before I set off, and evening by the time I got to Birdham. It was a Sunday, and my chief recollection of the journey is the weight of England-bound traffic near the border, due entirely to the Welsh licensing laws, which have the pubs closed on Sunday. A pub on the English side of the border must be a gold mine! After sitting in the car all day I felt like a half shut jack-knife, but after a meal and a few beers by the fire in the Yacht Club I straightened out enough to retire to my bunk.

Birdham Pool, separated from the river Itchen by a lock, is between Itchenor and the Witterings in low-lying country, so low indeed that at equinoctial spring tides the lock gates are submerged, the pool and the river merge and the approach roads are flooded. Originally the pool was constructed to store water to drive a cornmill, now defunct, and is now fitted out and used as a haven for a hundred or so yachts which can lie bow or stern on to the bank with easy access. The Birdham Shipyard which controls the pool has its slipway into the river close by. It was the ideal place for me to fit out, and a fascinating place for anyone interested in yachts, with a great variety of craft wintering within the security of its lock.

My life now became a combination of hard work, red tape and lists. Unless you carry a notebook and write down ideas and needs as they cross your mind they are lost forever, or so it seems. All my pockets had bits of paper in them carrying absolutely vital pieces of information, and even in the quiet of an evening in the local I couldn't be without paper and pencil, lest someone should think to tell me not to forget to take a spare sealing ring for the pressure cooker, or some other obscure everyday thing which within the bounds of the U.K. is easily replaceable, but the lack of which 3,000 miles from the nearest ironmonger would be a minor disaster.

The hard work began with getting all internal iron ballast out, chipped, painted and replaced. I got it up into the cockpit and cleaned and painted it, but before it could go back the whole of the bilges and lower part of the inside of the hull had to be thoroughly cleaned. The flooding resulting from the broken pipe had sloshed the contents of the bilges and the engine drip tray all over the place, leaving a filthy, greasy film which had to be removed before the ballast and floorboards could go back. For good measure, remembering all my pumping problems, I rove brass chain through the limberholes in the floors so that a pull would clear any blockage. Concerned that fifty gallons of water was by no means enough for the passages ahead, I searched for space for more tankage and found room for sixty-two and thirty gallon water tanks, and a fourteen gallon paraffin tank, under the cockpit floor and the doghouse bunk. I measured with great care and drew the tanks to scale and found a firm in Sheffield who would make them for me, galvanising them after fabrication. A week after I placed the order the Government clamped down on galvanising, but I had ordered just in time. There was no point in putting the bottom of the boat all back together again till the tanks arrived, so I lived in some discomfort for a while.

Sails had been on my mind. I had only one suit, in good condition, but that would not be a proper outfit for my voyage. I also wanted to be able to set twin staysails when running before the trades, so I commissioned a repeat set of plain sail, to be tanned brown, and my pair of staysails. Delivery in six to eight weeks was promised. *Simba* had no radio and I felt that I had to have a good receiver for time signals, weather reports, whenever they might be available, and so on. I chose Schooner Marine on the strength of accounts of long ocean passages which I had read which praised the make. In the event, after I had told them of my proposed voyage and perceived needs, they made me a set which performed perfectly throughout the voyage. My lost anchor was replaced by yet another secondhand one, found in the Birdham Shipyard with a bent arm which they straightened for me, at the same time taking my chain ashore and annealing it, and that nearly lost me half my cable. The yard returned it in two lengths in a wheelbarrow and ranged it on the jetty by *Simba*'s bow and I took one end on board, over the windlass gypsy and secured it down in the chain locker. When I hove it aboard over the windlass I found that I came to the end far too soon, and indeed, I had only one length of it. The shipyard were adamant that both lengths had been delivered, but searched their premises without finding the second length. It might have been stolen, but that was unlikely, so I assumed that it had dangled an end over the jetty and then slid into the pool. I fished for it with my magnet, one recovered from a wartime radar set which could lift a hundredweight and, sure enough, there was my chain below the jetty, easily recoverable now that, thanks to my magnet, I had the bight of it in my hand. That magnet has served me well, recovering tools and all sorts from the harbours of the Pacific!

Most of the time I lived on board, cooking for myself, having the odd meal in the Yacht Club and feeding the family of swans on the pool, who became so used to me that, if I didn't get up at my usual time and give them their scraps of breakfast, they knocked on the hull with their beaks. I like to think that they were concerned for my welfare, but it was just cupboard love. Breakfast was a bit of a problem. With bacon and eggs rationed it was, more often than not, fish, with the result that when bacon day came round much frying pan cleaning was needed. Solution, have two pans. About once a week I could have a night at the Dolphin and Anchor, or the Ship, in Chichester, as much to have a good hot bath as to be fed without cooking.

The expense of fitting out was beginning to run away when a man living in an adjacent boat showed me a list put out by a firm selling Navy and Air Force war surplus in Kingswear in Devon, so I got out the Ford and trundled down there on a glorious autumn day. The colours of the New Forest, lit by the weak seasonal sunshine, were magnificent, as was the countryside of Dorset and Devon along the way. I put up for the night in Torquay, a nice cheery place, even out of season, and went on next day to Kingswear on the beautiful river Dart, and found, in Devon Marine, an Aladdin's Cave of Useful Things. Heaped in glorious disorder was everything the prospective voyager could possibly want: gyro compasses and lifebelts; fire extinguishers and rocket firing pistols; lifeboat pemmican and lifeboat fishing lines; outboard motors, marlinespikes, toolkits and the proverbial shoes and sealing wax. I should not be let loose in a place like that, for, with the aid of a foreman who must have had the second sight, for he knew where everything was, I found what I needed, and more. I eventually came away with 100 fathoms of one and a half inch cotton rope, a grapnel, three lifebelts, a petrol generator, fifty fathoms of small stainless steel wire, an aeroplane compass, several electrical fittings and some electrical wire. I wish I had bought more of the rope, for it was a particular bargain. By 8.00 p.m. I was back in Birdham, in front of the bar fire, unbending from the jack-knife position and enjoying the company after a couple of solitary days.

Timber for making shelves and cupboards to hold all the things we had to take with us was a problem. Most of it seemed to be subject to Government controls, and private yachts going on extended pleasure cruises weren't high on the priority list. But some wood was uncontrolled and I had to make do with it. One evening after a day of joinery I thought to give the Kingswear generator a run, and charge the batteries, so I set it up in the cockpit with its vertical exhaust spouting fumes into the cold evening air, and retired below for a read on my bunk among the chaos of the day's work. As I read I thought that there was a strange smell but I put it down to the paint on the new generator scorching and thought not too much about it, until I started to doze off. Then it crossed my mind that it might be exhaust gases. But, with the motor in the open air of the cockpit I dismissed that thought, until I got up and immediately felt dizzy. I went into the cockpit and pressed the stop button, and the next thing I knew was that I awoke, very cold, lying across an oil drum by the stopped generator, having been gassed by the fumes which, in the still evening air, were falling straight back into the cockpit from the vertical exhaust and then draining into the cabin. Had I not woken when I did I wouldn't be writing this now. And I think I've said that before, or something very like it. Dangerous business, this yachting. I departed for one of my nights ashore after that experience.

In early December I took a few days off to visit my Mother and the rest of my relations up in the Manchester area. There was fog and there was snow and, despite the sparkle that the snow gave to the usually grimy North, coal rationing and food rationing made a hard winter even harder and a bit depressing, so I was not sorry to get back to the boat and on with the work with sunshine and blue sea in prospect. I had a new cabin door made, in two halves like a stable door, and a new cabin hatch cover, and battens and booms for the staysails, to fit into goosenecks on top of the windlass. I had

strong battens fitted outside the large doghouse windows to break the force
of seas coming aboard, tiled the galley and W.C. in green masonite,
obtained by dint of much letter writing, and swapped the Calor gas cooker
for a twin burner primus stove with an oven box on top, for Calor gas
would be unobtainable out of England. I took lessons in bread making from
the wife of my friend Bill Lindsay, but all my efforts to bake came to
naught. It was cold and wintry, and Christmas was coming, bringing with it,
on Christmas day, a visit by half a dozen friends and relations. After
Christmas eve in the Yacht Club with a good fire going and the ever
cheerful Len behind the bar mixing ever more wicked potions, I crawled
back on board and into my bunk at about midnight. At about noon the
party turned up and after snacks and drinks on board, we all went off to the
Dolphin and Anchor for lunch. A good Christmas. Almost the first at home
for thirty years.

The day after Boxing Day it snowed. Not much, but enough to make
things even more Christmassy, and at about 10.00 a.m. I was sitting in the
cabin, with the heater going full blast, reading about the stealing of the
Coronation Stone from Westminster Abbey when there was a knock on the
cabin door. I called 'come in' and the door opened revealing a large
gentleman in a blue suit, overcoat and bowler hat, who asked if he might
have a word with me. I said that he could and invited him to come in and sit
down, and asked what I could do for him.

He opened by saying, 'First of all, sir, I must inform you that I am a
police officer', so I hastily reviewed all the crimes I had committed recently,
and thought they were not worth such a visit, and as I did so the headline in
the paper about the stone caught my eye so I said, 'Well, it's not here.'

'What's not here?' said the policeman.

'The stone,' said I.

'That's what I've come for,' said the policeman, to which I replied,
'You're joking,' and he said he was not.

'It has been reported to the police that a black Ford car with a large steel
chest in the back of it has been seen around here. I have traced the car to the
pool, here, and I think you are the owner. Is that not so?'

Of course the car was mine, and I do keep a large steel chest in it, in
which I keep my decent clothes, as has been my practice almost since I first
went to sea. He got out his notebook, anticipated promotion shining out of
his eyes, and asked me what my movements had been on Christmas day.
Did I have any Scottish relations? Where did they live? He looked at my
passport, which wouldn't help him much as, though Scots, I was born in
Koslin in Pomerania, and he looked at my identity card and then asked if he

could look in the chest. I agreed, but we couldn't find the key (later discovered attached to my knife and lying on deck under the snow), so he settled for hefting the chest which, containing as it did just a few books and clothes couldn't possibly contain the stone; so he went away satisfied.

I had not yet selected a companion for the voyage and had been giving thought to the problem. I knew several acceptable people who would like to have come but who were tied down by jobs, or families, or both. Getting the right companion was of fundamental importance, for the voyage could only be successful if the shipmates were compatible; it is not easy to get along with one companion for long spells, often in adverse conditions, and my mind went to John Hoskins, with whom I had got on well on the dodgy passage round from Fishguard and who, though a bit slap happy, had done well then. He didn't seem to stay in any job for long, and so might be available, and when I asked him he jumped at the idea, and we arranged that he should join me a month before sailing day.

The battles with red tape in connection with timber control were as naught compared with the problem of getting *Simba* registered, a necessary step before going foreign and having to produce the ships 'Papers' at each new port. I asked Mr. Duff, the local surveyor, to do the job for me and he had quite a task. First of all the name wouldn't do, for it was already registered, and none of my alternative spellings were acceptable to the registrar. In the end I thought through the names in *Kim*, my favourite Kipling book, and tried to register Kim, but that too, was already on the books. So I eventually invented *Kimballa*, and under that name she made the voyage. The other major problem with registration was proof of ownership. My purchase was properly documented, but she had had about ten owners in all, and the registrar wanted proof of all the transfers, many of which were not properly recorded. There was even one deceased owner whose widow flatly denied that her husband had ever owned a yacht! I was glad that I had handed the problem to Mr. Duff.

By now my sails were already a month overdue, for the sailmakers could not get the canvas. The galvanised tanks arrived and, because I had measured so carefully to use up all the available space I had to take the ship apart to get them in. But fit they did. I struggled for three days just to get the exhaust cooler uncoupled to get the tank in behind it. The bolts were frozen solid and it took a lot of doing.

John joined me at the end of February and we both went to the doctor for T.A.B. injections and vaccination. We went up to London together with our passports and got visas for the U.S.A. and French Oceania, and I got my bank manager on the job of trying to get me a few dollars to pay for the passage of the Panama canal. More red tape even than for registration. The Bank of England wanted to know the route, the number of people on board and even wanted a document guaranteeing that I really would make the voyage, and in the end allowed me my £100 of foreign currency, then a year's ration, with $50 allowed only, and let John have his £100, with no dollars.

The sails arrived, so we had propulsion and we went seeking permission to buy stores for the voyage, for rationing still prevailed. After much study, of the regulations the Customs gave me permission to buy six months' full rations for myself, but only two thirds of that for John, who 'was only a passenger'. They gave no credence to my proposition that a forty-foot yacht with only two on board in the middle of the Atlantic was undermanned, so we had to settle for that. We gave our lists to the Lock stores who arranged to supply everything the day before we sailed.

Time was going by, so I went up North to say goodbye to the family and see the bank manager in Liverpool to get travellers cheques and currency and arrange my affairs for my absence. Both he and his assistant were most interested by the prospect and had a National Geographic world map on the desk, with the route drawn on it and the ports of call underlined. I think they wished they were coming too! On the way back I picked John up in Reading and we dashed back to Birdham, for I had arranged to go on the grid for a final scrub and the renewal of the rudder post at eleven that night. At 6.00 p.m. we moved over to the lock gate and retired to the Yacht Club to keep warm while we waited for the tide. By 11.00 p.m. it was blowing so hard as to make putting her on the grid that night impossible, so we postponed the job till the next tide. The following morning it was bitterly cold but the wind had dropped, so we locked out and put *Kimballa* on the grid, we scrubbed her underbody while the yard's carpenters renewed the rudder post. We also painted the topsides green, which I thought would be a good working colour, which was a mistake. Experience now tells me that the only colour for a yacht in the tropics is white. The carpenters finished the rudder post just before the rising tide overtook them and we floated off, locked into the pool, and returned to our berth. It was now the 24th March, I was determined to sail on the 31st, and the ship wasn't registered yet; but there was still a week to go.

The engine makers fitted me out with a stock of spares, and sent a man down to overhaul the engine. We put together a medical kit with the help of a doctor member of the Yacht Club, with added help to get drugs provided by another member's company, the International Chemical Company Ltd. We remembered vitamin tablets but it was not until we were half way across the Atlantic that we realised that we had no clinical thermometer. Fortunately we never needed one.

I was worried about the possibility of being pooped by a following sea which, with the large cockpit leading down to the cabin, would have been disastrous, so I decked the cockpit over but for a small square for the helmsman's legs. We fitted a Sestrel Major compass but didn't buy a chronometer, the cheapest secondhand machine being £40. My Rolex, and time signals, would have to be good enough, and so it proved. On that day, the 24th, I held a little dinner party at the Ship in Chichester to say goodbye to my friends the Lindsays and the Battersbys, all friends from schooldays. I hate goodbye parties, but I enjoyed that one. At yet another farewell lunch I was given a mascot for the voyage, a toy rabbit, called Harvey. He looks down on me now, with a beady eye and chewing a carrot.

The register arrived on the 30th, in the nick of time. We did our last-minute shopping and were cleared by the Customs, and took our stores aboard. I resisted the demands at the Yacht Club for a monster farewell party, being all too conscious of the number of voyages which have set out with a fanfare, only to end a week later in Falmouth or somewhere. But, intending, when we sailed, to anchor inside Hayling Island for a couple of days to get squared away, we spent the last evening in the Club in the company of a few friends and turned in at about 2.00 a.m.

Chapter 21

Away to a false start

High water on the morning of 3rd April 1951 was at 9.00 a.m., and, that being the best time to pass out of the pool, I decided to make it my departure time. Not only was it the best time to pass through the lock but the ebb would help us on our way down to Hayling Island.

At 6.00 a.m. the horrible jangle of the alarm clock woke us both and we hauled ourselves out of our bunks to a fine, misty, overcast morning. Breakfast was a hasty affair after which I took my car round to the Yacht Club car park and left it for a friend to take away and dispose of later. Back on board we hoisted the dinghy onto the cabin top and lashed it down, hoisted the Blue Peter, gave the engine a short run and tidied up below. The pool was quiet, just a few men going about their business, and John's parents, who had come down to see him away, on the bank.

At 8.00 a.m., 'The Toad', a youngster from the surveyor's household, came aboard and helped us hoist the Red Ensign, the Portuguese flag at the foremast head and the Birdham Yacht Club and Cruising Association burgees at the crosstrees and then, with the Toad at the helm, we cast off and motored across the pool and made fast by the lock entrance where we topped up our fuel, water and lubricating oil tanks. By this time, to my surprise, quite a crowd had gathered on the quay wall. Half the members of the Yacht Club seemed to be there though, after my late night, I was not so observant as to be able to take note of them all, I can remember Tony Ford and his wife and family, Mr. Gatehouse of the shipyard, Mrs. Atkinson and Les of the Yacht Club, Bill Lindsay and his two daughters and many more. I wished that Tony and his family, and Bill Lindsay and his and many others could have come with us, for we had spent many a happy evening together in boats and the Yacht Club talking Pacific Islands, which still seemed, and in fact were, a very long way away.

With the last of the fuel and water aboard John returned from the Lock

Stores with the onions and the morning paper, which had nearly been forgotten and, just on 9.00 a.m., the lock gates opened. I stepped ashore to say goodbye all round and, after a quick search to see that no female cooks had stowed away, we cast off and moved slowly into the river. The Yacht Club had its flagstaff dressed overall and fired a salute with their starting cannon so, when the assembled company gave us their rendering of 'O landlord fill the flowing bowl', we dipped our ensign to them, for we thought that, at last, we were away. But not quite, for as soon as we had cleared the lock the engine stopped and we had to anchor rather hurriedly to clear the air lock which had stopped it. This was soon done and we got under way again with the Atkinson's launch *Aimee May* in company, but quite soon another air lock stopped us and we had to anchor again to clear it. But that was soon done and we hove up and slipped downstream on the ebb, past Itchenor with all its yachts preparing for the summer, and through the lovely English countryside for what we thought was the last time.

At about 11.00 a.m. we arrived off Hayling Island, moored to an empty buoy and set about getting squared up ready for serious sea, setting up the rigging, getting the mooring ropes below and listening intently to the weather reports on the wireless. They weren't too favourable that day, but in any case we were not yet quite ready for sea. Came the dusk and we hung out our anchor light and had our evening meal and settled down to go over the route to Madeira, consulting charts, sailing directions, wind and current charts all for the hundredth time. We were happily immersed in this task when, at about 8.00 p.m., we heard the sound of an engine and were hailed by *Aimee May* with Les, Len, Tony and Albert aboard, all full of good cheer and equipped for a party, which promptly developed. The Pacific was only five miles closer than it had been when we last saw them, but we all enjoyed ourselves and at about 10.30 p.m. we said our farewells once again and they departed into the dark for Birdham.

The next day was overcast with frequent rain squalls, not a pleasant day to start the voyage, so we spent it re-arranging our stores and making the boat as comfortable as possible for the coming months. The weather report indicated that the wind should go into the north west the next day, which suited us, so, late in starting already, I decided to sail next day if at all possible. That day, 5th April, dawned fine and clear and, sure enough, the wind was a moderate breeze from the northwest. The outlook was not encouraging but I was determined to go at high water, 11.00 a.m. When that time came we started the engine, cast off from our buoy and motored out over the bar and into the channel. Half an hour later we stopped the engine, set all plain sail and laid our course to pass to the south of the Isle of Wight.

As we went on our way the wind backed into the southwest, which did not suit us at all, and was blowing a full gale by the time the French coast came in sight at nightfall, making our progress down Channel negligible. We tacked onto the port tack and took in the mainsail, continuing on our way under reefed jib and mizzen. With the gale continuing to blow all the next day we make very little forward progress and at midnight I decided that enough was enough and it was time to seek the shelter of Torbay, so we handed all sail and started the engine and made for Berry Head, whose light we sighted at 7.30 p.m. as we crawled slowly against heavy seas towards the shelter of Torbay. It took until 1.30 the following morning to reach Torquay harbor, and we crept in through the sleet squalls looking for a place to stop. Just after we had dropped our anchor we spotted a convenient buoy but, in accordance with McGonagle's law, the anchor was foul of someone's mooring chain and only by paying out our cable to the bitter end could we reach the desirable buoy. This we did and, leaving the foul anchor problem for the next day, we fell into our bunks without even making ourselves a hot drink. I recall that, just before I fell asleep, I said to John, 'If a customs man shows his face before ten in the morning, shoot him.' The man must have been blessed with second sight, for it was only at 10.00 the next morning, as we were getting the cabin heater going and breakfasting in our dressing gowns, that he appeared, saying that he had seen us earlier, but thought we would probably be asleep and left us to it, which I thought was very decent of him. He examined our papers, had us fill in the forms for the Census which had been taken while we were at sea, and went away, leaving us to continue our recovery.

We had sailed 336 miles to make good 110!

By noon we were active again and we went ashore and spoke to the harbourmaster, who found us a much more suitable mooring, to which we moved that afternoon after we had unravelled our foul anchor. There was quite a lot of work to do after even so short a passage. The mainsail was badly chafed in three places, so it had to be repaired and steps taken to prevent future chafe. The petrol generator was acting up because of damp in the ignition system and the fuel and water tanks were in need of topping up. Wet and damp clothing and bedding meant that on the first fine day our rigging was festooned with drying clothes. We must have looked like a floating laundry. I had had hardly any dry weather at Birdham and so had been unable to caulk the decks, and several bad leaks had shown up in the Channel. As the weather was still unsuitable for caulking we just had to put up with it, though we tried, without much success, to caulk the worst places.

Each day we listened to the weather forecast, hoping for a shift in the wind which persisted in staying in the west and at gale force. John had telephoned his parents to report our lack of progress, and this resulted in a visit from a friend of his, F. C. (Buzz) Perkins, a marine engineer at present home on leave. He was interested in anything at all unusual connected with the sea, and came down to Torquay to see John and the boat. We put him to work on the generator and he had it fixed and running in short order, and so we gave him other jobs to do to keep him occupied, all of which he successfully carried out. He had been to sea in all manner of ships, from trawlers to cargo liners, and could turn his hand to anything. I pondered the idea of asking him if he would like to come with us, because we had found that *Kimballa* was quite a handful for two in bad weather. Evidently John and Buzz had the same idea, so when they came to me and asked if he could I had no hesitation in agreeing that he should come as far as Madeira, when we would decide whether he should continue with us. I had hestitated a little, for in confined conditions on a long voyage three is not the ideal number. If any one pair of the three possible pairings get on better than the others, then friction can result, particularly if all are of an age. But here it was a little different. For one thing I was the boss, and for another the age range was considerable, 24, 33 and 44. And anyway, four on and eight off is a lot better than four on and four off.

Parts of our newly painted green topsides had shed their paint, and had to be touched up. The jib sheets were clearly going to chafe, so we fitted them with wire pennants in way of the fairleads. Chafing gear had to be fitted aloft, the lavatory pump had been giving trouble, and as we overhauled it we discovered that the pan was cracked and leaking. We fixed that with a metal band and common old pitch. We even got pestered by a reporter, a profession which I abhor, who started asking a lot of questions. For a number of reasons I wanted to keep our impending departure quiet, I didn't want hordes of people wanting to see the boat, I didn't want the authorities to come down and tell me what lifeboats, line throwing rockets and other equally unstowable gear I should carry, so he got the elbow and went away quite hurt. Later, in the local, I heard him telling his pals all about us.

By the 14th we were, once again, ready to go the moment the weather would allow. There were indications of a change on the way on the 16th, so we moved over to the harbour wall and topped up all our tanks preparatory to departure. The evening weather forecast offered an easterly wind for the next day, so that night we went ashore for what we thought might be our last night in England, and awoke the next morning to find an easterly breeze with only a few light clouds in the sky.

I decided to sail at 9.30 a.m. so we had our breakfast and washed up. Once more we got the dinghy aboard and lashed down. We got in the gangway, sent all the mooring ropes below and at 9.30 we slipped from the buoy and motored towards the harbour entrance. As we were about to clear it we spied a messenger from the harbourmaster's office running along the breakwater waving to us. We slowed down and took the message, which was a telegram from Buzz's parents wishing us 'Bon Voyage'. Would we get away properly this time?

Sailed Hayling Island 6th April 1951, arrived Torquay 9th April 1951. 3 days 14 hours 30 minutes. 336 miles. 3.9 knots.

Chapter 22

Westward Ho!

On a beautiful, bright spring morning, with only a few woolly clouds decorating a clear blue sky we motored out through the harbour entrance into a sparkling, equally blue sea with the fresh easterly breeze blowing the tops off the waves. Perfect conditions for the real start of the voyage, so, as we cleared the breakwaters, John and Buzz set about the last, essential tasks preparatory to settling down to sail the ship the 1,300 miles to Madeira. The chain was unshackled from the anchor and dropped into the chain locker and the spurling pipe securely plugged. The anchor was well lashed down and the gaskets cast off the sails so, half a mile outside the harbour, we stopped the engine, set all plain sail, streamed the log and set our course to pass a mile to the south of Berry Head. The sails were setting beautifully, looking as though cut out of cardboard, and I felt that *Kimballa* must have been a perfect picture as she shook the dust of England from her. All the trials and tribulations which I had suffered getting to this point seemed worth while, and I looked forward to the voyage with eager anticipation.

Rounding Berry Head we altered course to the westward to take us down mid-channel and out into the Atlantic, away from the land with all the dangers which it held for our small, frail craft and away, too, from the twentieth century's so-called civilisation, in which man is so rapidly becoming the slave of his own machines. We organised our little community. We set our watches, with John keeping the four to eight, the morning and dog watches, Buzz the twelve to four, the afternoon and middle, or graveyard, watch and with me doing the eight to twelve, forenoon and first watches. We arranged that we would each cook one day at a time in strict rotation, for this was the least popular of all the tasks which had to be done on a continuous basis. Cooking good hot meals for three fresh-air hungry men takes a lot of time and trouble, and is all time out of the cook's 'watch below'. I was not worried that we only had rations for one and two thirds persons with three persons eating them, for I knew that we could stock up, free of the problems imposed by rationing, at our first port of call. We settled into a routine of having a good cooked breakfast, usually bacon and eggs with fried potatoes and coffee, and a cold lunch with coffee again. Preparing a meal in the cramped quarters of the yacht's small galley was no easy task and it was only too easy to get a meal almost to the point of delivery only to have a violent lurch of the boat fling it all over the galley floor, creating a start-again situation. We cooked entirely in salt water, preserving our fresh for drinking only, and found it to be successful but for the fact that it rapidly corroded our pressure cooker to the point of it becoming impossible to clean. The dinner menu was left entirely to the imagination of the cook of the day and was usually tinned corned beef, or spam, or tongue or pork stewed or fried up with potatoes, beans, carrots, onions, turnips or parsnips spiced, if the boat was not bouncing about too much, with a sauce concocted by the cook. If the cook was feeling posh we sometimes started with tinned soup, soup being something which we never attempted to make, for the essential stock pot gets in the way and is hard to stow securely enough to guarantee that it won't decorate the cabin floor. Pudding was almost always tinned fruit and tinned milk, with the meal rounded off by the inevitable cup of coffee, sometimes Nescafé, which gets boring, and sometimes tinned ready ground coffee, which seems not to get boring. All in all we ate well.

The salt water regime prevailed with washing clothes, with the result that they were never really clean, or dry. Salt water detergents are only a limited success, and anything washed in salt water remains damp because of the hygroscopic properties of the salt which remains in it. At our ports of call the laundries or dhobey wallahs saw to it that we set off on the next leg clean and dry, but we just got dirtier and damper until the next port of call.

The ideal sailing conditions in which we departed Torquay prevailed right through the first day and night, with *Kimballa* bounding along in the freshening breeze with her lee rail under and making up to eight knots at times. At evening we ran through a patch of some hundreds of coconuts and wondered if we had made record time and reached the Pacific already! They must have been dumped by, or washed overboard from, some homeward-bound steamer. By nightfall the land was out of sight and we lit our lights and ran on our way. I was nervous in the crowded approaches to the Channel and off the coasts of France and Portugal where traffic is heavy, for the lights of a small yacht are very close to the water and difficult to see. In particular, our starboard light, visible from right ahead to two points abaft the beam on the starboard side was, with the boat on the port tack and running with her lee rail under, often obscured by the bow wave. Received wisdom has it that shining a powerful torch on the sails when another vessel is sighted is good protection, but, as our sails were tanned brown to reduce the glare of sunlight in the warmer seas for which we were bound, this would have been ineffective so we kept a 300 candlepower Aladdin pressure lamp lit and hanging in the cabin where the watchkeepr could get it quickly. As the watches changed the man coming on would rise a few minutes early and make a cup of cocoa for himself and the man he was relieving so, with that at each end of the watch, and coffee with every meal, we were not short of hot drinks.

The first night of the voyage proper passed without incident with the wind easing but, fortunately, holding its direction. The sun came up to herald another fine day and I had no trouble getting a good sight for longitude at breakfast time, and another good one for latitude at noon, to generate a noon position and a day's run of 138 miles for an average speed of 5.3 knots. Pretty good for a cruising yacht in the hands of somewhat inexperienced amateur yachtsmen, I thought. As the day wore on the sky became overcast, the wind began to veer and we were treated to occasional rain but this was nothing to worry about. We were well clear of the land by now, and a veering wind would only push us further away from the traffic jam round Ushant and, unless it went right round to the west, we could still make away from both the French and English coasts. The wind continued to drop and over the next few days our day's run fell to a paltry fifty miles in the light and variable conditions, but we continued to make ground in the desired south-westerly direction. I had intended to get well out into the Atlantic before turning more southerly in about the latitude of Finisterre, lest a series of westerly gales drive us towards the coast, but the B.B.C. weather reports, which we could still receive, promised settled weather. So I set our course to pass fifty miles off that cape, not quite clear of the commercial crowd, but on the outer edge of it. In the event we did not sight it, indeed we did not expect to at that distance, and anyway there was fog between us and the cape, a bank in which we could hear the steamers hooting even though we were in clear weather ourselves. I was more than glad that we were in the clear for, though we carried a hand-driven foghorn which made a remarkable amount of noise, steamers' horns are much noisier and steamers' masters are intent on not hitting other steamers, and will listen more carefully for their sirens. Many of the larger and better found ships had radar by this time, but it was not in general use and, anyway, a small yacht can easily get lost in the sea clutter on the screen. We were glad to be out of both the fog and the main traffic lane.

I felt by this time that I really would make my date with Fulley in the Pacific. As a result of my difficulties in getting hold of foreign currency, which were bound to affect him equally, we had changed the venue of our meeting from Tahiti, which is part of French Oceania, to Raratonga, which is administered by New Zealand and is therefore part of the Sterling Area. Raratonga lies 700 miles to the south-west of Tahiti, but what is 700 miles in 10,000? Yes, I was beginning to feel confident, even though we were only just clear of the dreaded Bay of Biscay! I was even dreaming of the trip we proposed to the island of Rapa, an island so far off the beaten track that it has only one European resident, a Frenchman, and which has stone platforms and walls similar to those on Easter Island. Dreams of the future, but with every mile we made good to the south and west, becoming more substantial.

As the latitude decreased the weather became warmer, though the communal duffle coat was still passed from man to man at the change of watch. One morning as I took over the watch from John I noticed a small squid on the deck, one which had, either by sheer accident, or in an escape from some predator, squirted itself on board during the night. I thought it was a revolting-looking creature, yellowy brown and with tentacles like spaghetti. Fortunately very dead. Now John and Buzz had done a lot of talking about fishing during the voyage, but had actually caught nothing at all, so I persuaded John, who was cook for the day, to put it on Buzz's plate for breakfast, which he duly did. Arriving for breakfast, half asleep, Buzz saw the revolting thing and his eyes stuck out nearly as far as the squid's. But it didn't put him off his breakfast at all.

Clear of Finisterre we altered course for Madeira, with the wind obligingly swinging into the east again to allow us to make good progress in the right direction. In about the latitude of Gibraltar we encountered a moderate gale, but managed to sail on without reefing and put up the voyage record days run of 150 miles, for a speed of 6.25 knots. As we made westing we altered our clocks, doing it in half-hour stages each time apparent noon strayed half an hour from ship's twelve o'clock. We found it better to do it this way, instead of a few minutes every day, as it made it easier to remember the time of wireless time signals and weather reports. We ran the engine for fifteen minutes each Saturday morning, and found that it got easier to start as the weather got warmer. Electric light we only used at the change of watch, using a wall-mounted Tilley lamp, which gave a good, warm light, in the cabin, so our batteries only needed charging once a week which was a very good thing, for our little generator gave us a lot of trouble. Apart from the disastrous effect which the damp, salt air had on the electrics the thing had been designed for land-based use, and the petrol tank was so shallow that if the boat was rolling the petrol sloshed clear of the pipe to the carburettor from time to time causing intermittent fuel starvation. Buzz cured this by adding a small header tank, but we found no permanent cure for the electrics.

We sailed on through empty seas. Of marine life we saw and caught none, but for one turtle which spotted us the day before we sighted the islands and promptly dived, never to be seen by us again, though we had birds with us all the way. The sea was empty of shipping and in the whole passage to Madeira nothing came within a couple of miles of us. Even so we were not idle and, though I had expected time not on watch to hang heavy, the opposite was the case. There is always maintenance work of some sort to be done and the continuous motion makes everything take a lot longer to do than it should. Firstly because you are permanently tired, for the motion makes proper sleep hard to get, with your muscles continuously at work trying to counteract the rolling and pitching. Chiefly affected seem to be stomach, ankle and calf muscles, but the rest of you is permanently weary too. Then there is the problem of errant bits and pieces. Anything, or any part of anything, that you are working on will, if not properly secured, be thrown somewhere else by the motion, and that somewhere is almost always the bilge, necessitating the lifting of floorboards and guddling about in the mucky bilge to find it. Whilst this is going on the screwdriver, or whatever tool you happen to be using, will become dislodged, making you go through the whole performance yet again. There is a lot to do, and it all takes a lot of time. There isn't time to be bored, only to be tired.

We made our first landfall at 6.15 p.m. on Wednesday, 2nd May, my niece's birthday. John sighted the peak of Pico de Fatcho at a distance of about sixty miles. The winds were light and it was not before 10.00 p.m. that we were up with the land. During the night the wind dropped away altogether, and 10.00 the next morning found us becalmed and so, having only thirty miles to go, we started the engine to get us in before dark with the chance of finding a good berth in daylight. It was a warm, sunny day and we busied ourselves getting the ship ready for arrival. The anchor chain was got up and shackled on, mooring ropes were brought out in case they were needed and the lashings taken off the dinghy. The sails were given a harbour stow, all as we slipped by the intensively cultivated land, dotted with brightly coloured houses. It felt good to be alive on such a day, having made a good landfall and with a secure harbour almost within sight.

At about 3.00 in the afternoon the Bay of Funchal opened up as we rounded a headland and we beheld the town spread out before us at the foot of the mountain. The harbour was empty but for a couple of fishing boats and as we approached the main pier we noticed a motor launch painted with the word 'Piloto' lying at anchor and, on approaching it, a man on board waved to us and told us to anchor nearby. A cast of the lead showed a depth of four fathoms and so, putting the engine slow astern, we took the way off the ship and let go the anchor at 4.00 p.m., completing the first, short, passage of our long voyage. An hour or so later the doctor, the police and the customs men came on board and in no time at all we had our pratique, the forms were all filled in, our passports impounded for the duration of our stay, and our 'Q' flag could come down as all the officials departed. Shortly after that we were visited by Mr. Olfonso Quelho, the manager of Messrs. Blandy Brothers' coaling station. He came aboard to see if there was anything he could do for us (we were unlikely to need coal!), being a yachtsman himself and in the habit of visiting all the overseas yachts which called at Funchal. His English was so perfect that I thought that perhaps, despite his name, he was English. But no, his mother had been English, hence his mastery of the language. Not only did he save us a lot of bother by sending us a water barge before we sailed, but he gave us a lot of useful information about Funchal, and sent us a stock of books and magazines. One of nature's gentlemen.

By the time the ship's chandler, one Cipriano Francisco B. Correia, arrived, John and Buzz were itching to get ashore, so I told C.F.B.C. that I would look him up the next day and packed the lads off to the beach. Once alone I was visited by a very seedy-looking individual with a sheaf of recommendations as a watchman, offering me his services in that capacity. These characters exist in every port and collect recommendations as a philatelist collects stamps. As most of them can't read they are unaware of the tone or content of the documents, some of which make amusing reading. Like the one carried by a man in Bombay who was a shoemaker and came round the ships looking for work. One of his read, 'This hooligan has completely ruined my best shoes. On no account let him touch even your engineroom boots.'

As dusk fell a very contented Jack Arnot wrote a letter or two and sat in the cockpit, admiring the evening scene, smoking a cheroot and sipping a glass of Maderia, completely at peace with the world.

Sailed Torquay 17th April 1961. Arrived Funchal 3rd May 1951. 16 days 7 hours. 1338 miles, 3.4 knots.

Chapter 23

Madeira and the Atlantic crossing

After the most comfortable night's sleep for two and a half weeks we awoke next morning to a fine, clear, warm sunny day. Nearly, but not quite warm enough to tempt us over the side for a pre-breakfast swim in the clean, clear water of the harbour. Over breakfast we planned our day, and at about 10.00 a.m. Buzz and I got dressed and rowed ashore in the dinghy, leaving John to look after the ship.

Not being tourists in the accepted sense of the word we didn't feel the need of the services of one of the crowd of gentlemen calling themselves guides congregated at the end of the pier. But it was hard to make them believe that, and even after numerous refusals one of them detached himself from the group and followed us. Must have been something of an optimist! The world runs on money, so our first call was at Blandy Brothers where, despite a crowded office, Mr. Quelho waved a magic wand and we had our travellers cheques cashed in no time and went our separate ways. Buzz to the market to weigh up the prices for comparison with those which the ship's chandler would quote for the same thing, and me to call on the British Consul.

I was greeted by the Consul's right hand man, and only after I had convinced him that I was in no sort of trouble did I get to see the Consul himself, Mr. Cox. I told him that I had called to make my number and see if there were any letters for the ship, and in the course of conversation discovered that Mr. Cox had been Consul in Rangoon immediately after the government of Burma had been handed over to the Burmese. As Rangoon had been my home port for many years we found a lot to talk about, and when Buzz arrived to meet me I got more evidence of what a small world we live in. Buzz knew him, for he, Buzz, had at one time been sent to Copenhagen, to bring back a ship which had been bought by a London firm, only to find that the owner's representative had disappeared, which left

151

Buzz stranded and with little money. So, a distressed British seaman, he turned to the Consul, Mr. Cox, for help. So they, too, had a lot to talk about, which took up so much time that I felt obliged to decline Mr. Cox's invitation to lunch.

At the post office I found a few letters for us and posted those we had written. A messy business, as Portuguese stamps have no gum on them, and gluepots are set about the counters. After stamping twenty or so letters one looks a bit like the cartoon of the cat and the flypaper! Outside again, with the sun over the yardarm, I found a handy cafe in which to enjoy a cool beer and watch the passing scene. I was importuned to buy a lottery ticket, but thought that I had probably used up my share of luck in that direction. Rich and poor passed by, women dressed all in black, children with no shoes, and wheelless carts or sledges, which are used in this hilly town instead of conventional drays. All very colourful; it was a pleasure to sit at ease after the hard work of the passage from Torquay. I found a barber and had a haircut which, even though I have only a small fringe round my bald pate, took three quarters of an hour, and put me in mind of the barber's shop in a P. & O. liner taking me out to India. It was also the ship's shop, and the barber broke off from cutting hair to serve customers when needed. I was in buying something for the fancy dress dance that night and H. G. Wells was in the barber's chair. When the man came to serve me H. G. remarked, 'You know, barber, it's growing all the time.'

Lunch in a small restaurant was very pleasant and tasty. A joy to eat food which you haven't cooked for yourself for a change, even though it was cooked in a surfeit of olive oil. A stroll in the park from which there is a glorious view of the harbour, and which has a memorial to Mecator in the form of a globe, with the meridians and parallels in wrought iron, and then back to the ship in mid-afternoon feeling that I had done a good day's work. Even so I turned to with the others to make a start on all the things which had to be done before we set sail for Trinidad. We had found that, running before the wind with the sheets well freed the mainsail in particular chafed on the spreaders and needed repair, and the problem had to be minimised. I had acquired some rawhide strips for this very purpose and, bound round the spreaders and well greased with tallow they did a good job. I had the benefit of advice from a Captain Nelson who, after retiring, had sailed a yacht called *Imatra* to New Zealand. He advised against the conventional baggywrinkle for chafe prevention as, in a small yacht it gets soaked with salt water and when dry acts like a scrubbing brush on the sails. I now believe that sheepskin with the fleece still on it is the ideal chafe preventer. On one of the days at Madeira I kept ship whilst John and Buzz went to lunch at the Consul's home, and occupied myself with moving and re-wiring the batteries, which were getting wet from our leaking decks. There was plenty to do.

Another day I visited the ship's chandler who was really a wine merchant, with chandlery as a sideline. As we sat at a table surrounded by enormous casks of wine, discussing, as one has to do, everything under the sun except the business in hand, we sipped a glass of real Madeira, not the stuff that they let the tourists drink. It was superb, and adds to the effectiveness of the preliminary chat, designed to weigh up the prospective customer and assess how far his tail can be twisted before he screams! We did a deal, and arranged for the stores to be delivered the morning before sailing day, which was to be Thursday, 8th May, at 5.00 p.m. I would have liked to stay longer in Madeira, but couldn't because of the shortage of hard currency. I had to conserve enough to get me through the Panama canal and to buy stores in French Oceania, so our stay in Funchal was, of necessity, short.

During the night of 7th/8th May a yacht which we had been expecting, *Katwinchar*, also bound for the Antipodes, arrived. She, too, had a crew of three and was entered for the Sydney–Hobart race the following December. The crew came aboard *Kimballa* on the afternoon of sailing day and we had a long and enjoyable chat about our projects and problems. Then, at 5.00 p.m., the police brought us our passports, and hung about until we sailed, just to make sure that we did. We hove up and motored out of the harbour to get clear of the lee of the land before stopping the engine and setting all plain sail. We were not truly out of the lee and into the prevailing east wind, and by noon the next day had only made good thirteen miles, but by dawn the following day we were out of sight of land and bowling along on our 3,000-mile leg to Trinidad.

We soon settled into our routine again, steering, cooking and working about the ship. Cook's specialities began to appear. Bread still defeated us, a soggy brick being the invariable result of our efforts. Buzz became a dab hand at pastry, and John was the king of the stews, marvellous dishes with a bit of everything in them. Curries, which I love, were my speciality, even though they did involve a lot of tedious washing up. The first attempt was a disaster, for I cooked the rice in the pressure cooker and, though I had followed the instructions to the letter, I made a mistake right at the end. Instead of cooling the cooker to reduce the pressure before opening the lid I, in my haste to see the result, lifted the safety valve with that object in mind. Instead of a gentle release of steam I got a solid stream of boiling rice water which shot up to the deckhead and then sprayed everywhere, coating the whole cabin and everything in it is a sticky, slippery paste, and in everything

I include myself. The cabin floor was so slippy you could hardly stand on it, and it took days to clean up the mess. Nevertheless my curries were appreciated, and my day as cook always brought out a stream of hints.

Our fresh fruit had to be eaten quickly for, in the warm climate, it just went on ripening apace, and most vegetables went the same way. Onions kept best of all, with potatoes a good second, though we found that we had to throw away about a quarter of our stock. We wolfed our radishes and lettuce, but weren't quick enough with the carrots, most of which went soft and had to be thrown away. None the less we ate well throughout the passage. The weather was kind to us and we had sunshine almost all the time and wore nothing but shorts in the daytime, though we still needed a blanket at night. The weather in England, and for the first part of the passage to Madeira, had been unsuitable for serious work on deck so we took advantage of the sunshine to scrape the dinghy inside and out and double up a couple of cracked planks and, after three coats of varnish, she looked like new. Then we set about scraping and varnishing all the brightwork on deck and generally sprucing the ship up. Running before the North-East Trade Wind the boat's motion was easy and so the work itself was less exhausting. Good weather makes everything so much simpler. With the clear skies and constant sunshine there was only one day on which I failed to get a good Noon position, and with everything being so pleasant and easy total harmony prevailed. Marine life was more plentiful in these warmer waters. Five days out from Madeira we acquired a shoal of pilot fish, seven or eight inches long and swimming along just ahead of our stem in their pale blue and black football jerseys. They stayed for a couple of weeks and then suddenly one day they weren't there. Another shoal of little black fish swam along just under our quarter and Portugese Men of War were always in sight, sailing along in the breeze, but never a flying fish did we see.

One day when the weather was fine and the wind was light, and as we weren't going along very fast we though we might take turns at going over the side for a swim, so we got a lifebelt handy and streamed a four-inch mooring line over the stern with a knot in the end of it to catch hold of if the swimmer couldn't keep up. But the moment we streamed that rope a shoal of large fish appeared astern of us. We were obviously being shadowed, and we didn't know by what else, so the swimming party ended before it began! We set about trying to catch one of these monsters, but with no success. What a good thing we don't have to make a living as fishermen, for it would be a poor living indeed.

The sea was still a vast empty circle moving gently along at our stately three and a half to six knots. It was twenty-three days out of Madeira that we saw our first ship, bound, I would guess, from the States to South Africa. She passed a long way off and may well not have seen us. At about this time we had a few rain squalls which we treated as a fresh shower bath and got ourselves clean; our fresh water was lasting well so we made no attempt to top up with rainwater. Our consumption was about two gallons a day for the three of us, so the stock would easily last the passage. About a week before our landfall the trade wind freshened and we suffered a few strong squalls, so we handed our large staysail and set a jib and took in the main and mizzen, using the opportunity to repair chafed places and re-attach track slides whose seizings had failed. The sky became overcast, but never totally so. The waterline was, by now, thick with shell from which grew a large, rubbery tulip-like thing which opened its scoop-like extremity to catch the waterflow and impede our progress. Shell even grew on the rotating log line where it entered the water. It all made us go a little slower, but we weren't all that fast at the best of times!

Our noon sights on the eleventh of June told us that we should make our landfall before sunset, and, sure enough, just as the sun went down we picked up the northeastern tip of Trinidad, and by 10.30 p.m. we had the Scarborough lighthouse on Tobago island abeam. Throughout the night and the following morning we sailed along the apparently uninhabited, thickly wooded and mountainous northern shore of Trinidad. The only indication of habitation was the occasional column of smoke from some invisible fire. Later we encountered a few fishermen in canoes propelled either by sails or outboard motors, and fishing with long, long rods. At noon we rounded the northwestern point of the island into the Dragon's mouths, a narrow passage with steep shores and sandy beaches, where we lost the wind and resorted to the engine to get us in, and handed all sail. By 4.20 p.m. on the 12th June we had entered the harbour of Port of Spain and were anchored off the Customs House. The Doctor and the Customs men soon came out to us and the formalities were quickly completed. Another passage was successfully under our keel.

Sailed Funchal 8th May 1951. Arrived Port of Spain 12th June 1951. 35 days 1 hour 20 minutes. 3,134 miles at 3.73 knots.

Chapter 24

Caribbean interlude

We were not left long in peace, for, shortly after the customs men had left us, we were asked by the harbourmaster to move elsewhere, our present anchorage being too close to the main deep sea shipping channel. So we moved to an anchorage populated by inter-island schooners. They were a picturesque collection of vessels, manned entirely by West Indians and mostly in an advanced state of shabbiness and disrepair. Their principal inter-island cargo appeared to be petrol and oil in drums, which they carried on deck as well as in the hold. How they managed to work the ship with the decks cluttered with drums I can't imagine, but they seemed to handle them very well. Music and song loomed large in the lives of these sailors, and every vessel had a mandolin or guitar on board and the singing went on late into the night and, with their tremendous sense of rhythm, the Trinidadian concert was really very enjoyable.

The press, who had been expecting *Katwinchar*, descended upon us, and after they had got over their initial disappointment that we were only *Kimballa*, concocted some fair to middling rubbish for their papers. We were 'intrepid', and making 'the most adventurous voyage of recent years', and had given up our jobs to make the pleasure trip to New Zealand. My twin staysails came in for flattering comment and the colour of our sails was described as sunset! It did no harm, but the inaccuracy of the reporting, and the imaginative interpretation of the facts, makes one wonder how much of what appears in the papers can be trusted. By the time they had gone it was too late to go ashore for our mail, so the lads went ashore to see the town by night while I stayed minding the ship, writing letters and writing up the log. As I sat in the cockpit watching the life of the harbour, the ocean-going ships loading and discharging, the flare of burners and clatter of riveting in the ship repair yard, the lights of the town came on. By night it looked much bigger than by day, with enormous neon signs dominating the skyline.

Just like any other port. So much for the romance of the Indies. But no, the music from the schooners was quite different from anything I had encountered before. After our long passage we were not late to bed that night.

Dawn brought an overcast sky with the threat of rain and after breakfast, dressed in our best tropicals and carrying raincoats, Buzz and I went ashore and, for the first time in my long seafaring life, I found myself staggering to the apparent motion of the land! We got the mail from the post office and Buzz returned on board with it while I went to Barclays to cash more travellers cheques, had a haircut and retired to a cafe to have a beer, read my letters, and watch the passing show. Whilst Negroes predominated there was a good leavening of Chinese, Indians and all manner of half breeds and in betweens whose ancestry would make an interesting study. Traffic was heavy with every type of British and American car to be seen, filling the air with their fumes. The currency was a confusing mixture, the basic dollar, worth about four shillings, being subdivided into shillings and pence which were also called cents, so one dollar fifty cents was in fact one dollar and two shillings. Makes life difficult for simple sailors. With rain still threatening I returned on board to find John scraping the shell and seed off the waterline. There was an amazing amount of it, though it had not, fortunately, grown on the copper sheathing below the surface.

Port of Spain was too busy a place to leave *Kimballa* unattended, so in the evening, after a visit on board by friends of John and Buzz who brought us up to date with life in Trinidad, they all went ashore, leaving me contentedly minding the ship and keeping up with my considerable correspondence. We had, by this time, acquired a young West Indian who, for the provision of an occasional meal, happily did our market shopping for us. No doubt he benefited also from backhanders or short changing us, but the amounts were insignificant and he could do better deals than we ever could. Worthwhile help.

My Mother's doctor back in Bury was a Trinidadian and, before leaving, I had visited him and he had suggested that I look up his brother who was a solicitor in Port of Spain, which I did the next day. In contrast to the slight doctor the brother was a large man who nevertheless moved about remarkably quickly and was full of good cheer and bonhomie. I asked if his brother had written to him about my probable visit, which he had not, letters from the English connection apparently coming at six-yearly intervals! He and his other brother and sister took me to a most excellent lunch in a large, modern Chinese restaurant, a meal served, unusually, by an efficient Chinese waitress. In the vast majority of Chinese restaurants there are waiters, not waitresses. Washed down with cold lager on this hot day the meal was a very pleasant interlude, after which they took me on a tour of the northern part of the island, showing me the abundant vegetation, the grapefruit, orange and guava orchards, the banana and coconut plantations and pointing out the many exotic and colourful trees and shrubs. I was amused to note that the Gold Mohur tree of Burmah is the Flamboyant in the West Indies. Afternoon tea in Mr. Nathaniel's lovely house with its garden full of English roses rounded off a most enjoyable day.

John had been keeping ship that day and, when I returned, he surprised me by telling me that he was fed up with the voyage and wanted to leave the ship and get a job in Trinidad. I told him that if he really wanted to go I wouldn't stop him, but I doubted whether he would find getting a job that easy, as most posts held by Europeans required qualifications, of which John had none. But he was determined and within a couple of days had landed a job as a rigger erecting plant at an oil refinery. His knowledge of rigging was minimal, but at £75 a month he seemed to have done well, and I wondered how long it would take them to rumble him!

Buzz was away in the south of the Island visiting Pointe a la Pierre, where he had a friend from his Royal Fleet Auxiliary days at the oil terminal there. When he returned I asked him if he would be willing to carry on with just the two of us and I was very pleased when he said that he would, with the reservation that he wasn't too fond of the idea of interminable watch and watch working. We talked it through and decided that that could be avoided if we slowed down a bit, and could make *Kimballa* steer herself when we got into the south-east trades in the Pacific. On that basis we agreed to go on together. I was more than pleased, for I had grown to like Buzz a lot. On another day I was taken by my solicitor friend on a tour of the southern part of the island, including the great pitch lake, which was nothing like what I had imagined. The existence of the lake has been known for hundreds of years and, whilst it was used by the buccaneers of old amongst others to caulk their ships, it really came into its own with the introduction of tarmac. I'd visualised a vast stretch of gleaming black pitch, but it was nothing at all like that, having a dirty brown-black surface scattered with scrubby patches of vegetation struggling for a living. It has no clearly defined shoreline and pitch oozes out of the surrounding countryside, killing off most of the greenery. It is dug out before being piped to storage tanks for shipment all over the world and is the centre of Trinidad's oil-bearing country, surrounded by innumerable oil derricks, each with its nodding donkey at its foot, and entangled by a maze of piping to take the oil away. Not attractive countryside at all, but our route also took us through the sugar cane plantations, dense masses of green laid out in vast tracts. We stopped for lunch at one of the clubs where I met a number of interesting people and sampled the local speciality, rum and lime which, for all that I don't really like rum is, appropriately iced, a marvellous drink in this climate. Onwards again, with a stop for tea at another house, hanging off a cliff above the sea, where the four-year-old daughter of the house took a long look at me and declared that I was, 'Quite nice.' We arrived back in Port of Spain in the tropical twilight and I managed to refuse an invitation to visit the 'Rainbow', Port of Spain's latest and best night club. I returned on board having had a very full and entertaining day.

Sunday followed, spent leisurely on board and exploring Port of Spain and its northern park, a vast tract known as the 'Savannah', and surrounded by the Governor's residence and the houses of the Chief Justice, the Bishop and such like notables. Full of brilliant flowers and magnificent trees it is a fine place to wander in and relax. Monday saw me fixing up stores with the chandler with more than usual care, for this lot had to last us through the hard currency area until we got back to the Sterling Area at Rarotonga, many thousands of miles away. I had intended to get the decks caulked but was advised that it would be done better and cheaper at Kingstown, St. Vincent, our next port of call. St. Vincent was off our direct track to the Panama canal, and we were going there for purely social reasons. When I was working on the Burmah coast I had become friendly with a pilot at Moulmein who, at independence, had decided that the street fighting, kidnapping for ransom and general mayhem made it an unsafe place to bring up a family. He had, as his wife came from St. Vincent, gone there from Burmah, and since it was only 200 miles out of our way I decided to visit him.

Apart from John's resignation our stay in Trinidad ended on a slightly sour note. The young West Indian who had been shopping for us had decamped, and a middle-aged chap offered to go marketing for us. I gave him three dollars and a shopping list and off he went. Four hours later he returned, very drunk indeed, with a few mouldy vegetables. We got rid of him with some difficulty, but he was back the next morning demanding more money. I told him that if he didn't clear off I would call the police and went below. I did not hear him rowing away so I came up to see what he was up to, just in time to see that he had taken the oars of our dinghy, which was lying astern of us, and they were drifting away on the tide. Strangely enough, when I told him to get them and put them back he did so without argument, but none the less I ran up the signal for the water police, and when they arrived I told them what was going on. What they did about it, if anything, I don't know.

When I went ashore to get our clearance papers I had my first encounter with the new-fangled steel band, oil drums tuned to different notes and being used to good effect to make very lively music. I had a bit of bother with the papers, for John had to provide assurances from his employers, Foster Wheeler, that they would be responsible for his repatriation, and this took a little time. With the papers in order we moved alongside, stored, fuelled and watered and moved back to the anchorage with a view to sailing at dawn the next day. I went ashore and said goodbye to my friends, after which Buzz did the same, and we turned in early.

Next morning we were up at daybreak in a hot, steamy overcast morning to get the dinghy aboard and everything prepared for sea. After a cup of coffee we started the engine and motored out to the sailing vessel control station, which was a wooden shack built on piles in the middle of the harbour. We made fast to the piles and encountered the second sour note. I took the ship's papers to a sleepy-looking Negro policeman who examined them, leisurely, and announced that because there was a date missing from them I would have to wait till 10.00 a.m., and then go back ashore to the Immigration Department to have the omission rectified. I didn't think this was a good idea at all, and insisted that he telephone the immigration people there and then, which he reluctantly did, getting equally reluctant responses from men who had been sleeping peacefully in bed. Six in the morning is not the best time to get action out of Trinidadians, but after a lot of seemingly aimless argument we were allowed to sail.

The distance in a straight line from Port of Spain to Kingstown, St. Vincent, is less than 200 miles, but takes you through the mostly low-lying Grenadines, separated from each other by narrow and intricate channels. To go on the eastern, Atlantic, side of the Grenadines would provide the best wind, but the islands would form a dangerous lee shore all the way, hazardous should an easterly gale blow up. I had in mind how the yacht *Tai-Mo-Shan* came to grief in these waters so I decided that, once clear of the Dragons Mouths, I would lay my course to pass to the westward of Grenada and the Grenadines.

Clearing the land we found a light easterly breeze, stopped the engine and set all plain sail, streamed the log and settled down to a couple of days of watch and watch. Drifting along at about two knots that afternoon we sighted what looked like a half-tide rock, and coming up with it found it to be an enormous turtle, old and covered in shell and all manner of marine growth, in need of a scrape and a coat of anti-fouling. He dived, and surfaced again much further away and we soon lost sight of him, or her. It was a miserable afternoon, hot and sultry with occasional light rain and I had the feeling that some nasty weather was brewing, for by now we should have been enjoying the trade wind. At nightfall we passed a schooner bound for Port of Spain, the weather did not break during the hours of darkness, and we continued on our two knot way.

Dawn came up hazy with poor visibility and an indifferent sight at noon credited us with a mere fifty miles made good, and as the afternoon wore on the wind increased until by evening it was blowing a gale from the southeast. I was truly glad that I had not attempted the windward passage for by now we would have had the Grenadines as a very dangerous lee shore. A heavy sea got up and the weather looked really ugly. We were close hauled on the starboard tack and overpressed, but with only the two of us on board we decided against venturing on deck to get in the mainsail, struggling though we were to keep her up to the wind. These conditions prevailed throughout the night and through most of the next morning, preventing us, for one of the very few occasions in the voyage, from making a hot meal. We lived on cheese sandwiches and anything else which came easily to hand as we crawled about the vessel as she crashed her way through the heavy seas. There was no chance of a sight that morning and my dead reckoning put us to the north of St. Vincent. At about 11.00 a.m. the wind dropped quite suddenly and we were left slatting about in a large swell. The sun came out and, although it was late for a longitude sight and the horizon was very poor I took a snap shot which put us to the east, not the west, of St. Vincent. The wind by this time had dropped completely away and we were rolling about most uncomfortably in a big, oily, swell. No land was in sight, so we set a course, southerly, in the hope of finding it. At about two in the afternoon the sun came out again and I got another, and better, observation which put us north of St. Vincent, in the St. Vincent Passage between it and St. Lucia. Just as I had finished working it out Buzz spotted the land, which turned out to be the northern part of St. Vincent and only two miles off. The highest peak in the island is over 4,000 feet, but all we could see at a distance of two miles was a shadowy coastline. Fortunately the island's coast is steep to all round, with no outlying obstructions, so we could safely follow it southwards. In improving weather, with life looking better and better, we motored southwards, made ourselves a meal and treated ourselves to a drink. Night fell, the haze cleared, the moon came up and at 8.30 p.m. the bay at Kingstown opened up. By 9.00 we were anchored 100 yards from the shore in five fathoms. I was glad that, with confidence in *Kimballa*'s ability to avoid being pooped in a following sea having grown, we had removed the plank and canvas cover of the cockpit, unshipped the tiller and engaged the wheel steering. This made life much more comfortable for the helmsman and markedly improved access to the cabin. With the anchor down and a nightcap under our belts we were soon in our bunks and asleep.

In the morning we awoke to find ourselves anchored in a beautiful bay surrounded by densely wooded mountains dotted with brightly coloured houses, with the town strung out along the waterfront on what little flat land there was. In our anchorage we had the company of a couple of island schooners, and out in the bay an ocean-going cargo liner was discharging into lighters. There was a wooden jetty for the use of schooners and lighters, with about nine feet of water, but no quay for ocean going vessels. Before the sleep had been rubbed from our eyes the port doctor, an enormous West Indian, arrived and we were soon able to take down our 'Q' flag. Everything in the boat was upside down after our two days of hard weather, so we spent most of the day getting things shipshape again, and by 5.00 p.m. were dressed and ready to go ashore.

As we were getting our dinghy alongside a boat rowed out and its occupants told us that a Mr. Gun, standing on the end of the jetty, was asking the name of the boat and whence she came, so we told them and they returned ashore. As we rowed in we met the same boat with Mr. Gun aboard and we asked him if he would like to come aboard, so we all went back to *Kimballa*. He turned out to be a yachtsman interested in all floating things and we found plenty to talk about. My pilot friend was living with his wife's parents, a Mr. and Mrs. Hazel', of Hazell & Sons of St. Vincent, so I asked Mr. Gun if he knew their address and, grinning broadly, he said that he thought he did, for he was a director of Hazells, and would take us to the house when we went ashore, which he duly did, and after a refreshing rum and lime, and having been told that my pal was away in London, we went looking for his wife who, by now, had her own home. We tracked her down and spent a very pleasant evening talking over the old Burmah days and remembering mutual friends.

The following day with Mr. Gun for a guide we saw part of the island, starting with a visit to one of the highest points which can be reached by car, from which the view, in the evening just before sunset, was magnificent, and the air distinctly cooler than it was down in the bay. Coming down from there through the endless coconut plantations we visited the swimming club, situated in a delightful bay with a palm-fringed white beach and a few yachts anchored off. We sat and watched the sunset, sipping our rum and limes the while, before Buzz and I repaired to the Blue Caribbean Hotel for dinner, to save ourselves the cooking! This very pleasant and hospitable hotel had just been reconstructed with a postwar influx of tourists in view, and we had an excellent dinner.

Next morning when I stuck my head out of the hatchway for my sniff of the morning air I noticed a large Negro hanging about in a dinghy, so with our Trinidad experiences in mind I asked him what he wanted. His face just split in half in an enormous smile before he replied, 'Ah's just exercising my limbs', whereon he rowed slowly away and we never saw him again. We were only too aware that anyone could steal our dinghy, which we kept tied up astern on two painters, so we got into the way of tying a light fishing line into it with the other end attached to a tin can in the yacht which, if the dinghy moved beyond the scope of her painters, would fall with a clatter. A simple burglar alarm which, on reflection, would only work AFTER the dinghy was stolen, though we might still be able to identify the thief.

With the aid of the invaluable Mr. Gun we found two men with the skill to caulk the decks, which they did very well for about a quarter of the price I had been quoted in England. Leaking decks had been a pest the whole way, for the constant seepage made the whole ship damp and ruined a lot of my books. And, free of the left-over wartime restrictions of Britain, we bought a small stock of timber for running repairs at sea. And we solved the soggy brick bread problem. One evening, at dinner with the Hazells and the pilot's wife, we described our problem and the ladies, despite their inborn scepticism on the subject of men cooking at all, sent for their cook, who gave us full instructions including specifying the type of yeast to use, a tinned American dried yeast. We bought a couple of one-pound tins before we sailed, determined to make bread some day, and we ultimately did! We were introduced to the family Siamese cat which had recently declined the services of its selected Siamese husband and mated with a tabby to produce a litter of six kittens, half of them Siamese looking and the other half showing their tabby ancestry. Of these more later.

Returning to the police station to collect the dinghy's oars, which we had left there for safety's sake, we found it locked, with the man with the key away and not expected back for a while, so we strolled along to the Blue Caribbean to fill in the waiting time with a drink. We were sitting peacefully doing just that when a stranger came in, looked at us, asked politely if we were from the yacht and, on learning that we were, said in a loud voice, so loud that everyone in the room could hear it, 'Oh, then you are the man that won the Irish Sweep.' Being in the oil business he had probably gleaned this information from the oil world's very efficient bush telegraph. Buzz, who knew nothing of this, looked at me in amazement, and the label followed me for the rest of the voyage. Finishing our drinks we recovered our oars and went back on board.

Our time in St. Vincent, exploring the island under the guidance of Brenda, the pilot's wife, visiting her friends on their coconut plantations, being terrified crossing the very narrow wooden road bridges, ambling round the large botanical garden with its prize exhibit, the first breadfruit tree in the islands, planted by Captain Bligh, was most enjoyable. We enjoyed the hospitality of the Blue Caribbean, and all our friends, new and old, visited *Kimballa* and enjoyed her hospitalility. But time was moving on and we must soon tear ourselves away, so we began the process of buying stores for the next two legs of the voyage, with 'Hard Currency, Shortage Of', printed firmly in our minds. On one of his marketing expeditions Buzz bought a sack of 1,500 limes and, borrowing a lime squeezer from the Blue Caribbean, we spent an afternoon squeezing limes and bottling the juice. With the addition of a tablespoon of alcohol as a preservative it made a very refreshing drink. We had, as usual, been adopted by a young West Indian, Selwyn by name, who helped with our shopping and brought us a block of ice each morning which generally lasted the day, and helped us to keep our drinks cool.

The time came for us to go alongside to top up our water tanks at the wooden jetty. As we were manoeuvering to get alongside with the whole of the juvenile population of the island watching and offering advice, the starboard main spreader caught the sunscreen on the window of an office on the jetty, and it came crashing down to the deck, barely missing Buzz who was up for'd with the bow line. Pandemonium broke out; every clerk in the office ran out and every one had his threepenceworth to put in. The chief clerk conceded that the screen should have been closed, for they had warning of our visit, but was adamant that we would, even so, have to pay for the damage. For the sake of peace I agreed, and a carpenter was quickly found and he borrowed a hammer and nails from us, a ladder from somebody else and soon had the shutter in place again. I reckoned that one dollar was the rate for the job, so I gave him that, provoking a discussion among all those present, and resulting in a demand for two dollars for the job. I told him no, and after a long further argument I asked him to give me the dollar back, which he did, and I told him to go away and we would get the harbourmaster to decide what the job was worth. Whilst we busied ourself with filling our tanks the crowd voiced their disapproval of my method of dealing with the matter, but before long we were full to capacity and prepared to move back out to the anchorage. In the nick of time I noticed that the shutter was open again, so we were able to get it closed and avoid knocking it down for a second time, and we motored away with the angry carpenter shouting and waving his arms at us. Before we sailed the Harbourmaster set the fee at fifty cents, which I paid him, so the carpenter was still cross with us when we left.

The day before departure, a wet one, Buzz returned from a marketing expedition with a damp paper bag in his hand from which came mewing noises. He had asked Mrs. Hazell for one of the kittens, and the frightened little mite in the bag became our 'Kim'. He was wet and full of fleas, so we filled a bowl with Lysol and set about fumigating him. As we pushed his body under the fleas migrated to the top of his head, so we had to sink that too. The fleas were hardy creatures and we had to repeat the process several times before pronouncing them all drowned. We dried him as best we could, gave him some milk and he was soon asleep in one of my slippers. Every time he woke he wandered about, falling all over the place and howling his head off for his absent mother. After a couple of days of this he realised that mum was gone, shut up, and settled down marvellously. The rain stopped later in the day, we went ashore and said our farewells, got our clearance papers, and then filled in the evening with dinner at the Blue Caribbean before turning in to Kim's intermittent howling.

The morning of sailing day dawned fine and clear. Selwyn brought us a nice large fish, which we saved on his block of ice for lunch. We prepared the ship for sea, started the engine, hove up the anchor and motored away from St. Vincent. Clear of the bay we felt the breeze, stopped the engine, and set all plain sail for Colon, 1,300 miles away.

Sailed Port of Spain 21st June 1951. Arrived Kingstown St. Vincent 24th June 1951. 3 Days 13 Hours 30 minutes. 302 miles at 3.5 knots.

Chapter 25

To the Isthmus of Panama

The route from St. Vincent to Colon at the *Caribbean* entrance to the Panama Canal falls into two parts. Firstly, 600 miles slightly south of west, past the islands of Curaçao and Aruba to Point Gallinas, the northernmost point of Colombia, and then 500 miles on a more south-westerly course past Barranquilla and Cartagena to Point Manzanillo in Panama, then yet more southerly for the last thirty miles to Colon.

The prevailing wind in July is the northeast trade, but July is the beginning of the hurricane season. I had hoped to be clear of the Caribbean by now, but had just failed to achieve that. We sailed from Kingstown on American Independence day, the fourth of July, and hoped to be in Colon by the third week of the month.

Screened from the trade wind by the island itself it was not until evening that the breeze began to fill in, and by 4.00 a.m. we had a fresh following wind and were romping along. As we left the land behind the sea and swell increased, and by the beginning of the forenoon watch we were rolling heavily in a quite considerable following sea, and half an hour later an extra heavy roll pitched one of our lifebuoys over the side and we turned round to try to recover it. Wanting to sail back directly over our course we started the engine and steamed directly into the wind, but half an hour's search found no sign of the buoy in the rough sea and swell, so we resumed our course and stopped the engine.

This little mishap gave us pause for thought, for we debated what would have happened had one of us gone over the side. If we couldn't find a brightly painted lifebuoy we were unlikely to find a swimmer. We both took extra care around the decks thereafter. When we left Birdham we had rigged two wires, port and starboard, from the cockpit to the forestay, and when on deck we wore leather belts with a rope tail with a snaphook on the end which we clipped onto the wire whilst working. But we found that the tail was always tangling with something and that, combined with our long run of good weather, caused us to unship the wires, though we made it a rule that no one ventured on deck without someone else being present in the cockpit.

In the high following sea steering was hard work, and everything called for close attention and extra effort, and after three days of watch and watch we were a bit weary. So, when the wind dropped to a moderate breeze we decided to try our twin staysails in earnest, and endeavour to make *Kimballa* steer herself. Handing the jib, the main and the mizzen we set out twin staysails only, to my disappointment, to find that the wind in the sails lifted the booms and the upper part of the sails wrapped themselves round the forestay. I had assumed that the sheets would have exerted sufficient downward force to prevent this, but that was not so, and for the time being we solved the problem by putting a strong lashing from the boom to an eyebolt at the ship's side. This was a mechanically unsound arrangement, the lashing, being only about four feet from the heel of the boom, allowing the sail to exert much too much leverage at the point of attachment to the deck. But we couldn't, at sea, make any better arrangement, and it seemed to work. Three turns of inch and a half cotton rope seemed to stand the strain, and there appeared to be little whip in the booms. We found that by adjusting the sheets the boat could be made to steer herself with the wind anywhere up to three points on the quarter. We later discovered that we could set the mizzen without upsetting her self-steering qualities.

This changed our lives, as we had hoped. We could now sleep, as best we could, during the day, though the heavy motion made that difficult, with every change in the movement of the boat bringing you quickly awake. During the hours of darkness, when we felt most at risk of collision, we kept watch and watch. The wind freshened again and we continued to roll heavily along, making good progress, until one morning the staysail halyard parted, the sails and booms fell into the sea and we had a wet half hour recovering it all and securing it on deck. We decided to defer the expedition up to the mast to replace the halyard until after breakfast and, left to drift, *Kimballa* lay with the wind and sea on the port quarter and was comparatively comfortable. Even so, with the ascent of the mast looming ahead of us, breakfast was a trial to prepare that morning in the still considerable motion, with everything sliding and rolling about. The cooker was not in gimbals, as it should be for ocean voyaging, and, worse still, lay fore and aft. Athwartships would have been better if gimballing could not be achieved. But eventually breakfast was eaten and washed up, the morning sun sight taken and position line achieved, and it was time to repair the damage.

Going aloft in a small yacht in a heavy sea is no fun at all, and so we took it in turns. Today it was my turn. We attached the boatswain's chair to the main halyard and Buzz took the hauling part forward to the anchor windlass and winched me up, carrying the end of the new halyard with me. The mast swung like an inverted pendulum, each swing finishing with a grasp-loosening jerk, but Buzz soon had me up to the truck of the mast and, for once, I rove the halyard through the block and hauled the end down to the deck without it fouling anything. We spliced a thimble into the end of it and soon had our twins up and doing their job and the mizzen re-set. That sail gave us less trouble than any other throughout the voyage. It was set almost all of the time and we only had to have it in for repair twice.

Kim, in the week he had been on board, had visibly grown and could now walk about without too much staggering, though a particularly heavy roll would knock him off his feet. He got his sea legs quicker than anything I have ever seen. Whilst we were up and about his bed was a slipper or an old hat, but when either of us turned in Kim moved to a comfortable position

Buzz, Kim and Jack

on the sleeper's chest, as close to the chin as he was allowed. We had a sand box for him in the cockpit which, in present conditions, was frequently a box of wet mud, but even if it was raining he never failed to use it. At a very early age he learned the signs and smells of cooking activity and how to let us know that he knew what we were up to. At this stage he was not fussy about his food, living on milk and corned beef or tinned fish, washing himself meticulously after meals. He didn't like being left in the cabin if we were on deck and he would sit at the cabin door and wait for us.

We were now running before a moderate following gale with a big sea on a heavy swell climbing mountains high behind us and often looking to fall upon and submerge us, but *Kimballa* rose, every time, to those large seas and never once did one come over her stern. We gained complete confidence in her ability to cope with following seas, and would sit in the cockpit with a wall of water twenty feet high towering over us without giving it a thought. Had we tried to increase our speed it might have been a different story.

All went well for a couple of days after the halyard broke, except that the motion was very exhausting and we found it almost impossible to stand up, crawling about the boat from handhold to handhold when, just before dark one evening, the port staysail boom snapped at the lashing. We had quite a struggle to get the wet and flogging canvas in and to get the booms on board and stowed and to set a small jib. Much to our disgust we were back to steering, a situation we did not relish, for we were getting little sleep in the violently heaving boat. We reviewed our situation next morning and decided to spend a day sewing seams in sails, for all three of our 'Plain' sails were in need of repair, and by evening the wind had dropped away and we were able to hoist all three repaired sails and go on our way, sailing, though well out of sight of land, through dark brown water, the outflow from the Rio Magdalena which enters the sea at Barranquilla.

In the better conditions now prevailing I fished the broken spar, and we were soon able to put the twins to work again and remove the need to steer, which was a great relief, though qualified by a greater need to pump, for an ongoing leak had suddenly, for no good reason, become worse. *Kimballa's* construction, with a canoe body with no reverse curves, meant that she had a very shallow bilge which meant, in turn, that a very small quantity, just a few gallons, of water in the bilge would be washed by the motion of the vessel over the floorboards, up the ship's side and into bunks, bookshelves and lockers, wetting everything. The water rushed about so violently that it frequently left the pump sucking air, so clearing it took an awful long time. The cabin floorboards were permanently wet, and we had to dump the linoleum covering them when it became rotten as well as slippy and dangerous. In these conditions a good wash down, or even a poor one, was impossible, so we just let ourselves get dirty, and we envied Kim his ability to keep himself clean. Perhaps yachtsmen should have longer tongues and suppler bodies! On damp and stormy days we found our daily dose of rum and lime more than usually enjoyable.

Not only were we dirty, but so too was the ship. I had imagined that she would be easily kept clean at sea, but that was not the case. Where the dirt came from I can't imagine, though the stove was responsible for a lot of it. If not sufficiently pre-heated with methylated spirit it would flare and smoke horribly, blackening the deckhead in the galley, a sooty deposit which salt water would not shift, so the galley stayed dirty until the proximity of our destination released fresh water for the clean-up job.

As we got closer and closer to Colon the radio broadcasts got louder and louder and stranger and stranger to we B.B.C.-conditioned souls. We still got our time signals from that channel, but the local stations seemed to divide their time between interminable advertising and 'Hot Gospelling' religious broadcasts, in which priests of all sorts of religions whipped themselves and their audiences to a frenzy which sounded for all the world like a madhouse. As the strength of the signals increased we knew we were getting closer to the canal, though of course we knew that anyway!

By now the weather had taken its toll of the ship's appearance. Much of the green paint had peeled off the hull, leaving large patches of the underlying cream showing. The varnish had nearly all stripped off the deckhouse and weatherboards, and the ship's wire rails were rusty, and frayed in places. The wind was falling lighter and lighter and our progress through the hot and sticky weather was getting slower. We wore nothing, going naked about the ship and dousing ourselves with buckets of cool sea water from time to time, and as we neared the land we began to see shipping again. With two days to go we sighted the high land of the Isthmus of Panama and as we closed it we saw the dense jungle which covers it, with smoke the only sign of habitation. Ultimately the wind died away to a calm and, with only sixty miles to go, we doused the sails and started the engine, motoring along the coast whose jungle came right down to the water's edge. Of fish we saw none, though they abound. We passed the bay where Drake lies in his lead coffin and, about noon, Buzz sighted the breakwater at the entrance to Colon harbour. My eyesight not being as sharp as his it was another hour before I saw it.

Except for one small coastal vessel we had the sea to ourselves. Settlements on the coast began to show up in the clearings, the masts of the radio station near Colon came into sight and by 3.00 p.m. the breakwater was a mere four miles away. The end of this passage was at hand. We used up our surplus fresh water in a frenzy of washing and felt much better for it. Arriving off the end of the breakwater we were passed close to by a large outward-bound British merchant ship and, not being sure exactly where we should anchor, we turned towards the main part of the town until a small outbound coaster waved and pointed our way towards the canal entrance, so we altered course in that direction and sighted a launch coming out, apparently to meet us. We slowed down and he came alongside and asked us whence we came and where we were bound. She was full of port officials going to meet an incoming ship, so one of them came aboard, showed us on the chart where to anchor, and left a monstrous pile of forms to fill in, saying that they would come back to us.

We went into the anchorage, as directed, let go in four fathoms and flew our 'Q' flag, some sixteen days, eight hours and thirty minutes from Kingstown, St. Vincent. Our berth was hardly inspiring with wharves, warehouses and sheds on the one hand and swampy, low-lying land on the other. It was overcast and very hot, so we drank to our safe arrival and set about the forms, whose multiplicity stemmed from the fact that in the Panama Canal Zone, probably one of the most efficiently run places in the world, 'ships is ships', and we were treated just the same as the largest of passenger liners. We even had to report Kim, though not by name. When and where were we last vaccinated, had anyone died during the voyage, where had we been since the voyage commenced; was there any unusual mortality among the rats, what was our cargo, and so on and so on. At about 5.00 p.m. the launch returned, everyone came aboard, and in short order they had sorted out the formalities. The surveyor took a few measurements and went off with the ship's register, and in due course brought us our Panama Canal certificate of Tonnage. They all stayed for a drink and a chat with us, during which we were introduced to a new meaning for the word 'grief', when the customs man explained to us that when we went ashore we should land at a certain jetty and go through a certain gate, or 'we would get a lot of grief, and we didn't want any grief did we?' Thereafter we found new uses for the word! They departed into the dusk and, in the oppressive heat, glad to be safely at anchor at the end of a hard passage, we fed ourselves and turned in.

Sailed Kingstown 4 July 1951. Arrived Colon 20th July 1951. 1,368 miles, 16 days 8 hours 30 minutes, 3.48 knots.

Chapter 26

The Panama Canal

The Panama Canal Zone may be efficiently run but that does not prevent some of its staff being less than efficient and helpful. We had arrived on Friday too late to collect our mail from the Post Office, and had to wait until Monday for it. Buzz went ashore bright and early before the heat got too sticky, only to return with the news that there was no mail for us, a most unlikely circumstance. He had done his best to insist that there MUST be mail for us, but the Panamanian gentleman behind the counter became quite rude, Buzz got very cross, and came away empty handed. I was cross too. Enquiring around we learned that if we really were sure that there was mail for us we should ask for a Mr. White who would sort things out, which Buzz did the very next morning, and came away with a sack of mail almost too big to carry. No mail, indeed!

After Buzz's fruitless return on Monday we rowed ashore to inspect the town, which was a longish row and very hot work, but lightened by the American troops in a large transport which had just arrived. The troops seemed to be amused by our pumpkin, a very small dinghy with two large chaps in it, and lined the rails to count our stroke for us as we passed by. We landed by the canal's administration building, colourfully set among gardens and flowers and green lawns, with the roads filled with the most enormous American cars, many of which had two-way radios so that the drivers could be sure that dinner was ready when they got home! Men not in uniform seemed to have a bizarre taste in dress, violently coloured sports shirts, looking for all the world like ladies' blouses, hanging out over their trousers and carrying gaudy pictures of farming or beach scenes, or love letters, or pictures of film stars and so on. Definitely not British. We called on the Port Captain and the Customs House, got permission to shift our berth to somewhere more convenient, and made enquiries about the canal passage.

Next, to the barber, with Buzz, who had long golden locks, kicking and screaming. It is his contention that as I am almost completely bald the haircutting routine is pure jealousy, but he did admit to being cooler after being shorn. A stroll round the shops which, unlike the shops of Britain, were full of goods for purchase, had we spare dollars to take advantage of them, though a lot of them were tourist traps containing only tourist-type junk. We ambled through streets full of folk of a myriad nationalities, most of whom spoke English, or what passes for that in the Western Hemisphere, or Spanish, and came to rest for refreshment at the Tropical Restaurant. The Americans really do understand the icing of drinks which, in climates like that of Panama, for we were only nine degrees north of the Equator, is not a luxury but a necessity. Our stock of dollars had been enhanced in Trinidad where a friend had taken me to the Government department which issued currency. They had heeded my plea that with the canal transit to pay for and only fifty dollars in hand any serious repair, or illness, or accident, would strand us completely, and let us buy another fifty dollars. Even so one can hardly go mad on 100 dollars, so we still had to be careful.

Refreshed, we called on the Commodore of the Yacht Club, who was expecting us, for Captain Nelson had written to him saying we would be passing through. He kindly offered us the freedom of the Club during our stay and showed us where we could anchor close to it. In the dining room we found the crew of *Katwinchar* having a meal, they having made a fast, ten-day passage direct from Trinidad which was pretty good sailing. Their time from Madeira to Trinidad was almost exactly the same as ours. We left them to their meal and went back to the Tropical, where we were well fed before returning on board to heave up and shift to the anchorage off the Club, where we anchored bow and stern about fifty yards off the jetty. Much more convenient.

As evening fell the sky was full of brightly coloured birds, parrots and macaws, and clumsy toucans flying some fifty feet up looking for fish and, when they found one, folding their wings and dropping on it like a stone to surface with the catch, shake themselves and swallow it before splashing back to hunting height. In the dusk we rowed ashore to the club and spent the evening yarning with the *Katwinchar*s, who were going to pass through the canal and spend a few days at Balboa before going on to the Galapagos, the Marquesas and Fiji, and then on to Sydney in time for the race to Hobart which was their ultimate destination. During our stay at Colon we exchanged many an evening visit with *Katwinchar*, sitting in our cockpits talking yachts and yachting and ocean voyaging, with Kim, were we 'at home', trying out his baby teeth on the unclad toes which abounded on the cockpit floor. We never did cure him of that habit and he could deliver quite a nip before leaping away from the anticipated slap. He had, by now, settled down to life aboard ship and was entirely at home.

At other times we visited the club bar and met a raft of interesting people, all with the common interest of boats. I suppose the bar must have had opening and closing hours, but I never discovered them for I never found it closed. It has plenty of fans to stir the air and the drinks were cooled to perfection. A place to linger, had the dollars permitted, but they wouldn't stand the drain of club life for long, so it was time to think of moving on. We learned that stores could be bought duty free at the Canal Company's commissariat, so we went shopping there. Our limited purchases included onions and potatoes, powdered milk and Quaker oats, all in tins, a little flour, tinned potatoes and powdered egg, and a tin of ham for some special occasion. Ten pounds of tobacco and, joy of joys, some 'Lava' soap, used by mechanics to get grease off their hands, and said to lather in salt water, which we found it did. The makers don't advertise that fact. They should. All these stores were delivered in immaculate condition to the Yacht Club the following day against payment to the van driver, which is excellent service. We loaded them aboard and hove up and motored over to the fuel jetty to get our paraffin and diesel and lubricating oil, which was a bit complicated as they were not used to dealing in the pennyworths which we needed. But with great goodwill the task was accomplished and we returned to our anchorage off the Club.

I had been advised to go through the canal on a Friday as that was the day of the week on which we might expect to have a number of the small, wooden, motor vessels which act as banana feeder ships to the ocean going vessels, for company. If we could get into the locks with one of them we would be able to tie up alongside it instead of to the lock wall, very desirable, for when the lock is flooded the water boils and churns and *Kimballa* would plunge and roll in the seething waters and, if tied to the wall, could easily damage masts or rigging. And there would be a bonus in that we would not have to handle our ropes as the levels rose, the banana boat would have to handle hers! I went to the Port Captain and made the arrangements. He would provide the pilot, and two negro deck hands to handle our ropes in the locks. He issued a certificate that we were carrying no cargo and proceeding through the canal in ballast, which I took to the accounts department and paid the canal fees. These were on the same scale, per ton, as any other ship in ballast, the rate being seventy-two cents a ton, *Kimballa*'s fees amounted to six dollars and forty-eight cents for the boat and pilot, and fifteen dollars for the deckhands. A real bargain.

1421—Balboa   MR 40875—Panama Canal—10-16-50—2,000

THE PANAMA CANAL
CANAL ZONE
PORT OF BALBOA

CLEARANCE

𝕿𝖍𝖎𝖘 𝖎𝖘 𝖙𝖔 𝖈𝖊𝖗𝖙𝖎𝖋𝖞 𝖙𝖔 𝖆𝖑𝖑 𝖜𝖍𝖔𝖒 𝖎𝖙 𝖒𝖆𝖞 𝖈𝖔𝖓𝖈𝖊𝖗𝖓:

That   J. M. K. ARNOT

Master or Commander of the   KETCH KIMBALLA (BRITISH)

burden 8.96 net *tons or thereabouts, navigated with a crew consisting*

of 2 (two) *members, and bound for* NEW ZEALAND via TAHAITI

has here entered and cleared his vessel according to law.

    GIVEN under my hand and seal this

    27th *day of* July

    one thousand nine hundred and fifty-one

        Y. N. West
         Captain of the Port

Panama Canal Clearance Certificate

That Thursday evening we spent in the Yacht Club, putting our story into the visitor's book and saying goodbye to the friends we had made during our stay and, since both *Katwinchar* and *Kimballa* were to pass through the canal in the morning, starting at 6.00 a.m., we went back on board early. To no avail, for *Katwinchar* hove up and came alongside us and the rum and lime lasted into the early hours, and it was pure good fortune that awoke someone at 5.40 a.m., just in time to receive a large block of ice, much appreciated, from the club bartender, and get the boats ready to move. Our pilot, Pilot Anderson, boarded with his deckhands promptly at 6.00 a.m. and we got under way.

The first six miles of the canal, from the harbour at Colon to the locks at Gatun, is a channel cut through the land, with jungle-covered hills to starboard and flat jungle to port. It was overcast and hot and the breeze created by our passage was more than welcome. The two deck hands busied themselves, preparing the mooring ropes so that they would not foul at the crucial moment, and generally making themselves useful. Pilot Anderson, stripped to the waist and wearing a pith helmet, found himself a place to sit on the coach roof, ignoring our cockpit awning, which we had made specially for him! His piloting so far had been to tell us to follow *Katwinchar*.

As we rounded a slight bend the great mass of the Gatun Locks loomed before us. There is a flight of three, and they raise ships eighty-five feet to the level of the Gatun lake. A concrete monster lying asleep in the jungle without a keeper in sight. As we approached we were overtaken by a medium-sized cargo vessel and one of the small banana boats and, as we were a shade early, the first locking of the day not being until seven, we stopped and hung about chatting to *Katwinchar*. Presently two enormous gates in the concrete wall ahead swung slowly open to reveal the first step of this wonderful ocean staircase, and the cargo steamer slowly entered and was made fast to her six 'mules', three on either side with their six wires holding her steady in the middle of the lock, which is 1,000 ft. long and 110 ft. wide. Room for a whole fleet of boats our size! The banana boat went in next and made fast to the lock wall on the port side astern of the steamer. We followed her in and made fast to her starboard side and *Katwinchar* came in and tied up to us. All this was done in silence. Nobody, be he lockmaster, pilot or ship's captain used a megaphone. The pilots and lock crews are so expert that they can do the job without shouting at anyone, and the number of people involved is small. When we were all secure the enormous gates, now behind us, slowly closed, the handrails sprang up on top of them as they did so, and great chains rose from the bottom of the lock to protect the gates themselves from mishap.

Then the sluices opened in the culverts in the bottom of the lock and the water boiled in, making the surface like a giant cooking pot, with currents and eddies swirling in all directions. It was this that I had feared had we been tied up to the wall. The big ship in the middle of the lock was less affected, and was held in the middle by the six mule drivers, who winched in their wires as she rose, holding her in place, playing her like a fish with six anglers attached. Twenty thousand tons of water a minute were pouring into the lock, all by gravity, lifting us at more than a foot a minute. Soon the water was up to the level of the next lock; the chain ahead of us sank out of sight, the massive gates opened to reveal the next lock and an expanse of water now more than 2,000 ft. long. The six mules on their rack and pinion mechanism, anchored to their tracks so that they cannot be pulled into the locks, moved forward in succession up the steep incline between the locks and ultimately, at a signal from the pilot, brought their charge to a standstill in the middle of the second lock. Our banana boat cast off and, under her own power and with the two yachts clinging to her like limpets, moved ahead and tied up in the middle lock. The chains rose, the gates closed and the whole flooding process was repeated. All our moorings stood the strain and in due course the lock was full and, when the gates were opened, we all moved into the third, top, lock, the last at the Atlantic end of the canal.

When that lock had filled, the chain lowered and the gates opened we beheld the Gatun Lake spread before us. The Lake forms a major part of the canal to the north of the continental divide, being formed by the damming of the Chagres river by the Gatun locks. It is full of small islands, formerly hilltops, and clumps of treetops standing on drowned islands. Wildlife proliferates, the islands being populated by the survivors of the flooding. The shipping channel is buoyed and ships keep strictly to it. The steamer cast off from her mules and moved out into the channel under her own power, the yachts cast off from the banana boat and moved out after her, and the banana boat emerged last of all. We motored along in *Katwinchar*'s wake, admiring the scenerey, easily keeping to the channel, and soon came up with the steamer which had stopped with steering gear trouble and was awaiting a tug, which we soon met. Our pilot pointed out the remains of the work done by de Lesseps in his efforts to build a sea level canal, a disaster in both human and financial terms which none the less paved the way for the present canal. We passed the Governor of the Canal Zone in his fine motor launch, with some of the lady guests playing bridge in the stern sheets. No time to be bored.

We made lunch for the five of us, and washed it down with canned beer iced on the block provided by the club bartender. *Katwinchar*, which was a little faster than us, chugged along ahead, gradually drawing away. She has relatively little freeboard and looked like a submerged log with her very tall pilot, pilot Hart, looking like an extra mast when he stood up on deck.

As we approached the continental divide the mountains loomed ahead of us and we entered the Gaillard cut, one of the world's great engineering feats, where, by the use of explosives and high pressure hoses, the mountain was cut away and dredged out to form the canal. Millions of tons of rock were moved and for many years landslides would occasionally block or partially block the canal. Work is still in progress cleaning up the more dangerous parts of the mountain. A monument to the skill of the engineers and to the many who lost their lives in the making of it. The cut is seven miles long and the mountains rise, in places, 500 feet above the surface of the canal. Onwards through this impressive scenery we went, into opening countryside towards the single Pedro Miguel lock, passing a couple of Atlantic bound steamers as we went. Approaching the lock we came to *Katwinchar* moored to the bank and we tied up ahead of her, broke out the iced beer and, crews, pilots and deckhands all, settled down to await the time to move into the lock. We had to be particularly nice to the deckhands, for Kim had disgraced himself. Having had his lunch he had spotted a deckhand's unattended plate and helped himself to a tongue sandwich, darting out of reach and scoffing it before he could be caught.

About 3.00 p.m. we got the signal to move into the lock. We had lost our steamer in the lake, so this time there were only the banana boat and the two yachts, so we let the banana boat in first and both followed her in and tied up to her. The going down process is much smoother, for the water simply drains out of the lock without causing the eddies of the filling process. Once in, the gate behind us closed, the chains rose from the lock bottom and, with the sluices open, we began to sink down the lock wall, soon losing sight of the surounding land. Once again the banana boat did all the work with the ropes while we just hung on, and when the surface levelled with the Miraflores Lake the lower gate opened, the chain sank and we motored out.

Miraflores Lake is some two miles long, and narrow, and we soon arrived at the two lock flight of the Miraflores locks, and repeated the downhill process twice more before emerging into the six-mile cut leading to Balboa and the Pacific. In the last of the locks we said farewell, over a rum and lime, to the *Katwinchar*s, for they were to pause at Balboa while we intended to anchor off, away from the fleshpots and the dollar drain, and spend a couple of days making ready for the Pacific crossing. The afternoon was overcast, with thunder threatening as we motored down to Balboa to disembark our pilot. Our clearance papers should have come out with his launch, but they didn't, so he said he would arrange to have them sent out to us next day and we thanked him, said farewell to him and motored out to the fairway buoy some three miles distant, where we anchored out of the channel. It was fresher out there, with the benefit of whatever breeze there was, and we made our evening meal, hung out the anchor light and turned in. It had been a long and fascinating day.

Sailed Colon 27.7.51. Arrived Balboa 27.7.51. 11 hours. 38 miles. 3.45 knots.

Chapter 27

Four thousand ocean miles

When I woke on the morning of 28th July the 5,500 miles between Panama and my date with Fulley, in Rarotonga, in October, felt like 10,000. There wasn't time to hang about so as soon as we had breakfasted we set about preparing *Kimballa* for the longest passage of the voyage. There was much to be done.

The winds in the Gulf to Panama are notoriously fickle, and the doldrums can extend many miles beyond the Gulf before the southeast trades fill in. So I had bought five five-gallon tins of additional fuel for the engine, and these had to be secured on deck so that they would still be there when we wanted them. All our other stores had to be properly stowed and secured, for the passage of the canal had not involved any heavy weather! The rigging was standing up to its task remarkably well but even so there was a lot to do to it. The mainsheet had to be renewed, a number of failing seams in the sails repaired, and all the track slides inspected and re-secured where necessary. The claw ring on the main boom, to which the mainsheet was attached, had chewed up the boom to some extent so we covered the boom in way of the ring with an aluminium sheet sleeve. I've never like claw rings, but our rig was such that the mainsheet could not be attached to the end of the boom, where it belongs.

We hoped to run for most of the passage under our twin staysails, so we had to find a mechanically sounder way of stopping the booms from skying. The solution was to loosen one of the screws holding on the stemband at the waterline and pass light stainless steel wires between the stem and the band, below the screw, one wire for each boom. These were shackled to the boom ends, and the free end brought on deck to a cleat so that, in conjunction with the sheet, the sail could be set to suit the wind. As we worked away a constant stream of ships, bound to and from the canal, passed us by and we were visited once by a military patrol boat which circled us and went away.

Our only contact with the outside world, apart from the launch which brought us our clearance papers, was a local yacht which passed close and spoke to us.

All our preparations took us three days, but by the morning of 31st July we were ready to go. As the forenoons were usually calm we decided to wait until after lunch to sail, when we hoped that the afternoon breeze would spring up. At 1.15 p.m., in a light northwesterly breeze we hove up our anchor, made all plain sail, streamed the log and set our course to the southeast. We were on our way towards Nukahiva in the Marquesas, more than 4,000 miles away. Even though it was an overcast and gloomy afternoon it was good to be under way again.

Our course was laid to take us six miles off the Pearl Islands in the middle of the Gulf. They are unlit, but steep to and usually quite easily visible, even at night, and we expected to be up with them at about 3.00 a.m. I kept the eight to twelve watch, with Kim assisting me; I got a time signal from Honolulu at nine, and the boat went gently along in the dark overcast, with occasional light rain damping the decks. I was not sorry when Buzz came up with the cocoa at 11.45 p.m. and, after handing over, I was able to retire to my bunk. I had not been asleep long when I was rudely awoken by Buzz's call, 'Jack, come quick', and I leapt into the cockpit in just the shorts I was sleeping in. Fortunately there was no light in the cabin, so I could see as soon as I got on deck, and what I saw was a dark line about a quarter of a mile ahead, looming throught the drizzle. Clearly we had got among the islands, which are cluttered with outlying rocks, so I told Buzz to put the helm hard a starboard and shot down to start the engine, which fired at once. We came round, head to wind, and took what seemed to be the logical option and retraced our course as exactly as we could under power. Fortunately we cleared everything and, after two hours of motoring into the wind we stopped the engine and resumed our passage, steering a rather more southerly course. A close call, and not a good beginning to the Pacific crossing. At dawn the islands were well clear on our port quarter, and our noon sights gave us a day's run of seventy-four miles, not bad for this part of the world. We still had the doldrums to cross before we felt the trades, so we reconciled ourselves to a spell of frustration, for not only are the winds fickle, but three major currents, the Peruvian, Mexican and Pacific meet in the Gulf, and their confluence both causes the variable winds and makes current prediction for navigation unusually difficult.

My objective was to make to the southwest and cross the Equator in about ninety degrees of west longitude, at about which point I hoped to pick up both the equatorial current and the southeast trades. On most days we saw the sun for a little while, enough to fix a series of disheartening positions. In the next ten days our run seldom exceeded thirty miles, and that frequently not in the desired direction. The light, fickle wind would die away, leaving the sails and sheets slatting and banging and, should we hand them, the wind would spring up again. If we left the sails up it refused to blow, with the sails and rigging doing themselves far more harm than is the case when they are full and drawing in the freshest breeze. It was a dreary time, with the water supply constantly in mind, for when you don't know how long it has to last you have to be mean with the rations.

Kim was growing at an alarming rate in both size and personality. He now had the courage to leave the cockpit and go on deck where he would stalk the mainsheet, or any other rope which might be drumming on the deck in the windless conditions. Except when eating he would come at the gallop to a whistle, or the call of his name, which is surprising, cats being the independent creatures that they are. He was a bit of a pest when cooking was going on, always present and hopeful, winding in and out of the cook's legs, which didn't make life easy, especially if the ship was rolling heavily, as she often did in the doldrums.

I had always been conscious that, were I to fall over the wall and not get back, Buzz would be left, lost, in the vast ocean, so at about this time I set out to teach him to take sights and find our position. He learned very quickly, and within a fortnight of our both taking morning and noon sights each day he was just about as accurate as I was, and thereafter we continued the habit so that he could keep his hand in. Our joint results produced disapppointing answers. It was ten days before we sighted the island of Malpelo, a bare lump of rock a mile long and 700 yards wide, and less than 300 miles from Balboa. Completely uninhabited but for sea birds, we had not intended to pass within sight of it, but the light winds and strong currents had done it for us. When, four days later, it was still in sight we wished it might sink into the sea, and when the wind began to blow from the south, the direction in which we wanted to go, I decided that enough was enough and it was time to use the spare twenty-five gallons of fuel.

So we decided to run south under engine for thirty hours and see how much southing we could make. No sooner was the engine going than the wind freshened and we were soon plugging into a short head sea which helped to limit our thirty hour run to a mere seventy-nine miles, but it was seventy-nine miles south, the right direction. I reckoned that we had used all the fuel that we could spare, so we got the vessel under sail again and in the evening of that day we saw, and spoke to, the only ship we saw between Panama and the Marquesas. She was the Shaw Savill liner *Delphic*, an almost new, elegant and workmanlike 10,000-ton cargo liner, bound from Panama to Auckland. She had taken a day to cover the distance we had spent twelve days on! Though we had sailed 600 miles so far we had made good a mere 300. Our slow progress was brought home to us one day when we had taken our noon sights and had our lunch with a little drink to cheer us up. The next day our sights showed that we had made good a mere four miles, so we decided to have a drink to celebrate the smallest day's run so far and, when Buzz ditched the bottle, it landed alongside yesterday's

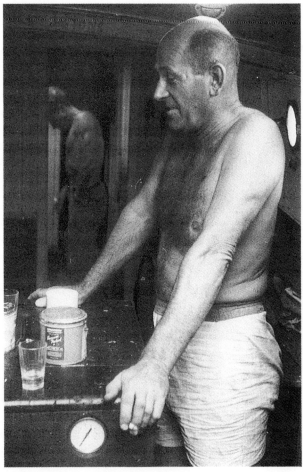

Jack in *Kimballa*, Buzz in forecabin

empty, still drifting along with us. As day followed day we crept south in mainly overcast conditions, with light rain at times, a long, low swell and a temperature of only about eighty degrees necessitating a blanket at night.

Three weeks out from Panama we had the pleasure and excitement of encountering a shoal of dolphin which stayed with us and kept us company. Buzz, the fisherman, was in a positive fever and got up the fishing line and hooks and baited it with a piece of shiny tin. But the dolphin were very wary, inspecting the bait but leaving it severely alone all day until, just at evening, one of them took the bait. It shot out of the water and plunged back again and we were sure the line would break, but after a struggle Buzz got it into the cockpit at last, with Kim leaping about in great delight, trying to avoid the thrashing fish without missing any of the fun. The little savage tried to eat it before it was properly dead. It was a beautiful fish, weighing about fifty to sixty pounds and as Buzz got him cut up I busied myself with the cookpots and we had a really good fresh fish dinner that night. Kim as well, who ate about his own weight before calling it a day. Dolphin has a pure white flesh, looking like and tasting a bit like cod. We boiled some of it and pickled it in vinegar, but we could never eat the whole of a dolphin before it went bad. This shoal of about thirty dolphin stayed with us for several weeks, and we found that they could be harpooned much more easily then they could be caught on hooks and the continuous supply of fresh food was invaluable. On the occasions that they temporarily left us we found that all we had to do to get them back was to heave to, and they came to see why we had stopped! Though we ate them, they became friends, identifiable by their scars, and to those we could recognise we gave names. And they bought us luck, for we soon found the wind and current we were seeking.

In these wearying conditions we couldn't do much work about the ship, the motion and dampness making work about the decks impossible. Even small repairs were a trial, and when the main spring in my typewriter broke it took a couple of days to dismantle it, get the spring out, trim the end of it, temper it in the flame of a blowlamp and drill a new hole to take the catchpin. Any minute screw dropped would have been irrecoverable, so the whole thing had to be done deliberately and with great care, which is why it took two days. Buzz filled in his time doing a tapestry which I had on board, and we both wrote a lot of letters. On the culinary front we, having eaten all our Panama bread, or that which didn't go mouldy, read through the various recipes which people had given us, all slightly different, and, choosing the most likely, we set about baking. The first loaf was a bit heavy but we gave the next a bit of extra kneading and it turned out well. Though the oven was not hot enough to brown the loaves properly they tasted very good. Even Kim thought so, for he would, given the chance, pirate them whilst they were standing cooling. Buzz reckoned that kneading dough was the best way he had yet discovered of getting his hands clean!

Our diet must have been a healthy one, for neither of us suffered a moment's illness at any time during the voyage. To make good any possible vitamin deficiency we took Multivite tables daily, and Phyllosan tablets until they ran out. Onions lasted well in the fresh vegetable stakes, but potatoes went soft early on. The bread made a great difference to us, for you can do a lot of things with bread. By now, in the southeast trades, we were running under our twins with the ship steering herself, allowing us to sleep at night with a light on deck, and work about the boat during the day. Sitting in the cockpit one evening yarning with Buzz we got onto the subject of lighthouses and I told him a tale from the times I was in merchant ships. In 1920, when I was an apprentice in *Kasenga* we were bound from Calcutta to Rangoon to load a cargo of rice. As we passed the Alguada lighthouse at the southwestern tip of Burmah the Second Mate noticed a flag flying, and on looking at it with a telescope found it to be the red ensign, upside down, a traditional distress signal. Attempts to contact the lighthouse failed, but a radio message to Rangoon brought out a tug with a doctor on board to investigate, and one of the keepers was found to have fallen and broken a leg.

Twenty-five years later, in command of a small tanker bound from Rangoon to Akyab with a cargo of petrol and kerosene, I passed the Alguada lighthouse at about 10.00 a.m., some distance off, and I thought back to that day in *Kasenga* and, though one does not normally examine lighthouses closely, I thought to have a look at it through my telescope. To my amazement I found the flags S O S flying from the flagstaff. My wee ship didn't have a wireless, and I was reluctant to send an unwieldy lifeboat manned by a scratch crew in to the light, for a month before the relief boat had capsized among the rocks drowning all nine on board. So I steamed on, wondering how to report the matter.

About an hour later I saw smoke over the back of Diamond Island which I thought was probably a steamer making up for the Bassein Pilot and asked the chief to pile on the power. Alerting the pilot cutter with frequent blasts on our whistle we caught him before he disappeared back up the river. He came alongside us, and I told the pilot in charge what I had seen at Alguada and he said that he would go there forthwith, and I went on my way.

On my return to Rangoon I went to ask the Port Officer what had been the trouble, and he told me that they had been having a lot of bother with the lighthouse keepers, and that the Alguada keeper had put up his signal because he was short of kerosene for the light, which was not true, and he was also short of tobacco and sugar. This amused me, for I had once heard of a young candidate for second mate, when asked by the examiner the significance of 'S O S', answering 'Sink or Swim', but I had never heard that it meant 'Short of Sugar'!

Though the wind was still light it was southeast, and we could make good a little south of west, and the equatorial current began to push us ahead of our dead reckoning each day. On 25th August, three and a half weeks out from Panama, we sighted Culpepper Island, an uninhabited rock, the most northerly of the Galapagos Island, about thirteen miles off. Our friends the dolphin were still with us, and a few bosun birds also kept us company. The wind shifted a little more east each day. The sky cleared and we felt, at last, the full benefit of the southeast trades which enabled us to run for the next six weeks with never a hand on the helm, pulled along by our twin staysails. The sea was moderate and seldom did any water come aboard. Though we had expected sharks we saw not a one, even when we threw the remains of a dolphin overboard. Day after day *Kimballa* looked after herself and carried us towards the Marquesas and, though we had only 400 square feet of canvas set, we were doing about eighty miles a day, just over three knots.

Varnish needs constant attention and we spent our days cleaning off the old, sanding the woodwork and applying fresh. A slow process, with scrapers and sandpaper, but one which kept us busy, an essential condition for two people shut up together in a small boat for a long period of time. Occasionally, perhaps once a week, we had to take in a sail and sew a seam, and one such repair nearly brought disaster. We had a sail down, and as usual Kim was everywhere, helping with the repair, and unbeknownst to us when we came to hoist the sail he was hidden in a fold of canvas. As the sail bellied in the wind he was flung overboard, and would have been lost had Buzz not seen him go, dashed aft and grabbed him as he floated past the cockpit. With the sail having been down we had little way on, so instead of being lost, Kim discovered that he could swim, and was none the worse for his wetting. After a good wash he soon dried himself in the sun. We would have been very depressed had he gone, for he was at the silly stage by now, prancing and darting about the ship and doing much to keep us amused.

Though water was our principal preoccupation we liked to eat well and were dismayed when we encountered problems with our corned beef supply. Much of it was stowed low down in odd lockers and one whole case was in the cupboard under the bedroom washbasin. One day I opened up this case and, to my horror, found that one of the tins was swarming with revolting white maggots, so we got the case up on deck, boiled gallons of sea water, added lysol to it and washed all the tins and the lockers they had been in.

The tins which had rusted through and swollen up we threw overboard before drying the rest in the sun and re-stowing them. To no avail, for within a week the maggots were back. More drastic treatment was clearly needed, so this time we got the tins on deck and went over them with a blow lamp before re-stowing them. But still the maggots returned. We were a bit short of meat by this time, so we had to persevere even though it might mean opening three tins at dinner time to get one good one, until one day we opened five without finding a good one and dumped the lot over the side. We never saw a maggot again. I had encountered maggots in my porridge on the *Conway*, but not armies of them! Cockroaches might have been another creepy crawly problem, but we sailed from England without any and never lay alongside subsequently for more than an hour or two when fuelling and watering. Three large ones came aboard in St Vincent, in a sail which had been ashore for repair, but we spotted and killed them, and never saw another until we acquired some in Rarotonga. The common housefly, which came aboard in every port, was easily dealt with by the occasional use of an insect spray.

After a few weeks of keeping company with us our dolphin left us. Being intelligent creatures they had perhaps noticed their casualty rate and decided that we were not friendly after all. We saw the odd octopus, but had expected to see more, having read the account of the *Kon Tiki* expedition. I had a horror of these creatures, being unsure whether they really could board a slow-moving, low-lying vessel like *Kimballa*, so we used to keep an axe handy in the cockpit to chop off any marauding tentacle. In one of our occasional nonsensical conversations it was suggested that we should hang a sign over the side saying 'place tentacle here', but discarded the idea when Buzz pointed out that even if octopi could read it would not, in this part of the world, be English. Two men alone in a small boat do develop catchphrases, which they work to death, and nonsense ideas. Being in the southern hemisphere, where many phenomena are reversed, we developed the theory that, if either of us did something wrong way round, it was for that reason and therefore excusable. It all helped to keep us amused. We had crossed the line after Kim had been over the side, so, both Buzz and I having crossed it many times, we decided that Kim was well enough initiated and that King Neptune need not be invited aboard our little ship.

Kimballa rolled along contentedly in typical trade wind weather. A moderate quartering breeze, the twins pulling manfully, the following sea breaking gently, not blowing off in spume, and a blue sky dotted with puffy white clouds to cover it all. Working by day and sleeping by night we reeled off the miles and by 13th September had made good 3,300 of them, leaving 1,000 or so still to go to Nukahiva. Another shoal of dolphin joined us and kept us company, so once again we had fresh food. Flying fish abounded, to Kim's delight for, attracted by the light which we left on deck at night, they would fly on board and land with a thud. Even if he seemed to be asleep Kim would prick his ears and he would be out on deck in a flash, to return with the fish in his mouth, eating all of it except for the odd bit of wing. We had some trouble persuading him that our bunks were not his fishmonger's slab. He was well fed, so he only ate them because he couldn't resist them.

By this time the hull was getting very foul again. The shell and tulip grew again along the waterline and on the logline, interspersed with green weed about six inches long. Even though the copper sheathed underbody was weed free the waterline growth impeded our progress considerably, but there was nothing we could do about it out here in the open ocean. But, though the weed slowed us, it didn't stop us, and the 1,000 miles dwindled day by day until on 25th September our noon sights placed us seventy miles from the island of Ua Huka, which lies a few miles East of Nuka Hiva. Through heavy rain we sighted the island at dawn the next day. Mountainous and heavily wooded, it loomed above us, a welcome sight after so long at sea. Our destination was Taiohae on the island of Nukahiva. We coasted the shore of Ua Huka without seeing any signs of humanity and, as we cleared that island sighted Nukahiva in the distance. Under the influence of the islands the wind became erratic, so we handed the twins and hoisted the main to make more speed and get into harbour before dark that evening. It was overcast with occasional rain squalls and quite a heavy sea as the coast of Nukahiva, steep to, backed by fantastically shaped mountains, and footed by heavy breaking seas, drew closer and closer. Presently we sighted the landmark for which we were looking, a large, flat cliff with a vertical and a horizontal vein of quartz making a cross on its face. We knew that beyond that was Taiohae bay.

Losing the wind in the lee of the land we handed our sails and started the engine. For the first time the motor, which we had run every Saturday morning, was reluctant to start, and once started seemed not to be developing full power but it did keep going. Rounding the crossed cliff the bay opened up before us, a half to three quarter moon-shaped bay hemmed in by a crescent of mountains. Ahead of us we could see one or two small houses, and in a corner of the bay two yachts, for which we headed, coming to our anchor close to them, about a cable off a black sandy beach, at 4.30 p.m. 26th September.

Sailed Balboa 31.7.51, Arrived Taiohae, Nukahiva, 26.9.51. 57 days 6 hours 15 minutes. 4,024 miles. 3.1 knots.

Chapter 28

Isles Marquesas

I had read more about the Marquesas than about any other islands in the Pacific, and wanted to see them more than any others. We chose a poor day for our arrival, and timed it wrong as well, arriving in the overcast dusk, the darkness and gloom being accentuated by the steep mountains which towered round the bay. Anchored, we found not a soul in sight but there was a wonderful smell of earth and tropical flowers which, to our salt-soaked noses, was very sweet and strong. Presently three figures appeared under a Flamboyant tree on which fishing nets were hung to dry. They launched an outrigger canoe and the three of them, a Marquesan pulling and another Marquesan and a European in the stern sheets, scrambled into the canoe.

When they came alongside the two in the stern climbed aboard and greeted us in French, speaking, as they did, only that and Marquesan. The Frenchman was the Gendarme and the Marquesan a male nurse, that being the nearest thing the island had to a doctor. They had brought us the usual forms to fill in and Buzz, being fluent in French as a result of a spell in Mauritius, soon had the forms filled in and the formalities complete. Monsieur le gendarme took our passports away to keep until we sailed, and told us to come to him if we had any difficulties at all. By the time they departed it was dark and so, feeling weary and contented after our long voyage, we made our dinner and then sat in the cockpit smoking and talking. There seemed to be only one light on the island, and that turned out to be in the house of the only Englishman on Nukahiva. Kim's ears and nose were in a constant state of twitch, though he kept his distance from the strangers who came aboard. We were not late to bed that night.

The next day was a better day altogether and we were up at dawn. The sky was clear, though the sun took some time to climb clear of the mountain tops which surrounded the bay. One of the other yachts had gone out at first light, and the other appeared to be uninhabited. Ashore, smoke was rising from the fires in houses hidden in the trees, and people could be seen walking about. We unlashed the dinghy and put it into the water to let it soak its seams tight, made our breakfast and, as we were finishing that, the absent yacht returned. As she moored a European in her gave us a cheery hail. Once secured, he came over in his outrigger with his man and introduced himself as Bob McKettrick and, though I did not know at the time that he was English, I thought I detected a trace of Liverpool in his voice. He must be the only Frenchman, for he is that by naturalisation, with a Liverpool accent. He has spent many years in the South Seas and owns the little store on Nukahiva, and had been out in his boat to catch some fish for breakfast. He told us that *Katwinchar* had left about a week before for Suva, Fiji, which meant that she must have made a very smart passage of about forty days from Panama.

Later in the morning we bailed out the dinghy and rowed ashore, leaving Kim, who did not seem to mind, to keep the ship. There being no jetty we landed on the black sand beach. There had been a jetty at one time, but it had been pulled down to be rebuilt in another position, but in the meantime the sea had washed away both the remains of the old and the beginning of the new. So, no jetty. Close by the landing place the elders of the village were sitting under a tree, talking, their occupation through most of every day. They all smiled as we passed and wished us '*Bonjour, messieurs*' and we walked on along the waterfront towards McKettrick's place, passing as we did the neat, small houses, each in a tiny garden, which lined the road at infrequent intervals. Here and there in grassy patches would be a horse tethered and grazing, looking well groomed and well fed. They were quite small, say fifteen hands, and are used only as pack animals, not for pulling carts, for there are hardly any roads for a cart to travel. Children were scarce, school being in, but those few teenage girls we did see were filling in their time playing marbles in the road.

Bob's store was alongside his house, which was a new one, its predecessor having been washed away in a tidal wave originated by an Alaskan earthquake a year or two back. His stock was a little of everything and he ran the shop with his wife, seemingly without the benefit of cash, for everything was written down and credit ruled. Lighting was by petrol generator and cooling by a fridge worked by a paraffin lamp. We had come looking for meat, which we got because it was killing day, and fruit, which we did not because everyone grows their own and never thinks that it might be saleable. When the word got round we got more than enough in gifts. We bought an iced beer which, though French, was very good and, pressed by Bob, stayed for a most enjoyable lunch. Onwards then to the gendarmerie, which also changes money, to convert the last of our dollars into francs, a tedious business involving the noting of the number of every bill; the backwash, I believe, of a large, recent, currency swindle in Tahiti. Thence to the Administrator's residence to make our number. A beautiful airy house with a sandy beach in front of it and the tricolour flying from the flagstaff. M. Rebul, the Administrator, was a young and charming man who spoke excellent English, and over a beer we talked of this and that and left shortly with an invitation to lunch on Sunday.

Stretching our newfound land legs we walked on to the lighthouse, a simple whitewashed hut containing a table on which stood an oil lamp which shone out through the front window. I don't know how often it was lit, perhaps every night, or perhaps just when a ship was expected, but it can't have been visible at much of a distance. Walking back the sun disappeared behind the mountains at about 4.00 p.m. and the children came out of school and, like children the world over, were dawdling their way home, the boys kicking footballs about, the girls playing marbles and all of them eyeing us with great curiosity and giving us some form of friendly greeting. They are fine-looking children who grow into fine-looking adults, the men being particularly powerfully built. Lazy by European standards, but cheerful and friendly. The entire male population seems to be football mad. Every valley and village has a team playing in what appears to be a continuous non-stop league, the game being played without such refinements as boots, for they never wear shoes in any event.

After fifty-seven days of salt and sunshine *Kimballa* was in a bad state overside, though on deck we had done up the varnish work and that looked very smart. Much of the green topside paint had come off and she looked mottled and fleabitten to say the least so we set about restoring her to her proper glory. To get at the waterline and the marine garden which grew on it we hung the spare anchor and a couple of kerosene cans full of water off the end of the main boom and swung it out to its fullest extent to give the ship a list. We could have done with a bit more weight on the end, but we got nearly the list we wanted and, getting into the dinghy, went round the uphill side scraping the shell and grass off with three-cornered scrapers before scrubbing her with sand soap and scrubbing brushes. We even found crabs at home in the cockpit drain pipes. A wash with fresh water and a coat of green paint and one side looked much more like the yacht she was. Swinging the boom over to the other side we repeated the process and felt that we had a respectable home again. Kim was all eyes and nose while this was going on, for he got a strong whiff of fish from the muck we were scraping off. At sea he would sniff every inch of the log line if we had to get it aboard for any reason.

While we were at this job the inter-island schooner *Viterie*, owned by A. B. Donald in Papeete, arrived and began discharging cargo into boats from the shore. She was carrying mail and Buzz was lucky enough to get a letter addressed simply 'Buzz Perkins, Yacht *Kimballa*, Marquesas Islands, Pacific'. Among Viterie's passengers were thirteen prisoners being taken to Papeete to be tried for rape and as *Viterie* was going to call at Taihoe again before returning to Papeete they were landed, and lodged at night in the local gaol. By day they were released, and I believe they formed a football team to play the local side. The whole affair seemed to be considered a great joke by the local population.

On Saturday afternoon we were invaded by what seemed to be the entire small boy population of the island. They came in all manner of little canoes, and those who had no canoe simply swam. Initially shy and timid they soon gained confidence and found their way all over the ship. Communication was a problem for me, for the only common language was French, and mine was not much better than theirs, so we did not go too deeply into matters. They were fascinated by my big magnet, and it held their attention for at least an hour, and everything else on board was thoroughly examined, investigated and discussed. Kim was disconsolate, not liking having all these people on board, and retired to a bower of his own among the sails in the forepeak. When the time came for them to leave we gave them a jar of cherries to eat, and a tin of Quaker Oats, with the best cooking instructions we could put into French, and told them that they would be twice as strong as they were now after they had eaten it. Then they either scrambled into their canoes or jumped over the side, and made for the shore.

The next day two men came alongside in a canoe bearing fruit. We had been expecting some to come from Bob's place, having placed a sort of order which was to include bananas, but there wasn't any so we asked why. Confusion reigned, there was no satisfactory reply so we thanked them for what they had brought and off they went. To our dismay we discovered later that our visitors were the fathers of some of the small boys who had visited us, and the fruit was a present for us. We felt most embarrassed, but got Bob to straighten things out for us later.

The mob of small boys were not all the same colour, mostly golden brown but some having finer features and being a shade paler. We tried to sort them out and establish who was whose brother but with no success, chiefly because in this part of the world it is common for children to be given away. If a family is too big, or if someone takes a fancy to a child, the family will readily let it go. It seems to be a happy, workable agreement, but it can lead to a mild form of child slavery, for the people all live in family groups, and the more children you have the more there are to help. Sorting out who can marry whom later on must be a bit of a nightmare. Perhaps they don't quite go by the Prayer Book.

With washing ourselves, and washing the topsides, the twenty gallons of water with which we had arrived was gone, so we had to fill our tanks. The bay did not boast a jetty with water laid on, but near the landing place there was a pipe and tap with good clean water and jerrycans which could be borrowed. So off we went with the dinghy for one of us to fill the cans while the other stood in the surf and held the boat. With the cans on board we returned to *Kimballa* and emptied them into the tanks. It was quite heavy work, but after three round trips the tanks were full once more. As we completed this task an American yacht came in and anchored nearby. She was manned by a party of young men, mostly fresh out of college, who had been wandering in their vessel for nearly a year, and were about to sail back to California. Tucked away under the mountains I hadn't been able to get a time signal since we arrived, and as their boat was a mass of radio equipment they invited me to come over to get one. They played the gear like the organ at the Tower Ballroom at Blackpool, but failed to produce a time signal, though I was able to get a time check from their chronometer. I expected to get time signals again when we got outside, so it wasn't a matter of great importance, but it was interesting to see how the other half lives.

Sunday lunch with M. and Mme. Rebul was most enjoyable. They must have great experience of entertaining visiting yachtsmen, and must get great pleasure from it, isolated as they are. We were introduced to their one-week-old son before sitting down to an excellent meal throughout which English was spoken for our benefit. Tablecloths and silver were not what we had become accustomed to, and seemed almost out of place in this remote spot. The house was decorated with many fine native carvings, the family dogs and cats had to seek us out to be petted and, when our lunch had settled, we went out into the garden to play table tennis under a thatch awning. To the outsider it seems an idyllic existence, but the absence of European company must make it a very lonely one.

There are Tikis on the island of Nukahiva, and one of my objectives in coming here was to see them. They are in the valley of Taipiivai, brought to the world's attention by Herman Melville in his book *Typee*. The seaward entrance to the valley is about nine miles to the East of Taiohae, and about twenty-five by the track over the hills. We asked Bob what was the best way to get there and he suggested that the easiest way would be to take *Kimballa* to the seaward end of the valley, and then use the dinghy to get as far up the river as possible. Bob had never seen the Tikis, so we asked him if he would like to come and he decided to take a day off and do so. So, at about seven one morning Bob, and his grandson Tebe (Marquesan Joe), his man Tuki, and Tebe's dog, all came aboard and we got under way. Kim took unkindly to the dog and they kept their distance from each other all day; after all, *Kimballa* is Kim's boat! It was a beautiful day with hardly a cloud in the sky, and not too warm. We followed the coastline of sheer cliffs plunging straight into the sea, passing inshore of many semi-submerged rocks that we would have gone outside of had we not local knowledge aboard. Gradually the cliffs gave way to gentler slopes, and before long we came upon the sandy bay which lies at the entrance to the valley of Taipiivai, and anchored in ten feet of water, close by the schooner *Viterie* which was loading passengers and copra. Putting our mob ashore took two trips in our little dinghy, with Bob's man doing all the rowing with such gusto that I was sure the oars would break.

Landing where the river flows into the sea we pulled the dinghy across the bar and waded upstream with the boat for about a quarter of a mile and then Tuki rowed away out of sight upstream while we walked up through the coconut groves on the bank. We were soon joined by the Deputy Chief of Taipi who is the grandson of a man from Hoboken who married a Marquesan. Meeting him brought to my mind the tragedy of the Marquesan people. Before Europeans found the islands they were populated by some 100,000 of the finest specimens of the Polynesian race, the people of Taipi being among the best and strongest. But the whites brought with them all manner of diseases against which the Marquesans had no immunity, and they died in their thousands. Many were carried away as slaves to work the fields and mines of Mexico and Peru, so that by now the 100,000 have dwindled to 4,000. At one time the population of Nukahiva was down to 200, but with many of the diseases, especially T.B., having been got under control the population is rising again. Today Nukahiva boasts 862 souls. So did the white man destroy paradise, for that is what these islands are. They are even free of distressing insects, though I was warned about a sandfly called the 'nou nou', but never encountered one in my brief stay.

I have never seen a more beautiful valley than Taipiivai. The river, about fifty feet wide, carved a path through the valley floor, bounded by flowering shrubs. Dotted about the valley floor were small houses, built on stilts, and each with a neat railed garden. The road, such as it was, ran alongside the river and beyond the valley floor the ground sloped up, gaining steepness and ultimately climbing up into the mountains. The valley floor and lower slopes were dense with coconut palms, giving way, as the ground rose, to breadfruit trees and then to all kinds of colourful shrubs. There was a little wooden church, and another building, and an atmosphere of utter peace prevailed.

The chief took us to his house where we sat on basket chairs on the front verandah, where his wife brought us a large bowl of mangoes, bananas and oranges, and a jug of cool, cool water. Hanging from a tree in the garden was a cage holding a brightly coloured land crab, an ugly brute despite its colour, being fed up for the pot. They are said to be unclean feeders, so after capture they are fed on coconut for a couple of weeks before they are considered fit to eat.

The chief, learning that we wanted to see the Tikis, volunteered to take us to them and led us upwards through the valley. As we left the village we passed islanders spreading copra to dry on raised wooden platforms, with the pack horses which had brought it in grazing nearby. The trail led upwards and upwards, and every time Bob, who was not a young man, asked how much further the chief replied 'just round the corner', but after about three miles of this mountain trail, and a scramble up a place where the trail virtually disappeared, we were there.

The Tikis were made from a rock rather like red sandstone and were so old and weathered as to be almost unrecognisable as carved faces and bodies. They had been mounted on a stone platform, from which some had fallen and on which others lay about with jungle growing over them. It depressed me to think that this marvellous product of a bygone people would soon be lost forever, for whilst now little is known of their origins, soon no one will even know where they are. The missionaries do not encourage the upkeep of these places, fearing, I suppose, the competition of paganism, though I doubt that it is far away right now.

We rested, but not for long, having chosen an anthill for our seat, and set off down the hill to the village, a much easier task than the outward journey. Tebe and the dog covered twice the distance walked by the adults, but we sailors discovered to our cost that two months at sea in a small yacht is not the best training for even minor mountaineering. As we wended our way back we passed a group of islanders building the new church, labouring for nothing to a pair of seemingly skilful carpenters. Past the copra drier, greeted by the cheerful people, and back down to the chief's house for more fruit and a welcome drink of water. Tuki had brought the dinghy right up to the village, so he embarked Bob and rowed him all the way back to

Kimballa, while Buzz and I, and Tebe and the dog, walked down to the bar to await our ferry.

Just as we prepared to weigh anchor we were asked if we would take a passenger, and we agreed, being rewarded by a present of fresh fruit and vegetables. On the way back to Taiohae, Buzz's fishing stories being not entirely believed, particularly his account of the school of dolphin accompanying us into the bay at Nukahiva, we detoured out to sea to demonstrate his skill, but not a fish did we see nor bite did he get. We reached Taiohae just as dusk fell, tired but satisfied by a long day in the most beautiful place I have ever seen, and by the visit to the Tikis, almost unseen by Europeans, or by Marquesans for that matter.

Rarotonga and Fulleylove beckoned, and it was time to move on, so we decided to sail the day after next, at dawn, spending the day preparing the yacht for sea and in particular changing the engine oil which, disturbingly, showed traces of water. Several trips ashore for stores of one sort and another, and by evening we were ready to say our farewells, retrieve our passports and get our clearance papers. I think Bob was sorry to see us go, for he leads a lonely life, looking forward to the day when his son will return to the island. He left during the war to join General de Gaulle's airforce and is still on his way back. But for an American survey for an airstrip the war passed the Marquesas by. Heavy surf made getting the dinghy away from the beach in the blackest of dark nights quite tricky, but, safely back on board, we treated ourselves to a smoke in the cockpit and turned in.

Chapter 29

Isles Marquesas to Tahiti

Dawn on the third of October found us breakfasting, eager to be off to make use of the moderate breeze blowing from the east southeast. With more hindrance than help from Kim we got the dinghy aboard and secured, hove up the anchor and, at seven, we sailed, under power, for Tahiti. Steaming past Bob's house we gave him a wave, and made for the open sea. It was a fine morning and once clear of the land we stopped the engine and set our twin staysails and the mizzen, with nearly 800 miles of sailing ahead of us. We were hoping to make the passage in about nine days and we soon fell into our seagoing routine, sleeping at night and working about the deck in the daytime. There was plenty to do if we wanted to arrive in Papeete, usually haven to numerous visiting yachts, looking at our best. Our varnish needed to be touched up yet again, and, that done, Buzz scraped the whole of our teak deck, making it look extremely smart.

As we progressed the wind fell lighter and we soon began to lose ground against our nine-day schedule, so it was a week before we arrived in the Tuamotu Archipelago, which lay across our path a fraction over halfway to Papeete. These islands are low lying, indeed the name means 'Low', or 'Danger', and they are not too well charted, with the charts and sailing directions full of warnings to the effect that some of the atolls might not be in their charted positions, or even that their existence is doubtful, and that there may be undiscovered atolls not marked on the chart at all. No place for blundering about without a good lookout. Approaching the first of the islands we expected to sight, Manihi, my breakfast time sight yielded a position line which ran right through the middle of the lagoon, but it was not until 9.30 a.m. that a white line appeared on the horizon, the glitter from the coral beach, and soon after that palm trees appeared to grow out of the sea and before long the whole length of the island revealed itself. As we sailed by we could see a schooner loading copra in the lagoon and away

to starboard across the bright blue sunlit sea lay the uninhabited island of
Ahe. The 200 or so inhabitants of Manihi 'farm' Ahe for copra. Their whole
economy depends on the coconut palm.

In the force four breeze and the sunshine and the warm but equable
temperature sailing was a real pleasure, what I had dreamed of on cold wet
nights on the bridges of merchant ships. The considerable current between
the atolls was in our favour and we sailed, and were swept along, at a good
rate and the following morning we passed the islands of Arutua and
Rangiroa on the southwestern fringe of the group, Rangiroa being the
largest and most populous of the Tuamotus. On we went, polishing,
painting and scraping, even using a little fresh water in our clean up, and
getting our brasswork into sparkling order. The repainted lifebuoy was
given gold lettering and looked very grand, and we looked more like a lady
and less like a tramp every day.

As we cleared the islands the winds fell lighter and became variable so we
handed our twins and set all plain sail to try to get a little more out of her.
Cloud cover increased and we had occasional light rain, but under full sail
our progress was reasonable, and at dawn on Sunday 14th October I sighted
the twin peaks of Orohena and Aorai, jagged and rugged and stabbing the
morning sky like cardboard cutouts. They are some 5,000 feet high and, at a
distance of seventy miles, were as clear as could be. By now the wind was so
light that we were barely making one knot and, not wanting to take three
days to get to Papeete, we started the engine after breakfast with a view to
getting in before dark. Taking in all our sail we stowed it harbour fashion,
and spent a lazy Sunday putting the finishing touches to our appearance,
taking it in turns to steer. As we drew closer, and the island rose out of the
sea, its jagged mountains became more and more Disney dreamlike, for
Tahiti is a clump of mountains with just a narrow, inhabitable, fringe of
flattish land round its perimeter. By noon the sea was like a millpond as we
motored on, and by 4.00 p.m. we could make out the town of Papeete
sitting at the foot of the mountains. Church spires and houses began to
show behind the barrier of palm trees and soon we could see the breakers on
the reef which surrounds the lagoon which forms the sheltered and secure
harbour.

We hoisted our Red Ensign, the quarantine flag and the flag for the pilot,
having been warned by the Americans in Taiohae that, even at our size,
pilotage is compulsory, even though unnecessary, the entrance being well
marked by leading marks and beacons. About a mile off the reef we turned
onto the leading marks and, as we did so, spotted the pilot launch coming
out to us. As she drew alongside the pilot positively rushed aboard as

though there was not a second to spare, volleyed us with '*bonjours*', shook hands all round, seized the wheel and shoved a fistful of papers into my hand with the instruction, 'Fill them in quick, captain, so that we'll have no delay with the customs people.' They asked the usual questions and, though it is hard to write in *Kimballa* with the engine running, I soon had them completed.

It was nigh on sunset as we motored across the lagoon towards the town, but even so the colours of the sky, the sea, the foliage and the houses were brilliant, a proper welcome to the most famous of the Pacific islands. Approaching our berth we stopped to allow the police, emigration and customs men to board us to count our money and question us as to whether we had enough to live on during our stay. The beachcomber syndrome. Everyone was very friendly and polite, but even so it seemed, to we simple sailors, to be quite a performance. Eventually they were satisfied and all but the police left us and we made for our berth. The simple manoeuvre of dropping an anchor, swinging and making fast stern on to the town's main boulevard was accomplished under a hail of instructions from the pilot, who perhaps thought that silence would not have been seen to be value for money!

One the way in Buzz and I had been speculating on the mail position, and had concluded that we'd probably have to wait till Monday before going to the Consulate to collect it, generating between us the quite unreasonable idea that Consuls should be required to keep a lookout for incoming yachts, and be on the quayside with the mail when they tied up! Chance is a fine thing, for we hardly had our gangway out when an old gentleman rode up on his bicycle, got off it, wished us good evening, and went on to say that he had been out for an evening ride and had met the British Consul out for a walk. Pointing us out to the Consul as we came in he got the response that he, the Consul, would take a walk down when *Kimballa* was tied up, and give us our mail! The old gent had called to warn us not to go ashore until the Consul had been.

Sure enough, in about a quarter of an hour Mr. Devenish arrived with our mail, and I was able to give him the letter which I had brought for him from a friend of his in England, so his visit was more than worthwhile. He complimented us on the appearance of the boat, the only yacht in the harbour flying the Red Duster, and we invited him aboard for a drink; to be precise, a glass of port, a bottle of that, given to me by my mother's doctor before we sailed, being the only drink on board. He, in turn, asked us to come up to his house for a drink and a shower when we had looked at our mail. We walked up there later, through the Sunday evening promenade on the Papeete waterfront, to a lovely cool whisky and soda, and a delightful shower with no thought of water rationing for a change, after which we went with him to the 'Les Tropiques' restaurant and hotel for dinner. The hotel is situated on the beach and the restaurant consists of thatched roofs attached to still-growing palm trees, and it all looked glorious on this moonlit night. Our host had a long and detailed discussion with the head waiter about what to eat and how to cook it, this being French territory, and we enjoyed an excellent meal. Quite a change from the hashes and stews to which we were accustomed. We discovered that we had many mutual acquaintances in the yachting fraternity in Britain, and found plenty to talk about. The moonlight, and the silver, and the spotless tablecloths, and the elegant ladies, made a dream come true setting for our first evening on Tahiti.

Returning to the quayside we didn't feel like going back on board just yet so we strolled along the boulevard and, near its end, came upon a cabaret in full swing, where we stopped and spent a while drinking cool drinks and watching both the cabaret and the multi-coloured, multi-national throng which frequented it. Our first few hours in Papeete had been full of incident and entertainment, but eventually we went home to bed.

We found Papeete to be a very sociable place, and entertained many a visitor. The Red Ensign attracted many and visiting among the yachts, mainly American and French, in the port, was a common and enjoyable pastime. We were moored between two Americans, *Ruana*, freshly arrived from the Galapagos Islands with four very pleasant Californians on board, and *Vega*, a schooner of 150 feet which had been used to make a film in the islands about the *Filaria* disease, more commonly known as elephantiasis. She still had the film crew on board, and an English navigator, and her owner Cornelius Crane, who was tickled pink by the story of two days' empty gin bottles floating alongside each other! During our stay the Englishman brought to visit us both Crane and a famous yachtsman W. A. Robinson, the author of *Deep Water and Shoal*, the book which had, to a great degree, inspired my voyage. Robinson was also wrapped up in the problem of *Filaria*. *Vega*'s navigator seemed to be the ship's social director as well as her navigator, and was a bit of a wag too, re-christening *Kimballa* '*Ginparlour*'. A name, I think, more appropriate to *Vega* herself, a magnificently equipped vessel which, though having only a small auxiliary motor for propulsion, had a very powerful generator to drive all the electrical gear. As well, a very elaborate kit of radio equipment electric capstans proliferated on her decks to make the handling of her massive rig relatively light work.

The Commandant of the French Naval Station called one evening with his wife when I was alone on board, and took me home to his house for a drink and a chat, and to show me his marvellous collection of photographs of the islands of French Polynesia. We struggled a bit, though his English was pretty good, and I wished that I had paid more attention to French lessons at school. We had a bonus in the form of cooked breakfasts when Buzz met two passengers in a French ship taking European emigrants to Australia which called at Papeete with cargo. The couple were an Australian girl who had gone to England to find a job and the Dutchman that she had married, who were making their way back to Australia. They found the quarters cramped and the food poor in their ship, and particularly disliked French-style breakfasts. They jumped at my suggestion that they could come to *Kimballa* for breakfast provided that they cooked it, and we did well at breakfast time for as long as their ship was in port.

All in all we received great kindness from everyone we met in Tahiti, and got great pleasure from all the visitors we had, and all the parties which developed in our own boat and in others. One evening at a party in *Ruana* we were given an authentic exhibition of the Hula by two island girls dressed in their authentic grass, or rather shredded bark, skirts. With flowers in their hair their dance was most graceful and the musical accompaniment truly of the South Seas, and they seemed possessed of unlimited energy and obviously danced for fun. Buzz was the organiser of this particular party. Where he finds the girls I can't image. The waterfront to which we were moored was always full of activity and interest, with frequent arrivals and departures of island schooners and all the visiting and seeing off which goes with them. Departing they would chase all the visitors ashore and motor across the very blue lagoon towards the apparently uninterrupted line of breakers on the reef. Once out through the pass they would hoist their canvas and sail away about their business. Our faithful Kim was immune to the delights of Papeete. Though all he had to do to get ashore was walk our short gangplank he never strayed ashore until, one day, we carried him ashore to a patch of grass. He was terrified, and crept back to the sea wall on his belly, climbed down it and swam back to the ship to be hauled, dripping, on board by Buzz. And that was all he saw of Tahiti.

Mr. Devenish set off one day to drive us round the island, starting out along the shore of Matavai Bay, a small bay with sandy beaches and volcanic rocks, where Cook first anchored his ships when he came to Tahiti, and then on to Point Venus, the northernmost point of Tahiti, where Cook set up his instruments to observe the transit of Venus across the sun's disc in 1796, an expedition sponsored by the Royal Society. The actual spot from which the observations were made is marked by a fifteen-inch square stone marked with a meridian line and nearby there is a stone column surmounted by a sphere to commemorate the event. There is, close by, Point Venus lighthouse, one of the very few in this part of the world. Onwards along the northern coast to a place where the rock formation has created a blowhole through which blasts of surf impelled air and water shoot upwards into the sky. Unfortunately our circumnavigation had to end a little further on for the Public Works Department, in blasting to improve the road, had inadvertently blocked it, and it looked like staying that way for a day or two. So we had to retrace our route and return to Papeete, to an excellent lunch at a restaurant with the unimaginative name of 'The Yacht Club'. We would like to have visited Moorea, a spectacularly picturesque island about nine miles away, but time was too short. Seen from Tahiti it has the appearance of being enveloped in a blue haze and its mountains, gigantic needles and massive precipices, are one of the world's scenic wonders. It is a favourite spot for Tahitian citizens to visit for picnics and bathing parties on its lovely beaches.

If there is an unpleasant aspect of Tahiti it is rats, which abound. The bund to which we were moored was alive with them at night and the local Pi dogs, which also abound, don't bother to chase them, just sitting and looking at them.

But time was moving on and hard currency was running out. I sent a cable to Fulleylove, who might well be in Rarotonga by now, to say that I expected to be there by 2nd November and resolved to sail at 4.30 on Saturday afternoon, 20th October. We purchased the necessary stores at Etablissments Donald Tahiti, a very efficient New Zealand firm, and at some of the local stores which all seem to be in Chinese hands. Tahitians don't work at all if it can possibly be avoided, and John Chinaman is only too happy to graft away. Saturday dawned and we spent the morning rushing about on our final errands, arranging for water, taking in stores, paying bills and, at the last minute before it closed at midday, getting our clearance at the Custom House. Lunch at the Yacht Club ran on into a farewell party aboard *Kimballa* so well attended that I thought she would sink. But all good things must come to an end and, at 4.30 p.m., we chased our guests ashore to stand, a vividly colourful group in rainbow-hued clothes including grass skirts, on the wall to watch us go. We started the motor and, with leis and strings of coral about our necks, prepared to sail. No one leaves Papeete without enough flowers to stock an English market stall! Buzz went forward and hove away on the cable while I let go the stern lines and soon the chain was up and down, and there it stuck, the anchor refusing to leave the bottom. I went forward to help, and we soon realised that the schooner *Viterie*, last seen in the Marquesas, had laid her cable across ours when she came in. So much for our spectacular departure.

Ruana and *Vega* both put boats in the water to help, but even with that aid it took a couple of hours to clear. Once we had it up we went alongside *Vega* to get things squared up once more, and the farewell party started up all over again and went on until two on Sunday morning, when we decided that we really had to go. Though we had paid for a pilot he was happy not to turn out, so we cast off and motored seaward. It was a bright moonlit night and the passage out should have been easy, but we none the less managed to get stuck on a coral head. A bit of ahead and astern on the engine and we slid clear, and made our way out through the pass in the reef. There was almost no wind, so we ran the motor for the rest of the night, stopping it at 10.00 a.m. when, though there was barely enough wind for us to make one knot, we thought we had used enough fuel. We made all plain sail and drifted along with lovely Tahiti and Moorea still in sight.

An author whose name I cannot recall once wrote: 'The magic of Tahiti is not to be caught with the point of a pen, or secured with a camera lens. It must be felt to be understood.' How right he was.

Chapter 30

Pacific Rendezvous

In the limpid, clear water off Tahiti we saw our first shark, cruising about looking like the marine equivalent of a heavy bomber. After our exertions in Papeete even Buzz couldn't be bothered to try to catch it, and it ignored the scraps of food that we threw over the side. We all, including Kim, just lazily watched it and eventually it swam away. We hoped it had gone for good.

We had come quite close to achieving a Saturday departure despite the Consul's assertions that nobody ever left Tahiti as planned, and of my statement that we hoped never to leave, but none the less we were going on Saturday. Even the suggestion of unsettled weather failed to budge me from my view, developed in less than a week, that Papeete was such a demoralising place that one could easily drift into staying there for ever. And anyway, I had an appointment in Rarotonga. We idled Sunday away.

During the afternoon, as I was chucking a cooling bucket of water over my naked self, I remembered that it was my turn to cook the dinner. As I went below to find a towel I thought to pre-heat the burners of the stove, and poured some meths from the bottle onto them and put a match to it, which resulted in a whoosh and a flash and before I could react I found myself on fire amidships. I shouted to Buzz 'I'm on fire' and he dashed down and while I put myself out he smothered the fire on the stove with a blanket. Liberal application of Tannifax from the medicine chest made light of what could easily have been a disastrous burn. We set about seeking the cause of the accident and found that the meths bottle held petrol, the result of language problems in Papeete.

The Consul's prediction of deteriorating weather was fulfilled and, though the calm prevailed and we were using the engine off and on, the barometer was falling and the sky was becoming overcast, indeed all the signs of impending bad weather were there. After two days it began to blow and we put the engine to bed and set our storm jib and the mizzen. In a few hours it was blowing a full gale from the southeast and, though we were making progress, it was not quite in the right direction, and I was frequently unable to get my sun sights and find our position. The next few days were very uncomfortable, not only because of the violent motion, but also because our leak had increased again requiring a quarter of an hour's pumping morning and evening. And the motion was sloshing water everywhere again, even to the extent of lifting the floorboards from time to time, making the cabin look like a battlefield. So much for our hope of arriving at Rarotonga all spick and span. The last of our Tilley lamp mantles had disintegrated and we were down to a hurricane lantern in the cabin at night. Several seams in the mizzen split and had to be repaired. All in all not at all what we had become accustomed to in the Pacific. We got a lot of amusement from watching Kim in the heavy weather. Wherever he wedged himself his body seemed to ooze from side to side like a jelly as the boat rolled and pitched, but he stuck it out with proper fortitude and never complained.

Kimballa (Jack Arnot)

Three whole days elapsed from the onset of the gale before I could get a proper fix. Sometimes the sun never showed itself at all, and sometimes it would be briefly visible, only to disappear before I could get the sextant or, alternatively, it let me get the sextant only to have the sea douse me and the instrument with salt water, with the sun going into hiding again after I had cleaned the lens and mirrors. I wanted to keep careful track of our position,

Jack and Buzz at Rarotonga *(Fulleylove)*

for Rarotonga is a tiny island, circular, and only six miles in diameter. Its name means 'The Floating Island', for Polynesian navigators had great difficulty in finding it, and concluded that it shifted its position.

Eight days out from Papeete I got a position of sorts and expected to see the island during the morning, and several times we thought we saw land only to have it turn out to be cloud. We had to wait until three in the afternoon of that day, 29th October, before we saw the island and were sure it wasn't just another cloud. By now the wind had eased to the normal trade wind strength, though the gale had left a heavy swell and things were still very uncomfortable. Though volcanic, the island is completely surrounded by a coral reef having only a few gaps in it, and only one of those navigable without local knowledge. It was obvious that we could not get in before dark, so I decided to lay off for the night and go in next morning. Probably a good decision, for when we did enter the pass what did we see but efforts being made to pull a small trading vessel off the reef. We handed our canvas and let the boat drift, the drift being away from the land, had our dinner, put a light on deck and turned in, bone weary after days of gale.

Daylight found us fifteen miles offshore with the wind blowing directly from the island, so we started the engine, hoping to reach Avarua by about 10.00 a.m., but the engine was not behaving itself and we had a number of involuntary stops on the way towards the land. The harbour at Avarua is small, very small, being in fact just a narrow gap in the reef, with a wharf at the shore end with about seven feet of water alongside. There are leading marks, and the main engines of a vessel which failed to find the gap stand on the reef marking one place where the entrance is not. It was a cloudy day, not the best conditions for reef navigation, so I kept a mile or so outside the reef until the leading marks came into line. As I approached I could see that the harbour was full, with two small vessels alongside the wharf and a schooner anchored stern on to its end. The current in many of the islands sitting inside lagoons is outward flowing, because the sea breaking over the reef tops up the lagoon to a level slightly higher than the surrounding ocean, and the current can be quite strong. At Avarua we had to go in at full speed to get in at all. We came in through the pass and anchored near the schooner with some difficulty, for our anchor did not bite first time, and we dragged a bit before it caught. Once secure I swept the shore with my telescope and there, sure enough, was Fulleylove, standing atop the wheelhouse of one of the ships alongside the wharf. Eighteen months after that night in Karachi our plan was fulfilled.

Fulley came out in a local rowing boat, but could not get aboard until the doctor and customs had visited us, a visit which was mercifully short as the

Kimballa at Rarotonga

Kimballa at Rarotonga

paperwork was minimal. Fulley had arranged for the master of a local vessel to pilot us in, so he came aboard and took us alongside one of the vessels at the wharf, and by noon we were tied up, many photographs had been taken and we were, as usual, garlanded with frangipani.

Once alongside Fulley, unable to board us at anchor, arrived, and I think he got a bit of a shock at the mess we were in below. All the small girls and boys in the island descended on us and just stood and gawped, while Fulley went ashore for the mail and we cleared up the mess in the cabin and dressed to go ashore. Once ready we repaired to the only hotel in the island, the Hotel Rarotonga, believe it or not, where Fulley was staying. It is government owned and run, and usually full of government folk, so Fulley was lucky to get in. I think they must have taken him for an Inspector of Taxes, or something. Mr. and Mrs. Lucy, managing the place, allowed us to have baths, a great luxury, after which we joined a party in Fulley's room, a large party of the people he had become friendly with in his stay in the island. Despite the fact that the island is officially dry the Principal Medical Officer is allowed to issue permits for a limited amount of liquor. Dr. Davies, himself a keen yachtsman, recognised our need for a relaxing medicinal draft and we didn't have to go thirsty! We dined in the hotel that evening and, after talking far into the night, I spent the night on the spare bed in Fulley's room.

Next day one of the vessels alongside sailed and we got alongside the wharf and Kim, for some reason best known to himself, went ashore, though no further than the end of the jetty, where he could find himself a piece of copra to play with, or stalk a cockroach or two. The water was crystal clear, and warm, so ideal for swimming, and I had to go in the next day anyway to attach a line to an anchor sunk in the coral with which to keep the boat off the jetty when the swell made her bump alongside. On the other side of the wharf was the trading vessel *Siren* (appropriate?), which had gone on the reef a few days before, and which had been filled with empty oil drums to give her buoyancy prior to being dragged by motor lorries and manpower across the reef on a fine day, into the lagoon. Later on she was hauled up on the beach to be repaired.

Mount Te Manga, height 2,140 feet, is most of Rarotonga and Avarua lies at its feet, spreading along the narrow strip of flat land between it and the sea with a fine fringe of palms between the town and the beach. Indeed, palm trees grow along the shore right round the island, as do many other magnificent trees and there are flowers everywhere which are worn by everyone. Women wear them in their hair or round their necks, and men wear them in their hats. English is the language of the island and these friendly people greet you on sight, whether or not they know you, and European dress is the norm. The cinema and dancing are the local occupations, with dancing competitions between the villages an important part of local life.

The lagoon surrounding the island is strangely short of marine life and the fishing beyond the reef is similarly poor. Though a few canoes do go out at night and harpoon fish attracted by the light of petrol vapour lamps, fish never seems to appear on the hotel menu. The dangerous stonefish, and a sea snail regarded by the natives as a delicacy, are the most notable inhabitants of the lagoon. And there are no sparrows, which surprised me, for they are everywhere else in the world I have been, and that is quite a lot of the world. The commonest bird is the Indian Minah which has been imported. And rats, but not so numerous as they are in Tahiti.

I spent my time in Rarotonga mostly with Fulley, keeping largely to and near the ship for the harbour is not the safest in the world. And I had to dismantle the engine, which had been misbehaving. We abandoned our plan to visit Rapa, the weather being too problematical for us to be sure that if

Off the Jetty, Rarotonga

we made the trip Fulley would get back from his leave on time. We were well entertained, and returned the hospitality as best we could in *Kimballa*, making many friends. One evening, at a dinner under a thatch awning at a private house, I sat next to a globe-trotting old lady who was pausing in Rarotonga. She was a most interesting companion, having been to an awful lot of places, many of them off the beaten track and seldom visited by tourists. When we came to the coffee and cigarettes stage I got out my makings, cigarettes being in short supply on the island, and, unskilfully, rolled myself one. I say unskilfully, for there was tobacco dangling out of either end, but I put it in my mouth and lit it. Bits of burning tobacco fell into my lap and I hastily brushed them off, whereupon the lady raised her lorgnettes, looked me straight in the eye, and said, 'What, on fire AGAIN, Captain Arnot?' So much for swearing Buzz to secrecy, and all credit to the powers of the grapevine.

I had a new staysail boom made by Ron Powell, the one broken in the Caribbean being in a sorry state. Ron Powell had been in a yacht in one of the Cook Islands when it was struck by a hurricane in 1942. The yacht was

Party time, Rarotonga; Jack and Buzz

completely destroyed and he and his companion only saved themselves by lashing themselves to palm trees. Having no yacht any more he settled in Rarotonga and runs a combined curio and ship repairing business, occasionally going to sea for a voyage in an inter-island ship as stand in for someone ill or on leave. He made me a fine boom.

Being the centre of the administration of the Cook Islands, Rarotonga is home to many a Government official and is also home to innumerable Missionary Societies, so many that the natives must have great trouble deciding which particular brand of Christianity to be persuaded to. Some of the 'blue' laws which they managed to get enacted, and only lately discarded, would have been funny if they had not been so repressive. A native who walked out with his girl was required to carry a burning torch in his hand and was fined if he let it go out. If found weeping over the grave of a women not a relative a native would be fined. Incredible, but true. The court records prove it.

I would like to have put *Kimballa* on a slip to try to sort our leak, but there wasn't one big enough, and, with the hurricane season approaching, it would be unwise for a small yacht to be hanging about here after the middle of December. With Fulleylove's leave coming to an end it was time to think of moving on and, with the engine rebuild complete thanks to assistance and the loan of tools from the Public works Engineer, I decided to sail on 30th November in the hope of reaching Auckland around Christmas. We bought stores including Taro Tarowa instead of potatoes, of which there were none, pineapples, oranges and bananas, and a couple of hula skirts in case we felt like a dance along the way. Storing was made harder because we had to move away from the wharf, which was needed for lighters, and lie alongside the schooner *Ornant* at anchor and everything had to be ferried by dinghy. The lighters come into use when a deep-sea steamer is working cargo, for they have to drift outside the reef and land their cargo by lighters towed by motor launches. Fulley was flying out on 1st December, on his way back to work, so our joint farewells began and ended, and at 2.00 p.m. on the 30th we cast off from *Ornant* and motored out of the pass, passing close to the Union Steamship Company's *Waitemata* as we got into the open sea. We stopped the engine, hoisted all plain sail and set our course southwest for Auckland.

Sailed Papeete 20th October 1951. Arrived Avarua 30th October 1951. 8 days 22 hours 30 minutes. 638 miles. 2.9 knots.

Chapter 31

Auckland is our destination

We were now embarked on the last, the third longest, passage of the voyage, and it opened with a good day's run of 120 miles in the twenty-one hours to noon. That gave five and a half knots which would get us to Auckland by Christmas day, but as the days went by the wind lightened, and day by day the runs halved themselves, until on the fourth day out we only managed thirty miles in practically calm conditions. Our Taro and Kumaras made good eating, but they don't really compare with potatoes. We still baked bread with Kim, who was glad to get to sea again, not approving of all the people rushing about his ship, stealing his share when it was still warm and smelling good.

For two days we had a glassy calm, and, to prevent chafe in the sails and rigging we took everything down and just let *Kimballa* drift. There was no question of running the engine, for it had shot its bolt getting us out of Avarua. The water in the oil that we had seen so long ago was the result of a leaking gasket, and the dilution of the lubricating oil had caused excessive wear in the pistons and cylinder liners, and we no longer had enough compression to ignite the fuel. We struggled with it, but completely failed to get it going. Poor, staunch, *Kimballa* was indeed running down and in need of more than cosmetic attention. We hadn't been able to get spares for our Tilley lamp in either Tahiti or Rarotonga, and had to use a wick lamp that I had bought in Avarua, along with a hurricane lamp, to light the cabin at night, a gloomy combination after the soft Tilley light we were accustomed to. Our petrol generator had finally succumbed to the damp, so there could be no question of using our precious batteries for electric light. At about this time the S.S. *Waitemata* passed us at 2.00 a.m. and signalled to ask if all was well. We never saw another ship in the whole passage.

Dolphin returned to keep us company and provide us with most welcome fresh fish, appreciated by all, including Kim. Several large albatross also kept station on us and became so tame that they would almost take fish from our hands. About the size of swans, but shaped like seagulls, they appear to fly without effort, riding the updraughts from the seas and seldom flapping a wing. Quarrelsome, though, among themselves, with the best meals going to the most aggressive. To Buzz's astonishment I said 'Good Morning' to them every day.

When the wind came away again it was from the west and so heading us, forcing us to run close hauled to make any ground at all towards Auckland. Sometimes we sailed for two or three days on one tack, and sometimes we would make several boards within the day, seeking the most advantageous heading as the wind shifted about. Although *Kimballa* sailed herself quite well on the wind it was slow and wearisome work, with the head seas giving her a quick, jerky motion as she butted into them. Our progess towards our destination was slow, and a day's run of sixty miles might only contribute fifteen towards Auckland. Even the simplest jobs were hard work in this sort of weather.

When we reached the latitude of the Kermadec Isles, thirty degrees south, we ran into gales and were often under jib and mizzen alone, and when, even under this reduced rig, the jib one day blew into irreparable tatters we decided that the only thing to do was to sew a big reef into one of our staysails and set it as a jib. The sewing bee was scheduled for after breakfast one morning and, being cook for the day, I was carrying two china mugs of tea by their handles when a particularly heavy lurch flung me across the cockpit, smashing the mugs and cutting me badly between the fingers of my right hand. So badly, indeed, that I couldn't use a palm and needle and Buzz had to sew the whole of the reef by himself. It rained a great deal, and the decks leaked quite a lot, inevitably over the bunks, and soon Buzz's bunk got so wet that we took turn about in mine. Our leak in the hull was getting worse, and our spells of pumping longer and longer. The whale bilge pump did a good job but did occasionally get clogged by the inevitable rubbish in the bilge, and needed frequent greasing if it were not to become too stiff to use. To add to our discomfort we ran out of reading matter, even including the two dozen copies of *Punch* that we had been given in Rarotonga, and which we read from cover to cover including the advertisements. Normally this would not have bothered us for there is always plenty of work to do, but in these conditions it was impossible to do anything other than essential steering and watchkeeping, with the motion of the boat knocking all the energy out of us. The final use for the *Punch* magazines was as the basis for evening sessions of 'Twenty Questions'.

On the positive side we made good use of the radio, for I had been able to get a couple of high tension batteries from the radio station in Rarotonga, and we could get New Zealand and Australia loud and clear. The stations being commercial we got a lot of amusement out of the advertisements and came to the conclusion that in the shops of Auckland, and particularly in the Karangahapi Road, practically everything is given away for nothing. The West Indies were playing Australia at this time and, for the first time in my life, I got pleasure from listening to cricket matches.

All in all this was not the sort of weather which I had been expecting at the height of the southern summer with, day after day, westerly gales and rain. The sun did put in an appearance for a few hours each day so we were usually able to get an accurate fix, fixes which showed so little progress as to be disheartening. Buzz had a birthday shortly before Christmas and in celebrating it we scoffed the last of our liquor, so it was perhaps a good thing that we crossed the 180th meridian on what would have been Christmas day, and so went straight from Christmas eve to Boxing day, for we had nothing but our monotonous old stews, and no grog, to celebrate with. All our cigarette papers had got soaked and were useless, though we had lots of tobacco, so we were reduced to making our fags with toilet paper and gum.

Crossing the date line reminded me of a tale I had heard about missionaries in the Fiji group, which lies on the meridian. The first missionaries came from the east, Methodists, and they established themselves in the islands. Later the Catholic missionaries came from the west and settled, and for many years they had their Sundays on different days! The foul conditions and lack of reading matter left us plenty of time for yarning and Buzz told me many an extraordinary tale of his youth, one of which in particular has kept me amused ever since. It is this.

At one time he had worked in a circus, and the older hands told him that a true circus man always wears a tiger's whisker in the lapel of his jacket. So, wanting to become a fully fledged circus man as soon as possible, Buzz made enquiries as to how to obtain one. He learned that tigers, before settling down to sleep, turn round three times to port in the northern hemisphere, and then lie with their heads against the bars and usually a whisker or two sticking through. The trick was to borrow a pair of electrician's pliers, creep into the tent at night, and extract a whisker. And run. So Buzz borrowed the recommended pliers and crept into the animal tent one night, found the tigers' cage but also found that the watchman was not asleep but on the prowl. It was several nights before he found the watchman asleep under a rug and peace reigning in the tent. All tense and excited Buzz crept up to a convenient tiger, grasped a whisker with the pliers, pulled and ran. Pandemonium broke out, with the roars of the startled tiger setting all the other animals off. Lions and tigers roaring, elephants trumpeting, dogs barking, the whole tented jungle making its displeasure known and the watchman dashing about seeking the cause of the disturbance. Not finding it, for Buzz had fled as though jet propelled.

Now Buzz had not kept secret his intention, and had contracted with a number of people for whiskers at five shillings a time, and so he had to repeat the performance on a number of nights as the opportunity arose, with the result that the tiger who slept nearest to the escape route had lost most of his starboard-hand whiskers. Now part of the tiger's circus act involved them walking round the ring in line ahead before mounting their individual plinths, and because a tiger uses its whiskers to guide it, and because Buzz's tiger was short of almost all the right-hand whiskers, he kept trying to go round the ring the wrong way, to the mighty annoyance of the trainer!

Kimballa at Auckland

On the missing Christmas day we were still 500 miles from Auckland, little knowing that we would sail more than 800 to get there. The southwesterlies prevailed and we were being driven further and further south. New Year's day came and went, with our discomfort increasing. Cuts and abrasions, of which we both had many besides those inflicted by my mug smashing disaster, would not heal in this climate, and we were reduced to using diesel fuel in the lamps to save kerosene. Though this gave not too bad a light it was a smoky fuel and the smoke added to the general gloom, and my worries were increased by our leak which was getting worse and worse, requiring more and more pumping.

On my birthday, 5th January, our sights showed that we were in the latitude of the East Cape of New Zealand and about fifty miles to the east of it, and the rain and poor visibility the following night prevented us sighting the light, so we went onto the port tack to take us away from the land. Came daylight, faced with the choice between standing on that tack and going about onto the tack which would close the coast, but bring us to it well south of Auckland, we stood on, northwards and away from the coast. On the 8th the wind eased and shifted, giving us a slant which took us in towards the north end of Great Barrier Island at the northeastern entrance to the Hauraki gulf. The sight of that island through the rain and overcast was very welcome. As we came under the lee of the island the wind hauled round to the northwest making it the first fair wind for weeks, and by noon we were just forty miles away from the entrance to Auckland harbour. The wind freshened to a moderate gale and *Kimballa* romped along as she had not done for many a long day, making between five and six knots over the last fifty miles. As we made for the island of Tritri Martangi outside Auckland harbour the rain came down in torrents and, though we could hear the diaphone, we did not see the light until we were within half a mile of it. With this danger behind us it was a straight run down to the harbour entrance which showed up as the rain began to clear.

Our chart, which was quite up to date, showed that the examination anchorage was off Rangitoto Island and, arriving there nearly at midnight, very wet and weary, we found two merchant ships at anchor. Rounding up into the wind we let go our anchor and brought up to twenty fathoms of cable. We had made Auckland our objective from our departure from Birdham, and we had arrived. We got the sails in and secured and went below. It was cold, so we put diesel fuel in our kerosene heater and got it smokily going to warm the cabin and dry some of our sopping clothing. We sweetened our cocoa with glucose from the medicine chest, our sugar being all used up, and turned in to our damp bunks.

At dawn the next morning it was still blowing hard, with a good sea running, but the rain had stopped. There was no sign of doctors or customs or the like, so we put up our 'Q' flag and a signal seeking a tow, for we were anxious to get ashore after our hard passage. At about 8.00 a.m. we began to drag our anchor towards the shore of the volcanic island of Rangitoto, so we got up our larger anchor from the forepeak and bent it on to a coil of inch and a half wire rope which we kept for this very emergency, hove the anchor over the side and made the end of the wire fast to the mainmast. And by the time we brought up to our two anchors we had dragged the best part of a mile.

All that day we awaited the doctor and customs, but no one came near us so, despite what the chart said, we had to conclude that this was not the examination anchorage, and that the two anchored merchantmen were there awaiting berths. It was blowing too hard, in my view, to go manoeuvering round a strange harbour under sail, so we waited patiently all day, with the wind dropping towards evening. After dark we tried to raise the signal station with a lamp but got no response, probably because we were too far off for our torch to be seen. So we turned in, determined to sail in next day come what might.

Next morning it took about an hour to disentangle our anchor wire and cable after breakfast, but eventually we got both anchors up and set sail. It was nearly low water when we started so, after a couple of hours, we began to feel the flood tide which helped, for, with the wind against us, we had to beat in towards the harbour, which was not a simple matter because, with our makeshift jib, we couldn't tack, and had to wear round at the end of each board which lost us a lot of ground. People ashore must have wondered what we were up to but by 12.30 p.m. we had gained the harbour proper and were wondering where we should go when I noticed that one of the ships anchored in the stream was signalling us with an Aldis lamp. I was keeping a keen eye on the chart, the tide and the wind and did not pay any attention at first but when I had time to read the signal it was an invitation to come and moor alongside if we wished. At last someone was taking some notice of us.

She was the Shaw Savill cargo liner *Fordsdale*, lying at anchor awaiting a berth alongside, and she thoughtfully streamed a lifebuoy astern for us to pick up. At our first attempt we missed it and had to wear round and have another go, there being a stronger tide than I had allowed for. The job was complicated by the fact that *Fordsdale*, being light, was lying to the wind and in picking up the buoy which was streaming on the tide I got too close under her counter and carried away our foretopmast stay. Once alongside, thankful to be fast to something solid again, the Chief Officer, Mr. Hutchinson, invited us aboard, but we could not accept as we had not yet cleared the doctor. But the invitation did not exhaust *Fordsdale*'s hospitality, nor their ingenuity, for they soon lowered a tin of cigarettes and a bottle of gin down to us, and we had a drink to the good old *Fordsdale*. They then got busy with their lamp to the signal station, and arranged for a launch to come out and tow us to the ferry steps at Queen Street, where the authorities would deal with us.

It took about two hours for the launch to arrive and take us in tow and we were quickly alongside the steps at the foot of Auckland's main street. A crowd soon gathered to look at us, and Kim got fidgety at the sight of all the people, but the doctor and the customs arrived and swifty cleared us and completed the formalities. After our long voyage we were free to go where we liked in New Zealand which, as New Zealanders are proud to tell you, is as far from Britain as you can get. If you go any further you are on your way back!

Mr. Leak, a customs officer, arranged for the launch to tow us to a less frequented berth later in the evening, and Buzz went up to the post office 200 yards away to get the mail. They gave him his, but wouldn't surrender mine, and I was just able to collect it before closing time. Strangely enough, we didn't go ashore that evening and spent it reading our mail, resting and yarning, and turned in early.

News travels quickly and in the ensuing days there was a stream of telegram boys bringing messages to *Kimballa*. We had been ignored on arrival for we were not expected, our voyage being unpublicised, and the examination anchorage shown on our chart was a wartime one, no longer in use. But word of the completion of our voyage went swiftly round the world none the less.

Sailed Rarotonga 30th November 1951. Arrived Auckland 9th January 1952. 38 days 11 hours 22 minutes. 2327 miles, 2.6 knots.

Total for voyage, 191 days 10 hours 27 minutes. 14,285 miles, 3.11 knots.

Chapter 32

The Pacific

The Odyssey was completed, the great adventure over, *Kimballa*, somewhat the worse for wear after the testing last leg of the voyage, required slipping, the renewal of two planks, and a lot of work to restore her to a yacht-like condition again. Even without 14,000-mile voyages yachts require constant attention if they are to stay in a seaworthy condition, and yet more to keep them yacht-like. Fibreglass has reduced the workload, but *Kimballa* was a wooden, pre-fibreglass, boat. By mid-March she was on the slip, with Jack working like a beaver and living aboard, after allowing himself a short holiday at Gisborne. By April the boat was back in shape and Jack was looking for something to do whilst making up his mind that he was not cut out to be a farmer. It is said that all seafarers want to leave the sea, and most fancy farming. The advice generally given to disillusioned seafarers is, 'put a pair of oars over your shoulder and walk inland until someone asks you what they are.' But seafaring is not so easy to give up: it is a demanding, absorbing life. A hard, underpaid life in those days, but still one which, whilst advising others against its pursuit, cannot be shrugged off. Jack's whole working life was spent at sea. His long 'holiday' was spent sailing *Kimballa* 14,000 miles across the world yet in 1943, when I myself was preparing to go to sea, he wrote to his sister Annie, my mother, in the following terms:

> 'I am afraid Ian's career will be fixed one way or another by the time you get this. I most sincerely hope it is NOT the Merchant Navy. There is no similarity at all between the life of an Officer R.N. and an Officer in the Merchant Navy. I have been seeing a great deal of His Majesty's ships and the people in them this last year or so and know what I am talking about. I have met several

'Old *Conway*' of my day in them and talked to them about it too. For a boy like Ian who is fond of games, sailing, etc., he would find the Merchant Navy like a prison, for his chances of any games are practically non-existent. As far as sailing goes it is very seldom indeed that a ship has time to spare to put a lifeboat in the water and sailing a lifeboat is a very poor kind of fun for they are not meant to sail well. During the three years of my apprenticeship I was out in a lifeboat once and that was all the sailing I got and is as much as the vast majority of apprentices get. Ships in the Merchant Navy work day and night in most places that they go to these days and I am talking about peace time at that. This company's ships never stop day or night year in and year out except for a fortnight's drydocking each year when the officers work longer hours than when she is running normally. You may think I am exaggerating but it is quite true. We do our two four-hour watches on the bridge at sea plus one or two hours of other work and in port we are on from 6.00 to 6.00 a.m. or p.m. as the case may be. I am fed up with all night work in port. And on sailing days you may have been on all night then you carry on with your watches the next day to say nothing of messing about for hours mooring and unmooring. If he does join the M.N. I have no doubt he will say he likes it, just as I did. But the day will come when he wants to get married and then he will think differently. Then if he does not get into one of the half dozen better companies who knows what kind of companions and officers he may get with.'

None the less, with what was the then vast sum of £20,000 of unspent sweepstake winnings in hand, Jack remained at sea, though not in the sort of ships described in his letter, not ships which ran round the clock 351 days a year and twice round the clock in drydock.

In the first part of May 1952 Jack was offered, and accepted, the job of navigating a yacht, *Lady Sterling*, from Auckland to Suva, Fiji, a voyage of which there is no record beyond the statement that it was made. The yacht must have been well found and the weather unremarkable or comments would have appeared in the letters home. What was remarkable about it was the fact that it appears to have put a damper on Jack's intention to settle in New Zealand, a fact which was to have far-reaching consequences. Extracts from a letter to Annie dated 17th May in Suva follow:

'I took the temporary job of navigating a yacht up here as Mother's letter will tell you. I like this part of the world very much and it has somehow upset my ideas of New Zealand. It is a little bit like India without the disadvantages of India.

'I had to attend a ceremonial feast on arrival here where I had to drink a bowl of kava off in one. During the drinking all the assembly clap their hands slowly and as the bowl is drained say "Oooooooh" in a long drawn out breath. I was then given a whale's tooth on a string, which is a great honour, for bringing the ship safely to Suva. Amongst the Fijians I can demand anything I want if I show the whale's tooth and no true Fijian can refuse my wish. Few Europeans ever do this but I am assured that if I did my wish would be granted.

'The weather is pleasantly hot compared with Auckland which is getting into its winter. The club life here is similar to that in India before the war and I have been made a temporary member of the three principal clubs where I have met a lot of interesting and useful people.

'Just before I left New Zealand I applied for a job as a pilot in Tauranga which was advertised the day we sailed for here in the *Lady Sterling*. I have all the necessary qualifications and then some, but I think a New Zealander will get it. Tauranga is a very pretty spot and a coming port. The job is casual and would just suit me.'

Jack was right about Tauranga. In 1982 it handled more exports than any other New Zealand port. He didn't get the job. He continued to live on board *Kimballa*, reading the job advertisements and exploring Auckland and the shores of the Hauraki Gulf until August, when yet another offer of a ferry trip to Suva came up, which he accepted. This one turned out to be no sinecure. Again, from a letter to Annie dated 17th August in Auckland:

'Just over two weeks ago I left Auckland in a scow (similar to a Thames barge) to deliver it to Suva. We had bad weather to start with and put into Whangarei for shelter. We were there three days and then sailed for Suva. Most of the way the weather was most unusual and we had head winds and gales nearly all the way, the vessel was old and with the heavy seas she started to open up and we had to pump for half an hour in every hour from then on to keep her afloat. She had no galley and no

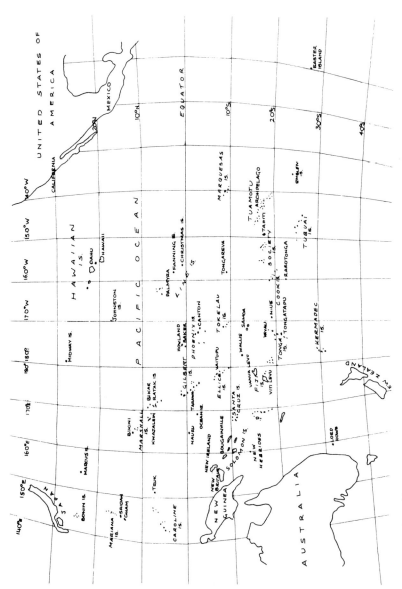

The Central Pacific

lavatory so it was a wonderful voyage. My ankles were swollen up when we arrived with long standing at the wheel. Two of the crew were so sick that they were almost useless. However we made it in ten days.

In Suva there is an island trading and shipping firm called Morris Hedstrom Ltd. They want a Master for a vessel they have recently bought. I saw their advertisement in an Auckland paper and applied for the job. I called on them at Suva and after two days of negotiations I managed to persuade them to pay a reasonable salary and have taken the job. I flew back to Auckland yesterday and will spend two weeks here settling up my affairs and then fly back to take command of the twin screw motor vessel *Altair*, at Suva. She normally trades around the Fiji group but occasionally goes to Tonga, Samoa and the Solomons. I will have to put *Kimballa* up for sale. I don't want to but I can see that I am unable to leave the sea and become a farmer as I had thought of doing, and I can't afford *Kimballa* unless I have a job of work. I could not keep her in Suva for many reasons, so she must go.'

And so was set the scene for the remaining twelve years of Jack's working life. The scene, but not the pattern, for outside of Morris Hedstrom's there were to be two other distinct ventures. But the venue was established, as was the size and type of ship. The venue was some five million square miles of the Pacific Ocean bounded by the latitude of the Northern Gilbert Islands, in 3 degrees North, to Nukalofa and Raratonga in 21 degrees south, and ranging from Port Moresby in 147 degrees of eastern longitude to Fanning Island and Raratonga in 159 degrees West. *Altair* was about 500 tons and 150 feet overall, and Jack only had one ship bigger than that in the rest of his career. And he didn't like her. Perhaps she was too big at 175 feet.

Chapter 33

T.S.M.V. *Altair*

Life in *Altair* can have been no picnic, for Jack's correspondence for the next year or two is sparse. The ship traded round the Fiji group carrying passengers and cargo, visiting any island or place for which the need for a call arose. The ship carried, besides humans and inanimate freight, livestock when required. The hazards of navigation among islands and reefs are very considerable, and photographs seem to indicate that *Altair* did not have the benefit of radar. Newspaper cuttings collected by Jack over the years are full of reports of strandings on the reef, by negligence, incompetence, drunkenness or even by design. Of disappearances, of canoes adrift and of blowings ashore in harbour in the hurricanes which sweep the islands. Difficult work but interesting and well within Jack's capacity.

The commonest cargo was copra, the product of the coconut palm which grows in profusion in the islands, and probably the most numerous group of passengers the schoolchildren, going home for holidays from school in Suva, and returning thereafter. Most of the islands were coral atolls, surrounded by a reef the passage of which was usually no easy matter. The small gaps in the reef which give access to the lagoon have to carry the tidal flow which fills and drains the lagoon twice a day, and the large volumes of water pouring through restricted passages make for very strong currents. Once inside coral heads dot the lagoon beneath the surface and can only be seen in certain lights. Not easy.

There was one island on *Altair*'s schedule which had a long and difficult channel through the reef and, once inside, through the lagoon to the anchorage. The channel was marked by perches, and so was not too difficult in daylight, but at night it was another matter. Jack's technique was simplicity itself. On approaching the reef he would put his launch, a large motorboat used mainly for ferrying cargo, over the side laden with paraffin lanterns. The launch would precede the ship into the channel, hanging

Altair (Jack Arnot)

Altair (Jack Arnot)

lanterns on the perches as she went, so that *Altair* had, effectively, a lit, buoyed channel to follow. When the last lantern had been hung the launch went out to sea again, passing the inbound *Altair*, then returned collecting the lanterns as she did so. Outward bound the procedure was reversed, with *Altair* hanging about outside the reef while the launch collected the lights.

From a letter to Annie, 26th November 1952.

'Yes, the reefs are coral. No, the Fijians do not deal in it except to sell some painted coral to tourists. In some islands it is cut into blocks and used for building. Fijians do not trade in anything as a rule. It is their custom that if they have anything that anybody else fancies they give it away, in fact in their code it is bad manners not to. Very few of them are in trade and very few have many possessions. The Indians who were imported years ago to work the sugar cane are the shopkeepers of Fiji today.

'The Coral reefs are the most beautiful colours, vivid electric blues and greens and, at sunset, all the colours of the rainbow. The coral itself is of many colours but soon fades when taken out of salt water for the coral bug dies.

'I am contemplating dedicating my declining years to the study of the mass destruction of the coral bug.'

There speaks the navigator. Perhaps he bred the Crown of Thorns starfish!

To Annie, 13th December 1952:

'We are on our usual round of the islands delivering cases of good cheer for Christmas, with a deck full of turkeys, hens, goats, pigs and three dogs for Suva. We are what I call the "brats special" this week. We had forty-one school kids aged from five to fifteen on their way back to their island homes from school, for the Christmas holiday.

'We are at the moment trying to arrange to be in Suva on Christmas day, without it seeming too obvious. The weather will have a lot to do with it.

'One meets a lot of interesting people around here. The other day I met a Doctor of Geology who is going out into the Pacific with a one and a half ton grab on the end of seven miles of wire to grab bits off the ocean floor to see what it is made of. He also

'Brats' aboard *Altair*

gave us a demonstration of water divining at a friend's house.

'We are in trouble this morning. We were loading a sling of eight sacks of shell valued at £95 when the sling capsized and we lost the lot in about thirty fathoms.

'This is the forty-third letter this Christmas, and I have written enough. Just one more, to Mother, and that is the lot. Wish you all a merry Christmas and a happy New Year.'

On 31st January 1953:

'We sail for Rotuma on Monday night, which is not looked on with favour by the crew, they do not like being out of sight of land, which we will be for nearly two days. We will also be jammed full of passengers on the way back, and she is not suited for so many. On top of all this my one and only cook has disappeared. No doubt it will all sort itself out.' (Rotuma is 350 miles North of Suva, open ocean between.)

Altair was a ship of which Jack became very fond. His pay was terrible, £800 a year wasn't much even in those days, and the work was continuous, but it must have been interesting for at about this time Jack decided that owning a ship trading in the Fijian islands would be more rewarding than driving someone else's ship and, in about April or May of 1953, he resigned from Morris Hedstrom Ltd. and formed a partnership, later a limited company, with three others, with a view to buying a suitable ship and trading her in the Pacific with himself in command.

In all probability the idea was older than that, for by June the ship had been found and Jack flew to Cyprus to complete the purchase of the wooden motor vessel *San Michele*, immediately renamed *Nukalau*.

Chapter 34

M/V *Nukalau*

Nukalau, an archetypal wooden Mediterranean cargo motorship, cost Jack and his three partners £9,000, so for the sum of £2,250 Jack became a shipowner, or rather sixteen sixty-fourths of a shipowner. The cadet from the *Conway* had come a long way both figuratively speaking and in fact.

The ship was entirely Mediterranean in appearance, her obvious ancestry being the Greek caique. She had a high, raked stem leading aft along a prominent forecastle with pronounced sheer dropping down to the main deck. There were two cargo hatches opening into one hold, with the single mast, fitted with two derricks, one for each hatch, and two winches, stepped amidships between the hatches. Abaft number two hatch was a short accommodation block perched on top of which was the bridge and wheelhouse, and the two lifeboats, and above that again the monkey island and standard compass. The short afterdeck contained a mooring winch, bollards and not much else bar gratings for storing the mooring ropes.

The engine was an eight cylinder diesel of unspecified make and horse-power, she was about 140 feet long and of 400 tons, capable of some ten knots when loaded. 'Not a thing of beauty, but my own.' The navigation equipment was equally rudimentary. A standard magnetic compass, a steering compass, a deep sea lead (not a sounding machine) and a hand lead. No radio direction finder, no radar, no echo sounder, no V.H.F. radio, just the basics used by seamen from time immemorial, with the master providing his own sextant and chronometer.

The purchase of such an insignificant vessel should, one would think, be a simple enough transaction, but the complications piled up upon themselves. Firstly, though Italian registered, the ship had been based at and had traded from Haifa, and even though the Suez Canal had not yet been nationalised there was a bar on its passage by Israeli shipping, so she was transferred to British registry, a proceeding which turned out to be far from simple. Then

230

there was the matter of the four Jewish members of the crew holding Israeli passports. More negotiations with the authorities of Famagusta, Cyprus, where the ship was lying, and eventually, after weeks of haggling, they were fitted out with Cyprus passports.

Then the sellers failed to provide a cargo for Port Sudan, the freight on which was to have been set against the purchase price. Then there was a minor delay while the ship earned a little cash lightening a Swedish ship which had gone ashore on Cape Andreas, not to mention the work which had to be put in to prepare the somewhat run-down vessel, accustomed to trading in the relatively sheltered end of the Mediterranean, for a passage half across the world including the Indian Ocean at the tail end of the southwest monsoon. So it was the end of August before *Nukalau* sailed for Fiji, light ship but with the prospect of a cargo at Aden.

A day and a half's run brought her to Port Said where the next bit of bother delayed them for a day. Even for a daylight transit of the Suez Canal the Canal Company requires that every ship rent a searchlight, which is hung over the bows in a large box. The light is beneficial at night, showing up the reflectors on the buoys marking the channel within the canal, and is demanded in daylight transits in case the convoy is delayed and does not complete the passage before nightfall. But *Nukalau*'s size and shape were such that the light simply could not be hung over the bow and stay out of the water, nor could it be perched on top of the stem. So, after the usual haggling and transfer of *douceurs*, it was agreed that, in view of her small size, *Nukalau* could make the passage without a light. She had, of course, to pay the rental of a light. It was in a letter to Annie at about this time that Jack remarked, 'I will be glad to see the leading lights of Suva Harbour again.'

Clear of the canal in the evening, with no searchlight to get rid of, *Nukalau* set course down the Gulf of Suez for Aden, 1,300 miles and six days away. She cleared the notorious bottleneck by the lighthouse on Ashraf Island in daylight the following day and, by nightfall, was clear of Shadwan Island and into the Red Sea proper. Southward she went down the length of that famous sea, past the Brothers reefs and light, past the Daedalus reef and thence down the long blank stretch to Jebel Atair and Zubair and Zuqar and Hanish Island, to emerge into the Gulf of Aden at Perim and the Gates of Hell, clear of which *Nukalau* turned East for Aden.

Rounding Steamer Point at dawn the ship was soon tied up to a buoy in the harbour, loading her cargo of salt for Bombay. With lighters full of the stuff queueing up to be emptied, and Arab stevedores crawling all over the ship, this did not take long. Two days later, after bunkering and watering,

Nukalau sailed on the longest passage of her voyage, the 2,200-mile haul to Bombay. Or so they all thought.

This time fortune did not smile upon *Nukalau* for, some three days into the passage, having been thrown about for a day and a half by the particularly strong tail end of the monsoon, *Nukalau* began to leak and, whilst the pumps could just control the inflow, the cargo was getting wet and more useless by the minute. So they turned round and returned to Aden where the cargo was discharged and the leak, found to be seams which had spewed their caulking, repaired by re-caulking the offending seams. What with that, examining all the other visible seams for incipient caulking failure, and loading a fresh cargo, the ship was in Aden for ten days, not only not earning but also costing harbour dues and repair bills, not to mention the cost of discharging one cargo and loading another. And there was a loss when the discharged cargo came to be sold. As Jack put it in a letter, 'Have you ever tried selling wet salt in Aden.' I suppose few people ever have!

So once again they sailed for Bombay. This time, the monsoon being that much nearer its end, the weather was better, the repairs held good and the passage was made in ten days without further incident. At Bombay, which I am sure Jack had selected when choosing his cargo with special care, there was something of a Burmah Oil reunion for Fulleylove, in command of one of their remaining ships, came into port after one of the endless Abadan–Bombay shuttles. Yarns were exchanged and bottles emptied before Fulleylove sailed for Abadan and Jack, by now loaded with spices and cotton piecegoods for Fiji, set off on the next leg of the voyage, from Bombay to Colombo.

Another 1,300 miles, another six days at sea and *Nukalau* came within the breakwater which makes Colombo harbour, tied up to a buoy and sent for the fuel and water boats. Ocean passages in small ships designed and built for coastal trades are hard graft so time was spent in Colombo on what in later times and places would come to be known as 'R. & R.' Essential maintenance work was done on board and in due course the ship sailed for Singapore, some 1,600 miles distant.

This passage was simple and straightforward. After passing the Pointe de Galle and rounding Dondra Head, three days due east to Pulo Weh, thence generally southeastwards into the Malacca Strait, past Port Klang, Port Dickson and Malacca before coming to anchor in Singapore Roads, through which passes the whole of the traffic from Europe and the Middle East to China, Hong Kong and Japan, not to mention the immense volume of local traffic generated by the enormous population of the area. They spent some days at Singapore, R. & R. again, enjoying the 'best run town in

Nukalau (Jack Arnot)

the East that I have seen since the war'. But all good things come to an end, time was moving on and Jack at least was getting nearer to home, the place which Suva by now occupied in his mind The navigationally more difficult part of the voyage was at hand, but it held no terrors for Jack, accustomed as he was to the problems of negotiating the coral reefs of the Pacific.

The choices open to a ship bound for Darwin from Singapore are legion. Leaving Singapore she can go through the Rhio strait between Bintan and Sambu islands, or simply go East of Bintan and turn south in the South China Sea, thence through either the Karimata or Gaspar straits in the Java Sea. From the Java, Bali and Flores Seas there are numerous exits into the Indian Ocean, the Timor Sea or the Arafura Sea. The Sunda Strait is too far west, and would both lengthen the journey and give greatest Indian Ocean exposure. The Bali strait is an option, particularly if combined with a passage of the narrow strait between Java and Madura. The Lombok Strait is wide and easy and the next to the east, Selat Alas, narrower and tending westwards. Next along is the Sape Strait between Sumbawa and Flores, which passage would involve either turning westwards to round Sumba island, or passing east of that island, through yet another strait, Selat Roti, between Roti and Timor before the road to Darwin was open.

Jack chose the Rhio–Karimata option. The Rhio strait is not too difficult and Karimata is hardly a strait at all, being some sixty miles wide between Karimata and Billiton Islands. Leaving Bawean Island close to starboard he entered the Bali Sea between Kangean and Raas and made out into the Indian Ocean through the Lombok Strait. It was the rainy season, so he hardly saw land at all during the passage but said in a letter 'but the sky cleared often enough for us to get our position occasionally', which must have been the case, for they debouched into the Indian Ocean without incident. *Nukalau* had left the northern hemisphere forever somewhere between the Rhio and Karimata straits. The open sea passage to Darwin went without incident and they arrived at that 'one horse town', as Jack unkindly described it, in good fettle.

From Darwin to Port Moresby, where they planned to bunker for the last leg to Fiji, is some 1,600 miles, or eight days and, though including the none too easy Torres Strait and the Northern end of the Great Barrier Reef, was accomplished without difficulty in fine, sunny, very hot weather. Bunkering completed, and with the fuel consumption figures clearly indicating that no bunkering stop would be required at Vila in the new Hebrides, *Nukalau* sailed in due course for Suva, Fiji, her new home port, where she arrived on 6th January 1954 after a voyage of a little over four months. A voyage which, after the sale of the cargo, yielded little or no profit, largely as a result of the incidents along the way. It didn't take long for Jack to decide that being a sixteen sixty-fourths shipowner was not his scene, for on 10th January he wrote to Annie:

'I am not happy about the way this company is being run and have advised the other directors to sell now while I think we have a good chance of making a good profit. I have decided to sell my share in her in any case even if they do not agree to wind the whole job up. Morris Hedstroms have already offered me the *Altair* again. They have had three masters since I left and none of them has been suitable. So when I get this lot wound up, which may take a month or so, I think I will take a couple of weeks holiday in the islands and then, perhaps, return to *Altair* if nothing better turns up meanwhile. I liked the job in *Altair* and I think I will again.'

Nukalau had not much longer to live. The *New Zealand Herald* of 14th June 1954 reported:

LAST MINUTE RESCUE FROM SINKING SHIP

NEW ZEALAND-BOUND *NUKALAU* GOES DOWN OFF N.S.W.

New Zealand Press Association, Reuters, Copyright. SYDNEY
'In darkness, 200 miles off the New South Wales coast, 13 men
were taken off the small motorship *Nukalau* early yesterday just
a few minutes before she sank.

'The Colonial Sugar Refining Company's steamer *Fiona*
picked up distress signals from the slowly sinking *Nukalau*, and
raced 65 miles to make the rescue.

'The wooden ship, 407 tons, 140 feet long, 28 feet beam,
sprang a leak and started to sink at 6.00 p.m. on Saturday.
When the *Fiona* reached her, a few minutes before 2.00 a.m. the
Nukalau's decks were awash.

'The *Nukalau*, under Captain Matheson, left Coff's Harbour,
Northern New South Wales, at 1.00 a.m. on Friday with a cargo
of posts, sleepers and poles for New Zealand.

'The Coff's Harbour berthing master, Captain D. Merritt, said
yesterday that she was not loaded down to her safety marks and
appeared perfectly seaworthy on leaving. The crew consisted of
four Europeans, seven Fijians and a Maori.

'The acting Deputy Director of Navigation, Captain N. Riller,
said yesterday that the *Nukalau*'s distress signals started at
6.15 p.m. on Saturday.

'When I learned of the emergency,' he said, 'I radioed all ships
in the vicinity. There were about nine or ten ships heading for
the sinking vessel. The *Fiona*, which was only about 65 miles
away, was the closest.

'At 9.45 p.m. we were able to raise the *Nukalau* again by
radio. The Captain said his decks were awash and that the ship
was still sinking. He said he didn't know how long it would last.
They were lucky to get the crew off in time.'

'The *Nukalau*, owned by the South Pacific Shipping Company
Ltd. of Suva, arrived at Auckland in March after an uneventful
trip from Cyprus. Until she was bought by her present owners
she was under the Italian flag as the *San Michele*.

'In the troubled years in Palestine after the war she was
employed in running the blockade. Under her hatches she

carried all manner of illegal cargoes, from firearms and ammunition to Jews trying to enter Palestine.

'The little ship was a successor to the freighter *Alexander* which was wrecked at Aitutaki in August 1951. After a refit in Auckland she sailed for Australia on 27 May.'

Note. Jack's letters show that *Nukalau* was, after arrival in Suva, due to dry dock in Auckland.

Chapter 35

Ai Sokula and *Altair*

So, at the beginning of April 1954 Jack rejoined *Altair* and, for the next two years, with only brief breaks for local leave, conducted her round the islands to his satisfaction and to the profit of Morris Hedstrom, fortunate shipowners to find such a competent master for such a small ship. The work in the islands was hard and the responsibility unrelenting, with no let up from day to day and week to week for the only foreign going qualified deck officer. The fact that in the twelve years that Jack had command of small ships he sailed in and out of the reefs and atolls of the Pacific without ever touching a reef or the bottom, unless deliberately to scrub the ship, testifies to his ability and powers of sustained concentration.

The first post-*Nukalau* spell in *Altair* lasted two years, years during which he learned the Fiji group like the back of his hand, making numerous friends among the planters, the schoolmasters and the traders living in the islands, friendships evidenced by a voluminous correspondence in his later years of retirement. His letters home were less frequent in this period than at any other time, which could be taken to indicate that he regarded himself as settled into a routine job of no particular interest to those at home. More's the pity, for detailed descriptions of his voyages would have made fascinating reading.

By the beginning of April 1956, after two years of toil in *Altair*, Jack told Morris Hedstrom that he was going on leave and flew home by way of New Zealand, Australia, Singapore and the Middle East, to spend the spring and part of the summer in England visiting family and friends throughout the length and breadth of mainland U.K. On 3rd August he embarked in the New Zealand Shipping Company's T.S.M.V. *Rangitane*, a cargo/passenger liner of 21,867 tons with a passenger capacity of 436 in one class. Built in 1949 and entering service in 1950 she was the last but one of the passenger ships built for the company, and remained in their service until 1968.

The N.Z. Shipping Company's passenger service succumbed to the aeroplane in July 1969, so *Rangitane* was almost the last of her kind. Shaw Saville's *Northern Star* kept a service going until 1975, but the days of a regular passenger service to New Zealand ended with the sixties. Thereafter the cramped, exhausting aeroplane was the sole means of getting there and back.

On voyage 17 *Rangitane* was full and the five-week voyage from London to Suva by way of the Panama canal was a thoroughly enjoyable part of the leave. There were all the usual passenger entertainments, deck tennis, shuffleboard, swimming, sunbathing, eating and drinking, horse racing, dancing, cards, cocktail parties, films and all the general sociability of a great passenger ship at sea. Jack had the added advantage of being himself a Master Mariner, and of there being other 'Old *Conways*' among the officers. The last call before Suva was at Pitcairn Island, home of the descendants of the Bounty mutineers.

In those days proper passenger lists were printed and that for *Rangitane*'s seventeenth voyage included, besides being a passenger list, a potted history of New Zealand, of Pitcairn and Curaçao, a brief seamanship and navigation manual and contained a most colourful section showing the flags and funnels of the major shipping companies, most of which have by now quit the stage. It documents a bygone age.

Arriving in Suva in mid October Jack found that as far as *Altair* was concerned his luck was out; her present Master was not, as so many had been, unsatisfactory, and showed no signs of leaving her. But Morris Hedstrom had another ship, the slightly larger 175-foot single screw motor vessel *Ai Sokula*, which they offered to Jack and which he accepted. Her trade was the same as *Altair*'s but, where *Altair* had been a happy ship for Jack, *Ai Sokula* was not. From time to time he made a voyage in *Altair*, but by 9th February 1957 he had had enough, as he made clear in a letter to Annie on that day.

'Many thanks for your last two letters and the enclosed one from Donald. I have not answered them up to now as I have been very busy shifting from ship to ship. I will be shifting from this one shortly. I don't like her a bit. I sent in my resignation yesterday. I may have to make one more voyage in her which will end about the end of the month.

'We had a hurricane on 7th January. It did a lot of damage to the islands in the Eastern part of the Group. I was in *Altair* at the time. We were in a small land locked bay anchored and lashed to trees and had no damage bar a few broken wheelhouse windows.

'I have managed to dodge the assessor's job; the trial comes up on the 19th and they think they can get two masters from overseas vessels in port at the time for the job. Yes, I owe Ian a letter. I'll have a go when I get out of this ship and have time to look around.

'You grumble at 1/6 for a half-ounce letter; we pay 2/6. What the government does with the money it gets I don't know. My friend the harbourmaster sent a broken chair from his office the other day to the Public Works Department to have it repaired and it was returned unrepaired with a note saying they had not got the necessary funds. I hope to have a bit of a holiday as soon as I get away from this ship. Eighteen months day and night seven days a week needs a holiday. There are one or two good places in Fiji and I have some friends who have asked me to go and stay with them.

'There is a job I have my eye on and that is Master of the Missionary ship *John Williams VI*. She is owned by the London Missionary Society and is based on Suva. She sails to all the odd, out of the way, little visited islands in the Pacific, carrying stores as well as parsons and often has two or three months in Suva. The present Captain is now a very old man and is said to be past the job. I have written to them and said I would be willing if they ever need a Master for her.'

Ai Sokula must have been hard work, for Jack had only been in her for five months, not the eighteen mentioned in his letter!

The resignation was not a tactical one, for Jack was willing to take his chance, and all his past experience led him to believe he would not be unemployed for long. Nor was he, for his holiday was barely finished when, surprise surprise, he was offered *Altair* again, and accepted.

Jack spent his remaining time with Morris Hedstrom in *Altair* working the Fiji group. His letters were sparse and family oriented with but few of his wry comments. His letter to his Mother on 19th October 1957 contains one of the few passages not related to family affairs:

'The Balolo has risen. The Balolo is a greeny brown worm that lives in the coral and twice a year at a certain stage of the moon it rises to the surface and in strong sunlight soon disappears. The

Fijians and others wait for it on the predicted night and scoop it up and make soup of it. I have never tried it and I don't think I will unless I am starving.

'Another ship went on the reef during the weekend. The ship that went to take off the passengers itself got onto another reef on the way back to Suva, but got off on the rising tide.'

By now Jack had been offered the Master's job in the Missionary ship, starting in May 1958 as Mate for a trial four months with a view to becoming Master in September. By April he had completed his last voyage in *Altair* and was living ashore in the Defence Club in Suva, and complaining that it wasn't a good place to live, for it was too easy for friends to drop in for a chat and a drink, though I cannot imagine the convivial Jack objecting seriously to that!

So ended the penultimate chapter in Jack's seafaring life.

Chapter 36

John Williams VI

The London Missionary Society was founded in 1795 with the principal and secondary objects of bringing the Gospel and Education to the natives of the islands of the Pacific Ocean, discovered or undiscovered. Much has been written about the work of missionaries worldwide: of late much of that writing has been less than complimentary, but it cannot be denied that the missionaries and their families were very brave and dedicated men and women. It is, perhaps, a little far fetched, but not too much so, to compare their departures from familiar Britain, or America, for the vast unknown spaces of the Pacific to the departures of modern-day astronauts for orbital flights or journeys to the moon. Voyages into the unknown, then or now, are not for the faint hearted.

From 1844 the society owned ships as providing the best means of enabling a limited number of missionaries to tend their flock in the innumerable islands of the vast ocean, for there was never any chance of providing a man for each inhabited island, or even for each sub-group of islands. The later ships all carried the same basic name, that of an early pastor, whose brief ministry illustrates the difficulties and dangers of the job.

John Williams was born at Tottenham on 27th June 1796 and was, at the appropriate age, apprenticed to an ironmonger. At the age of 18 he joined the Tabernacle Church and, shortly after that, in 1815, he received the call to become a missionary. Young men who had received the call did not hang about in those days, for he was ordained on 3rd September 1816, married Mary Chauner on 29th October of the same year, and the couple sailed for 'The South Seas' on 17th November, arriving in the Islands the following year.

The Society have been shipowners almost since their foundation, and they claim to have the longest established flag in the Pacific. With the vast

241

John Williams VI (Jack Arnot)

distances between the extremities of their parish the Society had need of their own vessel if they were to bring the Gospel to any significant proportion of the islanders. And they got about, for in 1823 John Williams discovered the southern part of the Cook Group of islands, including Raratonga, the northern part of the group having been discovered by Captain Cook some while earlier.

For the next sixteen years John Williams pursued his misssion in the Islands until, in 1839, both he and a companion named Harries were murdered as they stepped ashore in Erromanga in the New Hebrides. So ended a short and eventful career. History does not relate the fate of Mary, or whether there were children but from then on all the Society's subsequent ships were named *John Williams*.

The first ship, in 1797, was the *Duff*, probably a brig. She was followed by the *Messenger of Peace* in 1827 which in turn was succeeded by the *Camden* in 1837, probably the ship from which John Williams was lost. There is no record of the fate of these early vessels, but reefs and strandings no doubt accounted for more than one.

In 1844 the barque *John Williams I* was built at Harwich and served the Society for twenty years before being wrecked on Danger Island in the

Cook Group. Two years later the Barque *John Williams II* was built at Aberdeen and had the shortest career of all the ships, being wrecked on Savage Island, now known as Niue, again in the Cook Group. In 1868 *John Williams III*, also a barque, was built, also at Aberdeen, to far better fortune than *JW II*, for she never had an accident in her twenty-six years of service with the Society to whom she must have been very attached for, when sold to make way for the first steamer, she was lost on her first voyage in new ownership.

So in 1894 sail gave way to steam and Robert Napier & Sons of Glasgow delivered *John Williams IV*. She was a vessel of 663 gross tons, capable of ten knots, and served for thirty-two years before being sold to become a coaster on the China Coast in 1930. *JW IV* was to be the only steamer that the London Missionary Society ever owned, for her replacement broke new ground in two ways. Firstly *John Williams V* was described as an auxiliary motor schooner and secondly she was the first ship to be based on Suva. She served for eighteen years and had the misfortune to be wrecked on her last voyage for the Society at Christmas, 1948 on the island of Savaii in Western Samoa. Her replacement had already been bought, and preparations for her conversion to her new tasks were under way.

John Williams VI was to be the last but one of the L.M.S. ships and the first with which Jack Arnot was to be associated, though that association was still ten years away. She was a wartime designed standard coaster, built in 1946 as *Empire Sloane*, and converted to missionary use largely by the conversion of a large part of her hold to accommodation for passengers and crew and the stores which they would need, leaving the remaining part of the hold as cargo space; 140 feet long on a beam of 26 feet, she was measured at 380 gross tons and displaced 780. She was powered by a British Polar Atlas 300 horsepower diesel engine giving eight knots at 300 revs. Including her conversion at Doig's yard at Grimsby she cost the Society £70,000, and was ready, under the command of Captain Williams, for naming by H.R.H. Princess Margaret on 5th August 1948.

To help defray the substantial capital cost, and the £15,000 a year running costs, she left her naming ceremony at Tower Pier for a clockwise fund raising tour of mainland Britain. After a pause for tidying up and preparations for sea in the Shadwell basin she set off to show herself to the public and elicit subscriptions and contributions from them, calling first of all at Southampton. Thence to Torquay before rounding Land's end for Bristol, Cardiff and Swansea. Then up the Irish Sea to Liverpool and by way of the Manchester Ship Canal to that inland city. Out again into Liverpool Bay and the Irish Sea to Glasgow and round the North of

Scotland to Aberdeen, Dundee, Edinburgh, Newcastle, Middlesbrough and Hull where she prepared for the passage to the Pacific, where her ports of call would be infinitely more numerous and have much more romantic sounding names. The expedition raised £14,885, a worthy slice of a year's running costs.

This, then, was the ship that Jack joined as Mate 'on approval for Master' in May 1958, and in which he was to serve until she was sold and replaced. She was of a very suitable size for the job in hand, having sufficient accommodation for a goodly load of missionaries, for an adequate crew including a Mate, a Second Mate and an Acting Third Mate, with a suitable Engine-Room staff and room for provisions, baggage, and the materials required for the building of missions.

Chapter 37

John Williams VI at work

Jack's probation began with a voyage to the Gilbert and Ellice Islands, best described in his own words in a letter to his Mother.

'We sailed from Suva on 10th June. It was a rainy afternoon with very poor visibility. However, this ship is fitted with radar, which is a great help in poor visibility and on dark nights amongst the islands.

'From Suva we had one lady missionary, Miss Maxfield. She is a school teacher, really. The other twenty-two passengers were deck passengers, people returning to their homes in the Gilbert and Ellice Islands. We arrived at the island of Nukulaelae in the Ellice Islands at ten at night. There was one case of school books to land here and a canoe met us outside the reef. Then on to Funafuti, the Capital of the Ellice Group. This is a coral island about five miles long and half a mile wide, densely covered by coconut trees and nowhere more than twelve feet high, except at the top of the trees which are about eighty feet. The island is surrounded by a reef upon which heavy surf breaks. The ship enters through a narrow gap in the reef and then threads her way through patches of coral to the town of Funafuti, which consists of a church and a cluster of thatched houses. That's all. There are dozens and dozens of children, all dressed in gaily patterned lavlavs and that is all. They all seem to be happy and the visit of a ship is a great day for them. Many come out to the ship in dugout canoes, which they learn to manage as soon as they can walk, and they all swim like fish, never mind the sharks, of which there are many. We dropped a few bags of sugar, flour and rice here, and a tin or two of biscuits, and sailed the same evening

245

for Nukufetau, where we arrived at dawn the next morning. We anchored in the lagoon and, it being Sunday, nothing was done except the holding of a Church service ashore.

'The next day we landed some school books and a few stores. The ladies' Church Committee came off and sang for us. They had the most horrible voices I have ever heard come out of a female mouth. All the Ellice females are said to have harsh voices.

'We are calling at Tarawa, the Capital of the Gilberts, in a few days' time. A ship will be going from there to Ocean Island, where it will meet a ship loading phosphate for Melbourne, which will take our letters with it so that they can be sent by air from Melbourne to England. We do not expect to be back in Suva until 25th August.

'Another eight islands and we will have visited all the islands in the Gilbert and Ellice Groups, some of them more than once. We are at an island called Butaritari just now, and the missionaries are ashore holding Church meetings and examinations in the schools. This is called a "visitation". I always thought a visitation was a plague. I have little doubt that the schoolchildren are with me there! The missionaries mean well, and try hard, but I think that some of them are a bit cracked and unbalanced due to a great deal of loneliness.

'We have two on the voyage just now, the Rev. and Mrs. Lowerey. He is a young hothead from the north of Ireland, full of enthusiasm, but I'm quite sure the natives have no idea what he is talking about, and, being polite people, just put up with him. His wife is nice and is an ex-nurse from one of the Glasgow hospitals. Then there are a Mr. and Mrs. Blacklock from the Isle of Wight. He is not a missionary but is a chartered accountant and a lay preacher, who looks after the Mission's accounts (or tries to). I like him and his wife; they are good, sensible, people. The Missions are badly run from an economic point of view, and there is a great deal of money wasted just because the missionaries know nothing of the commercial world with which they have to deal for supplies, etc.

'The navigation in this part of the world is very tricky. The place has not been properly charted and many of the islands are as much as seven miles from their charted positions. The lagoons are full of coral patches which are not marked, and which can only be seen when the sun and sky are right for the job.'

Then, on 17th August, from a letter to Annie:

'We will arrive back in Suva on the 25th of this month after having been away two and a half months. We expect to be in for about three weeks before sailing for the Cook Islands on a two-month voyage.

'The Gilbert and Ellice Islands are all coral atolls and although they differ a little in shape they are in all other respects exactly like each other. It will be good to see a hill and a river again, things these people have never seen, nor even have words for. We have been to every island in the group. The people are much like other Pacific native people, the men tending to be more handsome and slimmer than the women. The children, of which there are many, are full of fun. I recently came across two things I have never seen before. One, people lie down to have their hair cut, and, two, coming into a clearing in a coconut grove I found two boys with a line stretched between two trees playing tennis, each armed with a lavatory seat covered with chicken wire.

'There are lots of fish, turtles and sharks, but the food is very monotonous in the islands. There are, of course, coconuts which are the staple diet, pandanas fruit which is horrible, a very few pawpaws and a few bananas, and that is the lot. Money is of no interest and of little use; most people go from the cradle to the grave without ever seeing any. A chartered accountant's paradise.'

That one voyage covered the whole of Jack's probation, his period as Mate of the ship, and on 31st August, writing to his Mother, he says.

'Captain Gaskin hands *John Williams VI* over to me tomorrow morning and sails for the U.K. in S.S. *Himalaya* on the 10th September. He was brought up in Sutton, in Surrey, but spent most of his life in New Zealand, and has two sons and a daughter. The two sons were Spitfire pilots during the war and one is now A.D.C. to the Governor of Fiji.

'We sail on 17th September for the Cook Islands. We go to Rarotonga first to pick up the Resident Commissioner and the Rev. Thorogood, and a flock (gaggle, pride or lamentation) of native pastors, to return them to their islands. They have all been gathered in Rarotonga for a conference. We expect, all being well, to be back in Suva about the 13th November, and to sail again for the Gilbert and Ellice Islands early in December.

'We are not expecting any passengers, except perhaps a few deck passengers, from here to Rarotonga. Our first call will be at Niue, four days from here, where we will discharge a small quantity of gelignite, carbide, acetylene and sugar. It is then another four or five days to Rarotonga. As in the Gilberts many of the islands are steep to and it is not possible to anchor, so the ship just drifts all day, steaming in to the land now and then to pick up the boats.

'In Suva the weather is wonderful just now, Sir Ronald Garvey, the Governor, left to retire yesterday, and will be replaced by a Sir something Maddocs. There is an outbreak of polio in Suva just now with some ninety cases. I hope they won't quarantine my ship in the Cooks.'

Jack had just moved from the Defence Club into his own flat, and goes on,

'This flat is quite nice. The Cathedral is 400 yards away and the swimming baths and the boy's grammar school about the same. The bowling club and the Defence Club are about 800 yards away. The Town Hall and government buildings are all in sight. Despite overlooking a scrap yard I have a better view from the flat than I thought, and I can see the ships coming in over the reef.'

Thus was Jack established, with command of *John Williams VI*, a flat in Suva to live in in the longest spells between voyages, membership of the Beaconing Committee of the Public Works Department of Suva, one of the panel of Assessors called from time to time to 'try' those responsible for accidents at sea and, all in all, a well-respected member of the seafaring community of the Islands.

The first voyage in command of *JW VII* was, however, delayed, for on 14th September 1958 Jack writes to Annie,

'Polio is so bad in Suva just now that the medical authorities have advised us against our voyage to the Cook Islands. We touch at every island, and every person on every island comes on board so, if we were an unconscious carrier everyone might get it. We could, of course, sail, and then go into quarantine for three weeks, but that idea is not well thought of. So we are staying here, and taking the opportunity to dry dock the ship and to give her a coat of paint. When and where we sail will be decided by the Ship Committee of the London Missionary Society in London.

'The weather here has been fine for the last three weeks, without a drop of rain. Water is in short supply, and when that happens they put a great deal of chlorine in it, which spoils the whisky and makes your morning shower smell.'

On 28th September the ship was still in Suva, for Jack writes,

'*JW* is in dry dock just now and comes out tomorrow morning. We then fuel and store and go out and anchor in the harbour to await orders. I expect we will eventually sail for Ocean Island, where an overseas ship has dropped a church, which has to be transported by us to the island of Vaitupu about 600 miles away. We can do that with very little contact with the shore, and by the time that job is done our quarantine period will be over.'

But that did not happen, for on 12th October 1958, writing to Annie,

'We are still swinging round an anchor in the harbour but come alongside to start loading stores on Tuesday. With all this time on our hands the Mate has had to keep the crew busy and the ship is looking a picture. The engine room is like a battleship and the Chief Engineer says it is a shame to let anybody walk in it.'

And on the management of the ship,

'I get my instructions from the Chairman of the Ship Committee in London in a vague sort of way, with plenty of latitude about when to sail. He might say, "I think a Gilbert and Ellice voyage is indicated." I proceed and then meet the missionaries up there, who say where they want to go in the group. I never know how many passengers are coming until they board, so the second officer, who looks after the feeding, has quite a job, and usually stocks up to the limit which is a bit wasteful. However, that is how they want it and I am here to see that it is done.'

He didn't add 'It's a bit like having a private yacht', but might well have
done!

The first voyage in command of the ship eventually began on 20th
October, for on the 19th Jack wrote to his Mother,

'There has not been much excitement this week except for an
eclipse of the sun, about one third eclipsed, and for the first time
I have felt an earthquake. I was reading in the flat last Sunday
morning, just after I had written Annie's letter, when the whole
building gave a sudden jolt and that was that; no-one seemed to
think much of it.
'Tomorrow is *Der Tag*. We sail at four in the afternoon for
Funafuti in the Ellice Islands. We take the Rev. Ranford there
with all his belongings (the Fijian word for belongings is "Ya
Ya"), and all his food for him and his family for six months,
together with a great deal of timber with which to repair his
house. His wife and three children come with us next voyage.
From there we go to the island of Nui, about a day's run from
Funafuti, to land 300 bags of cement to build a church. Then to
the island of Nukanau with timber for the same purpose, and
from thence to the island of Beru, where the L.M.S. headquarters are. We have stores and building material for Beru. For
passengers we will only have the Rev. Ranford and an A.M.P.
which, by the way, means Assistant Medical Practitioner. These
are islanders who do a four-year course at Dr. Edmond's
medical school in Suva, and then act as doctor on an island.
Generally speaking people say they are very good. They are
supposed to be good at surgery; this is said to be hereditary, due
to their cannibal ancestry!
'From Beru we return to Funafuti for a couple of days, and so
back to Suva where we should arrive about the 14th November.
We then expect to sail again on 1st December for the Ellice and
Gilbert Islands, and the Phoenix Islands including Canton
Island. This voyage should take about three months and we
should be back about the 1st March next year.
'I am enclosing a photo of *JW VI*. It is not a very good one as it
is a photo of a photo. I will send you a better one when I get one.
I had a cable yesterday from England (I always think you are

dead when I get a cable). It was from the Ship Committee wishing us "*bon voyage*".

'I have some friends here called Girvan. They have two boys, Roland, aged seven and David, aged four. They come down to the ship to play on Sunday afternoon. The first thing that happens is that they take their shoes off. Children here do not wear shoes except in the street, and will always take their shoes off when their parents are out of sight. Then they go straight to the galley, where the cook enjoys stuffing them.

'Polio seems to be easing up a bit; there have been fewer cases reported of late. The Chief Engineer's daughter aged eight was thought to have it but it turned out to be tonsillitis.'

Chapter 38

More of missionary ships

Captain Arnot signed a contract with the London Missionary Society, operative from 1st September 1958 as Master of their ship, at a salary of £1,300 Fiji, which approximated to £1,160 Sterling, rising by £25 at the end of the first, third and fifth years. Also provided was a bonus of £100 at the end of the contract, and leave at the rate of three months for each two years. Hardly a fortune, but Jack had settled in the islands and the job gave him lots of time in port, living in his flat among his friends in Suva, with voyages of very considerable navigational interest to justify his existence. He was one of those few fortunate men who had found where he wanted to be.

Despite the small size of the ship and the unusual nature of her trade, or rather her mission, she was, under Jack's command, to be run like a 'proper' ship, and one of his early steps to this end was to write his Standing Orders and have them signed by all those affected by them. Extracts from them follow:

M.V. *John Williams VI*

STANDING ORDERS

This is not the usual run of commercial vessel. As a Mission vessel in the employ of the London Missionary Society her first and foremost duty is to be as helpful as possible to the Missionaries with whom she works. Officers and crew will please remember this and do their utmost to make the Missionary's time on board as pleasant as possible. A happy ship is well on the way to being an efficient one.

CHIEF OFFICER

The Chief Officer will generally keep the 4–8 watches at sea. He will control the deck crew and keep the ship clean, tidy and in repair. All boats will be under his supervision. He will also help with the Radio Telephone work.

SECOND OFFICER

The Second Officer will generally keep the 12–4 watches at sea. He will be responsible for the keeping of navigational records passing each day the necessary information to the Chief Engineer and for the general maintenance of all navigational equipment including the weekly Radar check (with the exception of the generator unit in the engine room which will be attended to by the Chief Engineer). Also excepting the hand lead lines which will be the third officer's responsibility. He will control the ship's medicine chest the key of which is not to pass out of the hands of an officer. Charging of accumulators will be in his charge. He will keep the victualling books and generally supervise the steward's department. He will assist with the Radio Telephone work. All mail is in his charge.

THIRD OFFICER

The Third Officer will usually be a Cadet acting as Third Officer. He will keep the 8–12 watches at sea under the Master's supervision. He will keep a record of all life-saving equipment and make a weekly check of all lifeboat gear. He will be responsible for all signal flags. He will sound all bilges and water tanks daily and enter the soundings on the sounding board and in the scrap log book. He will be responsible for the maintenance of all lead lines. In port he will work under the directions of the Chief Officer.

*   *   *

Wind Pendant
On approaching an anchorage or reef passage pendant No. 6 is to be hoisted at the yardarm.

Boats on the Boom
All boats, when finally secured to the boom for the night are to be secured with two painters.

Lookouts
The lookout at sea will be posted on the forecastle head. He will also act as bridge messenger and will be called from his post at the O.O.W.'s discretion by whistle. He will report any object sighted by striking the forecastle head bell.

Drifting off

The O.O.W. will manoever the vessel while drifting off in accordance with the Master's verbal orders in the daytime or written night orders. The Chief Engineer will be advised as to the degree of readiness at which the engines must be kept.

Anchor Watches

Anchor watches will be kept when required, Officers will not normally be required to keep these on the bridge but MUST BE ON DECK. It will be decided after the vessel is anchored whether anchor watches are to be kept or not. The Chief Engineer will be advised as to the state of readiness at which the engines must be kept.

Watchkeeping

On taking over the watch O.O.W. will ascertain the vessel's position by any available means. He will check the course as laid down in the night order book or the log book. If there is any doubt as to the vessel being on a safe course the Master is to be called at once; a.m. and p.m. star positions are to be obtained whenever possible. The deviation column in the log bok is to be deleted and the allowance for wind and current shown there. Course must not be adjusted at any time without advising the Master.

Finally, this is a small ship and cannot be run on rigid rules as found on large liners, so I hope there will be give and take between departments and no interdepartmental bickering. Don't nurse a grievance, let's hear about it and get it sorted out as soon as possible.

These orders may be altered or amended from time to time. Officers will please read these orders and, when they are understood, sign below.

And the work went on. On 16th November 1958 Jack wrote to his Mother:

'We arrived back in Suva last Tuesday after a nice short voyage. Since then the rain has come down in torrrents and many of the roads are under water, polio has at last stopped. There have been 317 cases in all, of which four adults and four children have died.

'My old ship, *Ai Sokula*, is still laid up, but there is a rumour that they hope to get her running again, and are advertising in New Zealand and Australia for a Master for her.

'A yacht with a man and his wife and a girl of 17 bound from Samoa to Suva went missing some time ago. The yacht has been found sunk off a reef in Northern Fiji. It was found with the cabin door padlocked, under water. There is no sign of the people. The dinghy has been found, with no trace of the people, who have been given up for lost.

'We are lying at anchor in the harbour and do not sail again until 15th December. We go first to some of the Ellice Islands, taking a missionary's wife and three children to Funafuti. Then on to our headquarters at Beru in the Gilberts. From there we go to all the islands in the Phoenix Group, and from there to Canton Island, and back to Beru, before going on to Ocean Island to pick up the Rev. Jones, wife and child to take them back to Beru. After that we wander round the Gilbert and Ellice until we get to Tarawa, where we are to meet the Duke of Edinburgh who, if it can be arranged, will visit the ship. We do not expect to be back in Suva until 10th April, so it will be a four-month voyage.

'The islands have two things I don't like. Land crabs and big spiders. We have a spider in Fiji as big as your hand. People like them around the house as they eat other insects and are quite harmless, but they give me the creeps. One got into my cabin in *Altair* once and almost covered the porthole.

'I have been busy getting uniforms altered. They don't fit round the neck any more, and I have sent to New Zealand for two boiled shirts in case the Duke invites us to dinner. I don't expect he will but we will be ready. All the crew are getting new white shirts and shorts, which is their Sunday uniform. Normally we don't wear uniform at all. A turkey is on order for each of the missionaries, and I buy a live pig for the crew to eat on Christmas day.'

Then, on 7th December 1958.

'The yacht which sank with the door locked had only two people in it after all. There was mail at the American consulate in Suva for the girl, but she had left the yacht in Samoa and flown home to New York. The search for the other two has been abandoned. Now an Australian yacht has disappeared near Papua with twelve on board.

'On Monday there was a hurricane forming some 300 miles to the north of Fiji. According to the meteorological people it would not hit Suva. From previous experience I thought it might, so I shifted anchorage to a muddy part of the harbour and put out three anchors. By Tuesday morning at dawn it was windy and wet. No other ships had taken any action. At seven in the morning the hurricane had arrived in the North of Fiji and all the ships started to scramble for an anchorage. At three in the afternoon the centre of the hurricane hit Suva; two ships dragged ashore, and many others dragged their anchors with their engines going full speed ahead. We did not drag a foot, but were in danger of others dragging into us. We had several near misses, but did not touch. The wind reaching 120 knots in gusts. Our only damage was paint blown off the ship, down to bare steel in places.

'All the palm and other trees look the worse for wear now. Some of the palms are just bare poles with no leaves and very few coconuts left. The main Suva wireless mast collapsed, and floods have closed many roads. Galvanised iron roofs are lying all over the place and many telephone lines are down. When I got back to the flat I found one window blown in and a lot of leaves and water in the lounge.'

And in a letter to me on the same day:

'At four on Tuesday morning the storm recurved to south and then southwest. At seven there was a scramble of shipping for a good anchorage. One so and so without main engines was towed and the tug, which was too small to handle him, dropped him about a hundred yards away from me. At two that afternoon the wind reached 120 knots and practically all but *JWVI* started to drag, two missing us by about fifty feet. Two went ashore. It was impossible to see through the rain but we could watch the whole show on the radar screen and measure their distances to half a cable. Our only damage was paint blown off. At three there was a dead calm and half an hour it came away from the West but did not blow nearly so hard. By nine in the evening it was all over'.

Then in the course of the next voyage he wrote to his Mother:

'I seem to be fated to run maternity homes. Two years ago, if you remember, we had twins born in *Altair*; a few days ago we had another birth on board. Fortunately one of the missionaries' wives was a nurse and looked after it. He will be called Billeboo, which is the nearest that the Gilbert tongue can get to Philip. There are only thirteen letters in the Gilbertese alphabet, so it is difficult to copy all the English sounds. We have a case of mumps on board which I hope does not spread, but there is little that we can do about it and it must just take its course. The doctor can see to it in Tarawa.

'We are having a great deal of rain, for this is the rainy season in this part of the world. I got the present of a Muscovy duck the other day, for the table, but everyone likes it so much that we can't kill it, and it is now going to be given to the Mission Station at Beru. It has the original name of Donald. I don't know whether you have ever seen one; they are much bigger than an ordinary duck and have bright red embroidery on the part of the face just abaft of the beak and partly overlapping it. When you stroke them they wag their tails like a dog. Fortunately they do not seem to make any kind of noise.

'While we were at the island of Butaritari the King died. He was a very old and very fat man. The next king will not necessarily be his eldest son but will be one of his sons, chosen by the island people.

'The children of the West Wickham Sunday School sent a Christmas present to the crew which was spent on games, amongst which was a set of dominoes. Since Christmas they have played dominoes every moment of their spare time. We can hear the rattle of them till midnight and later.

'We have the Reverend and Mrs. Lowerey with us just now. He is a mad Irishman and as daft as a halfpenny watch. I had to go back twenty miles the other day to get some exam papers which he had forgotten. He spends pounds sending wireless messages to all the islands under his care, and a few days later altering them all. We landed twenty tons of cement for him the other day to build some new school building. No sooner had we got it ashore than we got a cable from London that he was not to build the building, so it all had to be loaded again!

'We will be in Tarawa on 25th and 26th March to meet the

Duke. He will not be coming on board but we will meet him ashore. He will be rowed slowly past the ship in his barge. He will only be in Tarawa for thirty-six hours and has not time to see everything, and if he came to see *John Williams* he would have to visit the other Mission vessels that will be there.'

Jack's letter of 22nd March 1959 well illustrates his life in *John Williams VI*. It was written at Tarawa.

'We are here painting ship ready for the visit of Prince Philip on Wednesday and Thursday next.

'At the moment I am trying to teach the crew to cheer. The Gilbertese idea of a cheer sounds like a Boo. They all think it is a great joke, shriek with laughter and hold their sides when I try to show them how. I am sure there are no other people in the world who can be made to laugh so easily. They really are the nicest and happiest crew I have ever had or heard of.

'At the moment we have on board Miss Maxfield, the head-mistress of the L.M.S. girls school at our headquarters in the island of Beru. We also have Mr. and Mrs. Blacklock. He is the accountant for the Mission and does all the business, collects the passenger fares and generally acts as O/C troops on board. And we have Mr. and Mrs. Lowerey. He is headstrong and impetuous, rushing into problems before he has considered them, and forever changing his mind. One evening he will want a launch to go to a certain village the next morning at nine o'clock. Next morning he is dancing about at six, wanting to know why the launch is not ready. They are away from the ship most of the time, and are usually sick at sea, so that keeps them quiet for a time. They are going on leave to Ireland after this voyage and come as far as Suva with us. From what I hear from London they will not be coming back. His temperament is not suited to this part of the world where everything must go slowly. The Lowereys have no sense of time and invariably arrive late for meals. Their church in the island of Abaiang has a tower with a clock in it which is always three quarters of an hour to an hour slow.

'As soon as we land him at an island there is a stream of letters, all typewritten. They go: "Dear Captain, Greetings. My wife forgot to bring a tin of sausages ashore so we have nothing for dinner. Will you please send a tin by the bearer." And then an hour or two later. "Dear Captain, greetings. One of our Pastors wants to know if he can buy a sack of flour." Later on, "Dear Captain, greetings. Please send the enclosed telegram to London." Later yet, "Dear Captain, greetings. One of my teachers wants to bring a pig to Abemama island, shall I charge him freight on it, and if so how much?" And so it goes on.

'We called at the island of Abemama the other day. This is an island where R. L. Stevenson spent some time and became a great friend of the King before he went to Samoa where he died. The entrance to the lagoon of Abemama is a bit of a nightmare and this is the largest ship that has been in. Great big coral heads stick up in all directions under water and can only be seen when the sun is high in the sky. Three voyages ago this ship was stuck on one for about three hours but managed to get off without any damage. I sent our motor launch ahead with the second officer and two buoys to put on the shallow spots in the entrance, and got in all right. While we were in the lagoon there was a very heavy squall one night which shifted one of the buoys, so coming out again was not quite so easy, but we managed it. The ship is really too big, or should I say deep draughted, for some of these lagoons. Most of the lagoons have not been charted and it is just a case of steering by eye amongst the coral reefs, and only doing that when the weather is right. Some of the missionaries think they are on a train, which should keep time to the minute. What a hope in these conditions.

'The missionaries (female) are all very busy making hats for the Duke's visit, getting stains out of and even making frocks. Old white shoes are being painted and handbags having all sorts of things done to them. One is busy re-lining her handbag and I pointed out that it was most unlikely that the Duke would look inside. We sail half an hour after *Britannia* departs on Friday morning for Abaiang, to land some people who have come to see the Duke, and then on to Onotoa for the same reason. Thence to Beru to land Mr. and Mrs. Blacklock and Miss Maxfield, after which we have only the Rev. and Mrs. Lowerey on board. On to Arorae to pick up one passenger for Suva, and then to Vaitupu to pick up the Rev. and Mrs. Ranford and children to take to Funafuti. Then from Funafuti we clear for Suva, which is another four-and-a-half-day voyage. In Suva we have the slip booked for 17th April so, as we arrive on the 9th, we will have just a week to get ready for the slipway. Owing to the ship's size we have difficulty getting onto the Suva slip and, in order to do so, we have to take all the weight we can out of her. All water is pumped out, anchors are put ashore, life boats are landed and fuel oil pumped ashore. It is quite a performance. First of all the ship has to be fumigated, for we have an alarming number of rats on board. Suva is the only place where we go alongside and that is where they come on board. They eat the cheese off the traps and then spring them and we have not managed to catch one so far.'

Chapter 39

Yet more *John Williams VI*

Last words on the Duke of Edinburgh's visit to Tarawa, from letters to Annie:

> 'Yes, I met the Duke a couple of times. The first time I was introduced to him he said "Ah, Master of the *John Williams*. Do you do a bit of preaching too?" He was so flippant and happy go lucky in his manner that I think he must have had a few. *John Williams* went into a special anchorage and he steamed past us slowly in his pinnace, and we gave him three cheers with all the crew manning the rails. I met him again at a reception on board *Britannia* and talked with him about the ship for a few minutes. He said, "Your ship looked very well, Captain." He is very good at being informal and chatty, and gives you the impression that he is really interested in what you have to say.'

On 26th May Jack wrote, before a very short voyage to Funafuti and before another short voyage:

> 'This is going to be a short voyage. I expect to be back in Suva about 20th June and sail again about 15th July for Apia, PagoPago, Manua, Niue, Rarotonga, Aitutaki, Niue and Suva, which will take four to five weeks, as we will only be one day at each place. We are taking plants and seeds to help build up again after the hurricane which has, by the way, flattened eleven of the fifteen churches on Niue.'

On 30th May, in one of his infrequent letters to me, from Nanamaga:

> 'At the moment, 8.30 p.m., we are drifting. There are few islands where one can anchor in this part of the world, only the ones with enterable lagoons have safe anchorages. We do anchor on the reef in places, with the bows in the breakers, but there is no swinging room and one is on tenterhooks all the time, so I prefer to drift.'

On 9th July 1959, from Oben Teunaia:

> 'Dearest my loving friend Captain J. McK. Arnot.
> Please sir, may I tell you for something before we going back to the Gilbert Islands.
> I want to tell you, but if we arrive at Beru, in the Gilberts, please sir I want to stay there at my home, and please sir, get one boy for working in the kitchen forever.
> I want to stay on ship about 10 or 20 years, but now I can't stay more because my job makes me too thin and tired, because in every days I was being in the kitchen with too much hot from 4.00 a.m. to 1.30 p.m. and 2.30 p.m. to 7 or 8 in the night for cooking food and cleaning everything for 70 or 60 passengers and 17 crew, in every trip, and nobody can help me. You know my captain that the cooker on deck making a hard work in every days for about 70 or 80 passengers, or 17 crew with no Saturday or Sunday. He had no holy day and can't to get be happy. Please sir, can you get another one to help the cooker? They must both working for all the passengers and the crew, and I believe that the cooker making very hard work, and sometime, something not clean and they make sick to the people, also sometime the crew can't to eat the food because the cooker can't to make any kind of food for the crew, but only biscuit give them for every days. Please sir, think of the cooker and help him. He can't get anything to be happy, because if he buy his clothes and he can't to play. But he got only £1-8-0 in a week and he got £5-12-0 in a month. He makes hard but he can't make to much happy and nobody can help him. The cooker is a very poor man because he working for about 100 people in every day on a trip. And working for 17 men on every day in Suva, but he can't be happy every night;
> Oh, poor cooker!

Please sir, if you can't to get another boy to help the cooker, and can you let me work in another job on your ship? And, then I can help the cooker in my rest, when my work is finished. I can help him in that way, but not in the time for working.

You know everythings, my loving Captain and you can make them in a right way. But please sir, don't forget me if you want your servant in another job, and also do not forget to get your new cooker when we arrive at the Gilberts. All the best of good wishes to you, and our God will save you on your work for him.

Beg my pardon my loving Captain.

Yours, Oben Teunaia

This, surely, is eloquent testimony both to a happy ship and to the educational efforts of the missionaries. Not all of the apparent grammatical errors can really be so regarded, for many of them merely reflect Gilbertese usage.

From a letter to Annie, 28th February 1960, from Suva:

'I have had a letter from Donald [Jack's elder brother], the first for years, I think. He starts off, "It seems a pity that the climate of Fiji is such that it dulls the qualities of imagination, of intellect or of human interest that enable people to communicate usefully with one another. Also it makes unco poor Scotsmen of them, ready to spend 2/6 to send 150 words half round the world." He then proceeds with a lecture on the duties and powers of executors. The rest is so abstruse that I don't know what he is getting at, except of course the Government as usual and Mankind in general.

'We had a wonderful voyage to Papua and really enjoyed it. We met some really good missionaries, right back in the never-never country, doing a good job, and returned to Suva by way of Apia (Samoa).

'We are off to the Northern Gilberts on Thursday with two missionaries and a house builder on board, and about twenty deck passengers.'

The reference to executors stems from the fact that Jack's Mother had died a few months previously. On 25th September, to Annie:

'The Rev. Craig ("the boss", out for a tour of the Missions from London, and having already visited the Gilbert and Ellice

islands) does not like bad weather and just disappears until he is
feeling better. He still has about 10,000 miles ahead of him in
JW VI. We are in Suva for ten days this time for fuel and stores.
Meanwhile we have left the Rev in Niue island. We sail from
here a week today, pick him up at Niue and then go on to
Rarotonga and all the Cook Islands, picking up delegates for a
big Church conference in Manhiki island. Then we take the Rev.
to Apia, Samoa, and return to the Cooks to deliver all the
delegates back to their home islands before returning to Suva via
Niue.

'I had a letter from my old friend Fulleylove. He is Master of
the *Burmah Star* of the Burmah Oil Company. He is the last of
the ones I was there with, and retires in April next.

'This is very secret at the moment, but the life of *JW VI* is
drawing to a close. They have decided on a smaller ship, which
will be stationed in Tarawa and which will only come to Fiji
every four years for repairs. I am busy on the specifications for
the new ship now. They expect to build soon, and sell this one in
two or three years time. They have asked me if I will go in the
smaller ship. I have told them that, as I have nearly four years to
go on my agreement with them that I will, of course, keep it, but
I am not prepared just now to say what I will do in four years
time. Meanwhile I might have the job of seeing the new one built
and bringing her out. Where she will be built is not yet decided.
She will be a wooden ship as they are easier to repair than a steel
ship if she gets into trouble in the islands.'

The months went by with *JW VI* wandering about the Pacific, going as far
afield as the cable station on Fanning Island. In November 1960, 'Great
excitement. We saw our first satellite last night.' The Rev. Craig, a popular
and well-respected man, completed his tour and went home after steaming
more than 10,000 miles in *JW VI*. New Year's day 1961:

'The Rev. Craig should arrive back in London today. He is
not a good sailor and we had more than usually bad weather
much of the time he was on board. There is no more news about
the new ship, but one of the missionary wives let the cat out of
the bag and everybody knows about it now. I have been thinking
it over and at the moment I do not like the idea of being based in
Tarawa. It would mean that I would never be out of sight of

missionaries, and one can have too much of a good thing. Here (Suva) I can go the clubs and see the lads about every three months, and live in a different atmosphere for a little while. I don't think I could manage without that break occasionally. I am feeling a bit stale and am trying to get a relief for this coming voyage, and if I can I will go to New Zealand for a couple of months. I will have been at sea for forty years on the 7th.'

By 23rd April Jack was back in Suva, not having got his holiday in New Zealand, He wrote:

'We have had a long voyage, just on three months, with quite a bit of heavy weather. We had two whaleboats overturn going over the reef on the breakers, one with our Edith (Miss Maxfield, who is a school teacher) in it with all the school books and accounts. She was lucky not to be drowned or knocked on the head by all the boxes that were turned out with her. There were some thirty people in the boat, some of whom had cuts and bruises but nothing worse. Miss Maxfield lost her glasses and her watch. The next day the same thing happened with another boat, which had its bottom stove in and is unrepairable.

'The preliminary plans for the new ship will be sent out by air to the Rev. Craig, who is back in Samoa, and we will go over them together. Where the contract will be placed I don't know, but I hope it is in the U.K. I am long overdue for three months' leave and feel I need it, so we will have to talk about that too. I have tried to get a relief but there seems to be none suitable in this part of the world at the moment.'

By the 18th May:

'The ship has just had her bottom painted and her engines overhauled. They have steamed over 26,000 miles this last twelve months. Our Rev. Craig has been out from London again to a theological conference and has been to see me. I may get my leave in December and I expect that I will spend some of it in Samoa and some in New Zealand. I have told the L.M.S. that I will not renew my contract when this one ends in 1964. (a) The new ship will be too small to be comfortable and (b) she will be stationed in Tarawa where I would never be out of sight of missionaries.

'The new Orient liner *Oriana* arrived in Suva on Sunday and sailed the same day for America. She is the biggest ship that comes here. Very ugly but I expect very comfortable. She can move sideways off the wharf and has the latest of everything including a telenurse.'

On 13th June 1961, approaching Tarawa.

'This is a Centenary voyage. It is just 100 years since the first Christian arrived in the Ellice Islands. The Christian was a Cook islander who was blown out to sea from one of the Cook Islands, and drifted for nearly 2,000 miles to fetch up on the island of Nukulaelae in the Ellice. He was only just alive and was a pastor by calling, so he set out to Christianise the islands. This is called a miracle by the L.M.S. I call it chance.

'The Hon Bernacchi, the Resident Commissioner, was to come to the celebrations, but we got a wire yesterday to say that there was another strike in Ocean Island among the phosphate workers, and he had to go there and miss the do. It is a pity for I have had to go to all sorts of means to get this ship here on time to meet him. The sole missionary in the Ellice Group is on board. He may be a Batchelor of Divinity but he is the most vacant creature I have ever come across. He gave me a list of islands in the order in which to call on them. I typed out a list of the islands with times and dates and gave him a copy and put one on the ship's notice board. We set off from Funafuti, the first island, and after having been at sea three hours, he remembered that we were due next day at an island he had forgotten to put on his list. And here am I pressed for time to meet the Resident Commissioner. Thank goodness for the strike.

'Although this letter is dated the 13th it is only the 9th. It is as dark as the inside of a cow tonight and raining. We hope to find the island of Nanumanga, which is just under a mile in diameter, at four in the morning. Thank God for the radar.'

Despite the fairly frequent breaks in Suva the lack of leave was getting Jack down; the gilt was going off the gingerbread. On 13th December 1961 he wrote:

'We have just come back from a very trying trip. The missionaries in London and the ones in the Gilberts are having a tug of war, with me in the middle.

'I was told by London to go on what is normally a 4,000 mile cruise. When I got to the Gilberts the missionaries there wanted me to do nearly 7,000 and I did not have enough fuel. I did as much as I could but it is a worry at this time of year with hurricanes about. They just would not believe that we really were short of fuel till I finally had to say, "Well, the ship is sailing for Suva at such and such a time and that is that." London is on my side.

'The new ship is to be built by Brooke Marine at Lowestoft. The order will be placed this month and she will be ready in ten months. This ship has been put on the broker's list and they hope to sell her next September. They have not promised that I will go home to bring the new ship out, but hope that it may be arranged. It all depends on when and where this one is sold.

'The ship is on the slip in Suva just now and I expect to get her off on Friday, when she will anchor until next mid or late March before her next voyage to the Gilberts. Meanwhile I am going on leave for a couple of months. I expect to leave here by air for Samoa on 4th January and stay in Apia for two weeks with friends. I then return to Fiji, and if all is well, may go either to New Zealand or Norfolk Island for a while.'

He did go to New Zealand. Writing on 2nd February 1962,

'On Wednesday we had a *Kimballa* reunion. Buzz Perkins, who sailed all the way with me, is now a radio announcer and does it very well. John Hoskins, who left us in Trinidad, is the coal foreman for the Union Steamship Company. Perkins has four children, the last two being twins and Hoskins has two boys. The party started at 11.00 a.m. and finished at 11.00 p.m. There was enough material at that meeting for several good books.'

The latter days of *JW VI* were difficult. A cracked cylinder head was cracked again during repair and the ship limped around without it for a while. Correspondence dried up, and the date of Jack's departure from Suva to oversee the fitting out of *JW VII* is not apparent, but he must have been in England by September, for the new ship had been launched, run her trials, and taken round to London in time to be christened on 29th November 1962 by H.R.H. Princess Margaret, who had done the same for *JW VI* fourteen years earlier.

Chapter 40

John Williams VII

Thursday 29th, the day of the christening of the ship at Tower Pier, was a cold, damp grey November day. The event was televised so those of the family not invited to London made sure of a handy television set, black and white, of course! Jack, resplendent in his best uniform, welcomed Princess Margaret aboard and, to the horror of the watching family and to his own embarrassment, had difficulty getting his glove off to shake hands, but that was the only crisis of the day. The christening was followed by a service of dedication, after which the Princess toured the ship. She approved of the galley and commented on its colourfulness and the quality of the galley stove. After inspecting the Captain's cabin and testing the bunk for softness, she and Jack went up to the wheelhouse and went over the charts of the route out to Tarawa before leaving the ship 'without tripping over a single door sill'.

John Williams VII lay in the London docks until 11th December before sailing for the Pacific. For a few days she was fogbound, and then delayed when the Society's Financial Secretary decided to take passage in the ship as far as Gibraltar. But on Thursday, 11th December 1962, she cast off and, emerging from the dock into the London River, set sail on her 13,000 mile, three-month, journey to work.

The ship which was about the embark on that long voyage was just 85 feet long by 23 feet on the beam. She had been built by Brook Marine at Lowestoft of Aformosia planking on galvanised steel frames and had two Gardiner diesels to give her nine knots. Navigationally she was well equipped with Radar, V.H.F. radio, echo sounder, radio direction finding gear and an autopilot. For her work in the islands she carried, besides her lifeboat, a whaleboat. Her hull was nylon sheathed against worm.

The only record of that voyage still extant is contained in a letter to Annie dated 3rd March 1963:

Captain Jack Arnot and Mate Rosea, *John Williams VII*

'We arrived here at 2200 hours on 24th February and anchored, and came into the harbour the following morning. We made good speed from London having covered the 13,195 miles in two months and fourteen days, an average speed of 9.276 knots.

'We had a moderate gale in the Channel and she all but turned upside down. All the cabins on the main deck were flooded, and we did not manage to have a proper meal in the saloon until the day before we reached Port Said, which was Christmas day, and even then it came out of tins as it was impossible to cook.

'Shortly after leaving Gibraltar our port stern tube started to leak oil badly. I had thought of going into Malta to have it looked at, but it was too rough to attempt the harbour entrance so we carried on.

'Port Said was hell. They were getting ready to celebrate the sixth anniversary of the last British soldier leaving Egypt, and made as many difficulties as they could. They were rude and insulting and we had a job to stop the thieving on board. We had to put the ship on the slipway to have the stern tube examined by Lloyds surveyor, who was an Italian, for the Egyptians won't have a British one. Our agents, Cory Brothers, have been nationalised, and an Arab who knows little about ships does the agency work, and makes all kinds of difficulties, and you have to employ two watchmen, a policemen and a garbage boat day and night. It is unsafe to go ashore so, although we were there for four days, we did not get off the ship. When the time came to put her back in the water something broke in the shipyard and we were in the water in fifteen seconds. Fortunately there was no damage and we were able to pull up with two anchors before we rammed a passing ship!

'We got into the Canal after a long wrangle about the search-light, which we could not put aboard because it was too big. Shades of *Nukalau*. Then a long legal form in Arabic had to be made out for me to sign, saying that I would go on without one at my sole responsibility. Two hours after we entered the canal a fog came down and we tied up for twenty-four hours. The first pilot was a Greek and a halfwit and the second was an Egyptian who did not even know the helm orders. There are many Russian, Yugoslav, Italian and American pilots. The canal is working all right and there is a constant stream of enormous tankers in both directions, indeed we had a 63,000-ton P. & O.

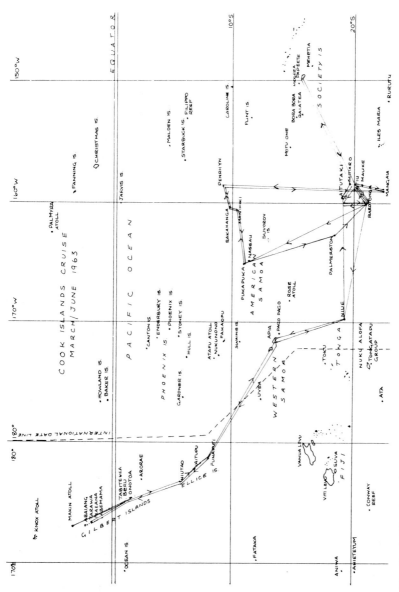

The Cook Islands cruise

tanker ahead of us. She was a quarter of a mile ahead of us and, when she gave an extra turn of speed to her screw, the current caught us and we were facing in the opposite direction before we got sorted out. The pilot just did not know what had happened, or what to do except that I thought he would jump over the side, and I wish he had. Owing to the fog the whole passage of the Canal was at night so we did not see much and I was glad when we dropped the last pilot at Suez. The agent failed to turn up, but I did not wait for him. We made a good passage of the Red Sea and arrived in Aden in under six days which is not bad. The automatic pilot steered all the way. One of our missionary's sons is in the Air Force at Aden, so the crew were well looked after. We arrived there on a Saturday night and I stayed until Monday night to give them a bit of a break and to let me see some old acquaintances and swallow some beer.

'Aden to Colombo took ten days in variable weather and with the motion violent most of the way. We stopped and bought some fish from a local fishing boat at Minicoy Island in the Laccadives, and then carried on to Colombo. It had been ten years since I was there. What a change. Motor cars parked on the pavements in the main streets, windows broken and, by the look of it, no paint used for those ten years. The ships in the harbour were half empty and there was a general air of shabby decay and a sort of hopeless apathy.

'I had dinner alone at the Galle Face where the menu was much as it would be in a similar class of place in England, so I got hold of the head waiter and got one of the best prawn curries I have had for many a year. The ship rolled a good twenty degrees all the time she was in harbour.

'From Colombo to Singapore the weather was moderate, and from the time we entered the Malacca Strait we hardly saw the sun for the next three weeks. We arrived in Singapore at midnight on a Friday night, and the next day found that it was Chinese New Year, so nothing could be done till Monday. There was a swell in the roads and the ship rolled heavily at her anchor.

'Singapore, with its change of government, has not gone back like so many other places, at least not as appears to the casual visitor. It looked and seemed much as it was before, swarming with people, mostly well dressed, with clean-looking shops bursting with goods and anything you want readily available.

'I dealt with an old firm of ship chandlers that I have known, on and off, for many years. The Chinese are very nice people to deal with. Tell Margaret (Jack's niece) that if I ever marry outside the U.K. it will be to a Chinese.

'It took a week to get through our work in Singapore as I had to put her into dry dock for the same stern tube was giving trouble again. This is all at the builder's expense, thank goodness, as there is a year's guarantee on the machinery.

'From England to Singapore we were seldom out of sight of a ship. From Singapore to Port Moresby we saw only two. We had overcast weather most of the way; it was hot with but little sea so we made ten knots for the passage. There was a lot of rain in the Torres Straits but with the help of the Radar it was not difficult. We arrived in Port Moresby one evening at about five and there was the usual big crowd to meet us, and some 800 people saw the ship there. Lady Cleland, the Governor's wife, came to see us and, of all people, the Catholic Bishop. The Rev. Craig arrived by air one morning and we sailed at ten that evening for Tarawa.

'We made such good speed for the first few days that, when we found ourselves unable to make radio contact with Honiara in the Solomons, we decided to go into Honiara to have the radio put right. Having anchored there we called the radio station, which was only a quarter of a mile away, on the distress frequency on full power, but got no answer. We at last got a technician off and, when we could find nothing wrong, he went ashore to the wireless station, which keeps a twenty-four hour watch on the distress frequency. When he got there he found that the reason that we could not make contact was that they were just not listening. Then we knew that we had arrived back in the Pacific Islands!

'We arrived at Tarawa late at night and came in the following morning. The entire population of 3,000 have been on board.

'We will spend about a month around the Gilbert and Ellice Islands and then we are off to the Cook Islands and Tahiti, returning at the end of June. That will be another 11,555 miles.

'The Chief Engineer who was on loan from the shipyard left today for Ocean Island and home via Australia. The Chief Officer leaves us in Apia for his home in Fiji and then I will be the only European left on board. Our main fridge has broken down, as I told them it would before we left London; they will just not listen to any advice from people on the job, believing that the makers of the machine know everything. So we will, I am afraid, be without a fridge for a very long time. My routine of six hours on and six hours off, plus calls at all times gets a bit wearisome. I won't be sorry when the eighteen months I still have to do are up.

'There is going to be fun and games in a day or two. They are thinking of reducing the crew's already small pay to bring it in line with that of the native pastors. They think, or pretend to think, that the crew's one object in life in being here is the love of God, whereas in fact it is because it is one of the very few jobs in the islands which pays cash wages.'

So *John Williams VII* was delivered and ready (more or less) to begin her work in the islands. From the account of the voyage out it is clear that Jack's early impression that she would be too small to be comfortable was borne out. Because she was so small she would roll at the least provocation, and there is nothing so wearisome as the cramped conditions of a small ship which rolls incessantly. Only when she was in the shelter of a lagoon would the rolling stop, and then only if the swell was not breaking over the reef. At anchor, or 'drifting off' outside, or on passage, she would roll her heart out to the exhaustion of all on board.

Departing Tarawa on 4th March on her first cruise of the Gilbert and Ellice Islands, the Cook Islands and Tahiti she made, in four months, what was a typical cruise for an L.M.S. ship. The extract of the log gives the detail of it and it does not require much imagination to appreciate the work involved in taking an 85 foot ship nearly 13,000 miles whilst visiting 54 islands in 118 days. The extract reads:

From	To	Dist. Miles	Time D. H. M.	Av. Speed Knots
Tarawa	Abaing	40	4 53	8.2
Abaing	Beru	263	1 8 02	8.2
Beru	Onotoa	43	4 56	9.1
Onotoa	Beru	41	5 28	7.5
Beru	Tarawa	255	1 00 51	10.3
Tarawa	Abaing	40	4 18	9.3
Abaing	Tabiteuea (N)	215	1 1 19	8.5
Tabiteuea (N)	Beru	81	11 11	7.3
Beru	Niutao	297	1 6 48	9.6
Niutao	Vaitupu	118	14 05	8.4
Vaitupu	Funafuti	70	8 27	8.3
Funafuti	Apia	611	3 3 07	8.1
Apia	Niue	343	1 13 07	9.2
Niue	Aitutaki	590	3 12 03	7.0
Aitutaki	Rarotonga	138	16 33	8.3
Rarotonga	Pukapuka	718	3 13 27	8.4
Pakapuka	Manihiki	268	1 11 18	8.1
Manihiki	Rakahanga	22	2 27	9.0
Rakahanga	Penrhyn	204	1 00 21	8.4
Penrhyn	Atiu	663	3 6 05	8.5
Atiu	Aitutaki	118	14 25	8.2
Aitutaki	Atiu	118	13 40	8.6
Atiu	Mitiaro	23	2 43	8.5
Mitiaro	Mauke	22	2 15	9.8
Mauke	Mangaia	110	12 32	8.8
Mangaia	Atiu	115	14 00	8.2
Atiu	Rarotonga	115	12 53	8.8
Rarotonga	Atiu	120	14 08	8.6
Atiu	Rarotonga	120	17 00	7.1
Rarotonga	Atiu	124	15 50	7.5
Atiu	Papeete	498	2 13 40	8.1
Papeete	Moorea	10	1 05	9.9
Moorea	Rarotonga	613	2 23 31	8.6
Rarotonga	Atiu	120	14 40	8.2
Atiu	Penrhyn	661	3 6 58	8.4
Penrhyn	Rakahanga	192	21 50	8.8
Rakahanga	Manihiki	23	2 40	8.6

From	To	Dist. Miles	Time D. H. M.	Av. Speed Knots
Manihiki	Pukapuka	286	1 9 25	8.6
Pukapuka	Nassau	50	6 38	7.5
Nassau	Palmerston	425	2 4 26	8.1
Palmerston	Rarotonga	267	1 13 17	7.2
Rarotonga	Atiu	120	15 47	7.6
Atiu	Mauke	45	6 33	7.0
Mauke	Mitiaro	24	3 15	7.4
Mitiaro	Mangaia	125	15 57	7.8
Mangaia	Atiu	115	14 00	8.2
Atiu	Aitutaki	124	14 00	8.9
Aitutaki	Rarotonga	140	16 30	8.2
Rarotonga	Niue	589	2 19 33	8.7
Niue	Apia	345	1 13 35	9.2
Apia	Funafuti	630	2 20 51	9.2
Funafuti	Niutao	196	20 31	9.5
Niutao	Beru	300	1 10 22	8.7
Beru	Tarawa	245	1 4 00	8.8
Lagoon passages & drifting		580	3 00 30	8.0

This voyage generated totals of 12,730 miles, 63 days, 9 hours and 46 minutes at sea and an average speed of 8.365 knots, with 54 islands visited the total time for the voyage accommodates a day at each island. Hard graft in anybody's language.

Jack kept a file of extracts from the Admiralty and local sailing directions. Typical of these is the entry for Vaitupu, Ellice Islands.

'Lat.   7°–28″ S.
Long. 178°–41″ E.
'Vaitupu is an island about thirty-two miles north north eastward of Nukufetau, is densely wooded and is fringed by a reef. There are two lagoons in the island into the southern and larger of which there are two entrances, one of which is practicable for boats at high water; an islet separates the two entrances.
'The southern lagoon is surrounded by a belt of coconut palms sixty feet in height. Landing can best be effected in canoes.
'H.M.N.Z.S. *Hawera* anchored in 1945 off the southwestern side of the island in a depth of ten fathoms, sand over coral, with the

church at Vaitupu village bearing 021 and the southern extremity of the island 100. This anchorage should only be used in settled weather.
(Chart 766, plan of Vaitupu.)
'The village is situated on the southwest side of the island. It is possible, with an offshore wind, to anchor with two sets of two beacons in line. Whaleboats can work the reef down to half tide.
'Pastor: Peni.'

Letters home from now on reflect the very different conditions which prevailed in *JW VII* as compared with *JW VI*. In July, after the conclusion of the cruise last described, Jack wrote:

'We have done 26,500 miles in a little over six months and we are beginning to feel it. I am certainly going to slow the pace down this next year, for we just can't keep it up. Six hours on and six off, plus many extra hours each day, month in and month out is a bit much at my delicate age (56). In the last ship I had no watch to keep at all.'

The problem had been foreseen and recognised, which is why Jack had, so early, announced his intention of not renewing his contract. For a long time after he had retired the L.M.S. sought his advice on matters connected with the ship and, in January of 1966, in response to a letter from the Rev. Craig about the staffing of the ship, Jack wrote as follows:

'I have read your letter and thought about it and in the main I agree with what Captain Harrison says. I have never met, and know nothing of, Captain Harrison.
'As regards staffing the engine room this goes back a long way. In *John Williams VI*, which was of the same horsepower as the present ship and had less machinery, there were three engine-room hands and the Chief Engineer. This was when she started her life in the islands. When I took over from Captain Gaskin she had six engine-room hands and a Chief Engineer. On my first voyage from Suva the Chief Engineer asked for another hand in the engine room. I told him that I thought the engine room was already overstaffed and that we would not increase it and that, provided there were no complaints from London, I would not reduce it. It is easy enough to increase numbers

but it is when it comes to reducing them that the trouble starts.

'As you know the difficulty of getting a Chief Engineer is very great, and to get one these days who will keep a watch is almost impossible. That is why, in manning the new ship, I had one hand for each watch and a Chief Engineer.

'There is, in my opinion, no reason why, when the Master is keeping watches of twelve hours and more a day on the bridge, the Chief Engineer should not keep eight hours of watches in the engine room each day. I think that with an unqualified Chief, such as you have now (and who belongs to no union which might complain) he should be made to keep a watch in the engine room. The ship could then be run with a Chief and two hands.

'In my time in both ships the engine-room hands always helped the deck hands when there was a shortage of manpower. I hear that Rosea, Tangaroa and Tuisani are the only ones left of the old crew who worked so long together. This is a pity and there may be a different spirit among them now.

'Manning on the bridge is another long story.

'When you told me the Society was going to build a new ship I suggested a bigger one. You said it had been decided that the new ship would be a smaller one.

'A ship, irrespective of its size, needs a man on watch on the bridge and one on watch in the engine room throughout the twenty-four hours when she is at sea. I could not see how we were going to man a smaller ship properly and still have enough cabins for missionaries.

'I pointed out that a smaller ship would not be able to carry the number of people, or the amount of cargo and baggage, that the old ship could carry, and that the temptation would be to run the new ship twice as hard to carry out the same tasks.

'You said that this would not be so, as the whole pattern of the itineraries was to be changed. In future pastors were to work in their own islands so that there would not be the constant shifting of pastors and all their goods and chattels from one island to another, and so there would be fewer pastors travelling. You visualised the ship in Tarawa for comparatively long periods, and that the ship would sail to an island with the missionary and schoolteacher, and stay there for perhaps two weeks, before returning to Tarawa to work other islands in the same manner.

'In view of the above I decided that the ship could be worked with a Master and one Deck Officer. The passages would mostly be short and there would be long spells between the long hours we would have to work at sea. There was one snag, and that was the Cook Islands voyage, but as this is only undertaken every three years, and lasts only three months, I thought that keen people would be willing to put up with it.

'When we got back to the islands with the new ship and settled down to our work I found that not only were the pastors not going to work in their home islands, but that we had to shift them about just as much as we had with the old ship, and that there was not room for all their belongings. And the ship was running harder than the old one did.

'I wrote to you at the time and pointed this out. Your reply was that it was one thing to get the islanders to agree to a plan, but quite another to implement it.

'So that is the crux of the whole matter. If the ship is going to be at sea a great deal, then she needs a Second Mate. I am not afraid of long hours, but even I felt that it was getting a bit much by the time I left. As Rosea has much work to do on arrival at an island I used to keep two hours of his watch, as well as my own, so that he could get some sleep, which meant, very often, fourteen hours a day plus being called for astronomical observations and landfalls.

'If you take on a Second Mate it means one less cabin for missionaries, leaving only the two saloon cabins for them. If this is insufficient it would appear that you have too small a ship for the work you wish to do.

'I am sorry that I cannot be more helpful, but these are the facts.'

The letter from Captain Harrison which prompted the Rev. Craig to seek Jack's advice sought a Second Mate, and made unfavourable comparisons of the staffing of the bridge and engine room. It is interesting that Jack's disillusionment began when, after the 13,000-mile delivery voyage, the first cruise was the Cook Islands tour, which lasted four months, not three, and which included no substantial spells in port.

The Cook Islands voyage seems to have taxed the organisation, and there

John Williams VII (London Missionary Society)

John Williams VII (London Missionary Society)

"The John Williams VII, the new ship of the London Missionary Society, moored at Tower Pier in the Pool of London. The ship, which is designed for work in the Pacific Ocean, is to be named by Princess Margaret on Thursday." (Daily Telegraph)

are a number of letters from the L.M.S. detailing their staffing problems,
which problems should surprise no one considering the conditions under
which the Master and Mate were required to work. A number of Masters
followed Jack, but none were satisfactory and, in February 1965, Jack was
called on to advise a man being sent out to the job at that time, with
particular reference to a Cook Islands voyage. He wrote to Mr. Craig:

> 'Sorry to hear of all your staff troubles in *John Williams VII*. I
> am afraid that these days of full employment are not helping
> you.
> 'I tried to phone Captain Jenks at six last night hoping that I
> would be able to get this letter away on the night mail. However,
> owing to a break in the line I was unable to get through to him
> till ten that night, so this letter missed the mail.'

After some sentences about a proposed meeting, Jack goes on,

> 'As regards fuel, water and stores for the proposed Cook Islands
> cruise much depends on the itinerary. If there is going to be
> a call at Tahiti, as there was last time, there is no problem.
> All that has to be done is to look back and see what we did last
> time.
> 'If the ship is not calling at Tahiti then she will have to refuel at
> Rarotonga.
> 'I think, but I am not sure, that there is a fuel storage tank at
> Rarotonga. If this is so there should be ample fuel for the ship,
> which will require about 5,000 gallons.
> 'The Master should, either through his agents or direct, advise
> Rarotonga of the amount required and the approximate date.
> This should be done as soon as possible and certainly not less
> than six weeks before the oil is required. This also applies to
> Apia and Papeete.
> 'Fuel oil requirements at Apia should be cabled to our agents,
> Burns Philip, who will make the arrangements.
> 'At Rarotonga and Papeete the agents are A. B. Donald & Co.
> 'Even if Rarotonga has an oil tank the oil will probably be put
> into *John Williams* in drums filled from the bulk tank. There will
> probably not be a pipeline from the tank to the jetty. I would
> also advise you not to put the ship alongside the jetty in
> Rarotonga. She has been alongside but the weather changes so

quickly that it can become dangerous. I had a near squeak last time I was there.

'The ship has a range of 4,500 to 5,000 miles so that it should not be difficult to work out where and when the oil will be required once the itinerary is known.

'Water is obtainable by barge in Apia and Rarotonga and alongside at Papeete. Most stores in the food line can be obtained at Apia and Papeete and, to a lesser extent, at Rarotonga.'

The consultancy continued with another question illustrative of the problems of operating the ship. Mr. Craig wrote to Jack:

'The problem is this. What is the maximum depth of water in which you would expect *John Williams VII*, engaged on our particular service, to anchor. We know, of course, the problem of certain islands where the coral goes sheer down to the ocean bed without hope of anchorage but the question I have asked relates to the performance of the windlass and the weight of the ground tackle.'

To which Jack replied:

'At the island of Avatele (the landing place of the first missionary) we anchored in a depth of nineteen fathoms. We found on this occasion that nineteen fathoms was just about as much as the windlass could lift and I took care in the future not to exceed this depth when anchoring.

'If I remember rightly we anchored in fifteen fathoms in the North Sea. As the windlass wears it may become a little less efficient.'

The problems of operating the ship were becoming greater as the legacy of Jack's sheer hard work and capability wore off, and the Society's shipowning days were already numbered.

Chapter 41

John Williams VII, Jack's final year

And so Jack entered his final year in command of *John Williams VII*. The routine of hauling missionaries around the islands went on as before. When a passage was to be made the steaming time had to be assessed so that the departure time could be fixed so as to produce the most suitable arrival time. Where there was a lagoon with an entrance in the reef and coral heads within, the sun must be well up. If there were no such problems a morning arrival, to give the landfall the benefit of morning stars, was a good idea, for Jack reported that the currents in the islands were so erratic that a difference between the position at morning stars and the D.R. of twenty or more miles was not unusual, and the islands were mostly small and low; getting to the island at dawn, after a night's steaming, was not recommended practice.

At sea, the eternal business of watchkeeping, a pastime not usually indulged in by shipmasters. Morning and evening star sights for position, as well as the more traditional and less accurate breakfast time and noon sun sights. Plans to be made for the loading or unloading at the next island, and the ship to be kept in good repair, and that did not mean sending for a manufacturer's technician. A missionary once wrote of Jack:

'In the Pacific, somewhere near the Cook Islands, on her maiden voyage, a fault in the automatic pilot sent the ship in circles. The Rev. Stuart Craig told of his wonder as, without fuss and, with the aid of the instruction book, Captain Arnot dismantled, investigated and finally repaired this piece of equipment.'

On arrival cargo, baggage and missionaries had to be discharged and loaded and the plan made for the next passage. The ship was almost never alongside, so everything had to be done with boats, sometimes in the shelter of a lagoon, but as often as not hazardously over the reef. Stocks of stores, water and fuel had to be monitored, for the opportunities to buy the latter were sparse, though it seems that food was less of a problem, at least it was not on the maiden cruise of the Cook Islands. Jack wrote from Rarotonga:

> 'The ship, as usual in the Cooks, has been swamped with presents of food. Over a ton of bananas, breadfruit, pawpaws, oranges, mandarins, guavas, tomatoes, yams, taro, kumalas and coconuts. Whole pigs ready cooked. The crew are getting so fat they can hardly walk. Frangipani, hibiscus and bougainvillaea pour on board and are wrapped round our necks. All quite overwhelming.'

Overwhelming, but in no way reducing the difficulty of the task confronting this particular shipmaster, working on his own with no qualified mates.

The return to Tarawa at the end of the Cook Islands cruise was followed by a quick dash to Nauru, 500 miles to the west southwest, for the opening of a new church, and back. Then another dash to Ocean Island, 240 miles to the southwest to land homeward bound missionaries. Ocean Island is solid phosphate and there is a ship to Australia about twice a week in which missionaries could take passage. Transport in the Pacific is now vastly changed, with the map showing hundreds of islands, including Nauru, with airport signs against them, but in those days only the largest islands had air communication with anywhere.

Engine trouble persisted, with the spare pistons being found to be the wrong size, and Chief Engineers hard to come by. On 6th October 1963 Jack wrote that he was off to Ocean Island again tomorrow to pick up a new Chief Engineer, an Icelander by the name of Johnsson. 'We are preparing a bunk in the main fridge for him.' Then, having picked him up he writes in November, 'My polar bear is called George Jonsson. He is about twenty-eight, small and fair and typically Norwegian, very fussy about his food, and has never managed to arrive at a meal less than twenty minutes late. His English is quite good with a strong accent. What his abilities as an engineer are I have yet to find out. He has no qualifications and gets £200 a year more than me and is only on a six-month contract. Ah well, one more on a six month contract will see me through.'

The Ocean Island expedition was followed by a three weeks' cruise of the Gilbert and Ellice Group, marred by the fact that the two and a half year old son of one of the missionaries came aboard with dysentery and still had it at the end of the cruise. 'Some people should never be allowed to have

children. Our next passenger will be 'the dream', The Rev. X. The natives
pull his leg all the time and he can't see it. We expect to be back in Tarawa
on 20th December and will have two or three weeks there.'
  From Tarawa on 22nd December 1963:

> 'We have a strike on Ocean Island just now, so no ships are
> calling and that is our main inlet and outlet for mail. However,
> there is a Dutch ship due from London tomorrow so I hope to
> get this away in her. It should go by air from the Solomon
> Islands in about a week's time.'
>   'Our polar bear lives mostly on milk; I reckon he costs about
> eight shillings a day for milk. He has a bee in his bonnet about
> crayfish and never stops talking about them, otherwise he is all
> right. He runs down Iceland and everything to do with it. There
> are no polar bears in Iceland, much to my disappointment.
>   'The canoe I told you about that went adrift from Manihiki
> has arrived in Erromanga in the New Hebrides (the island where
> John Williams was eaten). Of the seven on board only three
> arrived alive and one died after landing. They drifted 2,000 miles
> in just over two months, and must have just missed many islands
> on the way.'

Life in the remote Pacific was indeed very different from Western European
experience and required deep seams of self-sufficiency if anyone was to
survive, let alone do an effective job of work. On the hazards of the Ocean
Jack wrote on 5th April:

> 'Last Sunday we spent at sea looking for a canoe which
> disappeared from here. We searched for twenty-four hours but
> found no sign of her. A radio message today tells us that it has
> arrived at the island of Nauru, about 500 miles from here with
> both boys alive. A chance in a million.
>   'Another tragedy at Fiji. A sailing cutter which, if I remember
> rightly was licensed to carry twenty passengers, sank with a loss
> of ninety people. There were only three survivors.'

In May *JW VII* made a passage to Suva for dry docking and to transport
the Rev. Thorogood thence. They expected to be there just a week, but
stayed longer to await the arrival of Captain Chapman, Jack's successor.

Letters at this time were scarce so one can only surmise that Captain Chapman joined the ship sometime in June for a short period of probation, for Jack left her and handed over command on 27th July 1964 and retired from seafaring, ultimately to a bungalow at Geldeston near Beccles, where he enjoyed thirteen years of retirement.

Apart from a number of holiday cruises with members of the family his last voyage was from Suva to London by way of Pitcairn and Panama to London where he arrived to 'hang up his boots' on 11th October 1964.

Chapter 42

Tarawa

Saturday, September 16th 1978, dawned clear and fair over the Island and Lagoon of Tarawa in the Gilbert Islands, a dawn such as might well have prompted Magellan to give the Pacific Ocean its oft unjustified name. The light breeze chased ripples over the surface of the water and the palms nodded their satisfaction with the newborn day. To all outward appearances just another day in the unending series in the life of the islands and the ocean, but it was to be a day different from any other either preceding or succeeding it.

At the Tangitenbu Theological College at Bikenibeu the biennial general assembly of the Gilbert Islands Protestant Church, long associated with the London Missionary Society, was in session, and today was to be, for all the pastors and trainee pastors attending, a day different from any other, encompassing a religious ceremony quite outside the experience of all those without first-hand knowledge of the Western European culture. Senior Minister Baraniko Teiti, who was to conduct the ceremony, a man long experienced in the Gilbertese Church and the conduct of its work and services, awoke to the prospect of a day which was to be unique in his life's experience.

The morning passed in the accustomed way at Tangitenbu in the conduct of the affairs of the assembly; meetings and conferences, services and prayer and instruction for the trainees, but as midday approached minds relaxed their grip of affairs and began to be more and more occupied by the prospect of the afternoon's unique event, the scattering in the lagoon of Tarawa, at the anchorage of Antebuka, of the ashes of the late Captain Jack Arnot, for seven years in the fifties and sixties Master of the Society's ships in the service of the Church, and highly regarded by all who knew him both for his professional capability and simply as a man.

Cremation, and therefore the scattering of ashes, is a practice unknown in the Pacific, and so the lovely lagoon at Tarawa was on this September day to add to its long chapter of experiences; canoes or rafts or vessels unknown and unimagined by us bringing the ancestors of the Gilbertese; white men bringing their blessings and curses, Christianity, technology, disease, firearms and drink; the acceptance and settlement into a new way of life then unsettled by one of the bloodiest battles of the Second World War, followed by another difficult period of acclimatisation to the entirely new conditions following that war. Tarawa might be thought to have seen it all, but not quite.

The ceremonies of that September day are best related by The Reverend Tom Hawthorn's 'Taeka tabueta i bukin te Taramouri aei' which, when translated from the Gilbertese, is simply 'An explanation of the Service', a statement made to the assembled company to put the service and ceremony into context and which went as follows.

'John McKenzie Arnot, who died last February in East Anglia, had spent much of his professional life in the Pacific and had been Captain of two ships of the London Missionary Society. The *John Williams VI* had been bought secondhand after the Second World War when there was an urgent need; but *John Williams VII* was designed for the work and the area, even to slipping in the Betio dockyard on Tarawa. In this planning Captain Arnot played a large part and the result, as an islander put it, was "a very clever ship". He brought a Gilbertese crew to London to bring her out after the naming by Princess Margaret. In the Pacific, somewhere near the Cook Islands on her maiden voyage, a fault in "George", the automatic pilot, sent the ship in circles. The Rev. Stuart Craig told of his wonder as, without fuss, Captain Arnot dismantled, investigated and with the aid of the instruction book finally repaired this piece of equipment.

'Such quiet competence in the ordinary work as in the emergencies of his profession led his crews to trust him and learn from him. The solitude of the ship's master, the vast unpredictable Pacific, the multifarious responsibilities – none of these wore down Captain Arnot's even-tempered confidence from which others drew strength.

'On his death Captain Arnot's family, mindful of his love of the Pacific, suggested that his ashes might be scattered there and so were guided to send them to the Gilbert Islands Protestant Church Headquarters in Tarawa.

'In the Pacific anything new is talked about, so much had to be explained to the Church Executive Committee: the practice and nature of cremation, unknown here; the urns of the ashes and their disposal. But once understood and accepted the Executive decided that the honour was great and that it would be fitting for the scattering at Antebuka anchorage to be done in the presence of the Assembly of the Church when, once in two years, representatives of all the islands come together. So on Saturday, September 16th, trucks took the members, and those of the women's organisation, with the students of Tangintenbu Theological College to Bairiki to board the chartered landing craft *Mocambo*. We took with us the funnel flag of *John Williams VII*, the last of the line, honoured in the Pacific as senior in service even to the Navy. Around it, sitting or standing, we sang, and the harmony of 100 Gilbertese voices carried over the lagoon. After half an hour we anchored. Letters from Captain Arnot's nephew and from the Council for World Mission were read which explained the background and then the Rev. Baraniko Teiti conducted the service. Baraniko, himself honoured by the Colony for long service, had been in close touch with the ships and their Captains. After a hymn and prayer of thanksgiving the congregation read from Genesis the story of Jacob's death in one land and burial in another. Baraniko spoke of Captain Arnot's faithfulness, his content to work in the Pacific and of his gifts from God passed on in the service of the islands. Then, reverently, the ashes were scattered in the waters where "Captain Arnot brought the ship to anchor at the end of many voyages".'

So, seventy one and a half years after his birth, Jack Arnot's ashes were laid to rest, among the friends with whom he had worked for many years of his life, upon the waters of the Ocean which had captured him a quarter of a century earlier.